EXPOSITORY
COMMENTARY ON THE
VIMALAKĪRTI SUTRA

BDK English Tripiṭaka Series

EXPOSITORY COMMENTARY ON THE VIMALAKĪRTI SUTRA

(Taishō Volume 56, Number 2186)

Translated from the Chinese

by

Jamie Hubbard

Bukkyō Dendō Kyōkai America, Inc.
2012

First Printing, 2012
ISBN: 978-1-886439-44-3
Library of Congress Catalog Card Number: 2012931040

Published by
Bukkyō Dendō Kyōkai America, Inc.
2620 Warring Street
Berkeley, California 94704

Printed in the United States of America

A Message on the Publication of the English Tripiṭaka

The Buddhist canon is said to contain eighty-four thousand different teachings. I believe that this is because the Buddha's basic approach was to prescribe a different treatment for every spiritual ailment, much as a doctor prescribes a different medicine for every medical ailment. Thus his teachings were always appropriate for the particular suffering individual and for the time at which the teaching was given, and over the ages not one of his prescriptions has failed to relieve the suffering to which it was addressed.

Ever since the Buddha's Great Demise over twenty-five hundred years ago, his message of wisdom and compassion has spread throughout the world. Yet no one has ever attempted to translate the entire Buddhist canon into English throughout the history of Japan. It is my greatest wish to see this done and to make the translations available to the many English-speaking people who have never had the opportunity to learn about the Buddha's teachings.

Of course, it would be impossible to translate all of the Buddha's eighty-four thousand teachings in a few years. I have, therefore, had one hundred thirty-nine of the scriptural texts in the prodigious Taishō edition of the Chinese Buddhist canon selected for inclusion in the First Series of this translation project.

It is in the nature of this undertaking that the results are bound to be criticized. Nonetheless, I am convinced that unless someone takes it upon himself or herself to initiate this project, it will never be done. At the same time, I hope that an improved, revised edition will appear in the future.

It is most gratifying that, thanks to the efforts of more than a hundred Buddhist scholars from the East and the West, this monumental project has finally gotten off the ground. May the rays of the Wisdom of the Compassionate One reach each and every person in the world.

NUMATA Yehan
Founder of the English
Tripiṭaka Project

August 7, 1991

Editorial Foreword

In January 1982, Dr. NUMATA Yehan, the founder of Bukkyō Dendō Kyōkai (Society for the Promotion of Buddhism), decided to begin the monumental task of translating the complete Taishō edition of the Chinese Tripiṭaka (Buddhist canon) into the English language. Under his leadership, a special preparatory committee was organized in April 1982. By July of the same year, the Translation Committee of the English Tripiṭaka was officially convened.

The initial Committee consisted of the following members: (late) HANAYAMA Shōyū (Chairperson), (late) BANDŌ Shōjun, ISHIGAMI Zennō, (late) KAMATA Shigeo, (late) KANAOKA Shūyū, MAYEDA Sengaku, NARA Yasuaki, (late) SAYEKI Shinkō, (late) SHIOIRI Ryōtatsu, TAMARU Noriyoshi, (late) TAMURA Kwansei, URYŪZU Ryūshin, and YUYAMA Akira. Assistant members of the Committee were as follows: KANAZAWA Atsushi, WATANABE Shōgo, Rolf Giebel of New Zealand, and Rudy Smet of Belgium.

After holding planning meetings on a monthly basis, the Committee selected one hundred thirty-nine texts for the First Series of translations, an estimated one hundred printed volumes in all. The texts selected are not necessarily limited to those originally written in India but also include works written or composed in China and Japan. While the publication of the First Series proceeds, the texts for the Second Series will be selected from among the remaining works; this process will continue until all the texts, in Japanese as well as in Chinese, have been published.

Frankly speaking, it will take perhaps one hundred years or more to accomplish the English translation of the complete Chinese and Japanese texts, for they consist of thousands of works. Nevertheless, as Dr. NUMATA wished, it is the sincere hope of the Committee that this project will continue unto completion, even after all its present members have passed away.

Dr. NUMATA passed away on May 5, 1994, at the age of ninety-seven, entrusting his son, Mr. NUMATA Toshihide, with the continuation and completion of the Translation Project. The Committee also lost its able and devoted Chairperson,

Professor HANAYAMA Shōyū, on June 16, 1995, at the age of sixty-three. After these severe blows, the Committee elected me, then Vice President of Musashino Women's College, to be the Chair in October 1995. The Committee has renewed its determination to carry out the noble intention of Dr. NUMATA, under the leadership of Mr. NUMATA Toshihide.

The present members of the Committee are MAYEDA Sengaku (Chairperson), ICHISHIMA Shōshin, ISHIGAMI Zennō, KATSURA Shōryū, NAMAI Chishō, NARA Yasuaki, SAITŌ Akira, SHIMODA Masahiro, Kenneth K. Tanaka, WATANABE Shōgo, and YONEZAWA Yoshiyasu.

The Numata Center for Buddhist Translation and Research was established in November 1984, in Berkeley, California, U.S.A., to assist in the publication of the BDK English Tripiṭaka First Series. The Publication Committee was organized at the Numata Center in December 1991. In 2010, the Numata Center's operations were merged into Bukkyō Dendō Kyōkai America, Inc. (BDK America) and BDK America continues to oversee the English Tripiṭaka project in close cooperation with the Editorial Committee in Tokyo.

MAYEDA Sengaku
Chairperson
Editorial Committee of
the BDK English Tripiṭaka

Publisher's Foreword

On behalf of the Publication Committee, I am happy to present this contribution to the BDK English Tripiṭaka Series. The initial translation and editing of the Buddhist scripture found here were performed under the direction of the Editorial Committee in Tokyo, Japan, chaired by Professor Sengaku Mayeda, Professor Emeritus of Musashino University. The Publication Committee members then put this volume through a rigorous succession of editorial and book-making efforts.

Both the Editorial Committee in Tokyo and the Publication Committee in Berkeley are dedicated to the production of clear, readable English texts of the Buddhist canon. The members of both committees and associated staff work to honor the deep faith, spirit, and concern of the late Reverend Dr. Yehan Numata, who founded the BDK English Tripiṭaka Series in order to disseminate Buddhist teachings throughout the world.

The long-term goal of our project is the translation and publication of the one hundred-volume Taishō edition of the Chinese Buddhist canon, plus a few influential extracanonical Japanese Buddhist texts. The list of texts selected for the First Series of this translation project is given at the end of each volume.

As Chair of the Publication Committee, I am deeply honored to serve in the post formerly held by the late Dr. Philip B. Yampolsky, who was so good to me during his lifetime; the esteemed late Dr. Kenneth K. Inada, who has had such a great impact on Buddhist studies in the United States; and the beloved late Dr. Francis H. Cook, a dear friend and colleague.

In conclusion, let me thank the members of the Publication Committee for the efforts they have undertaken in preparing this volume for publication: Senior Editor Marianne Dresser, Dr. Hudaya Kandahjaya, Dr. Carl Bielefeldt, Dr. Robert Sharf, Reverend Kiyoshi Yamashita, and Reverend Brian Nagata, President of Bukkyō Dendō Kyōkai America, Inc.

John R. McRae
Chairperson
Publication Committee

Contents

Translator's Introduction

The *Expository Commentary on the Vimalakīrti Sutra* (*Yuimagyōgisho,* hereafter *Commentary*), attributed to "Prince Jōgū" (Shōtoku Taishi, 574–622), is a three-fascicle commentary on Kumārajīva's translation of the *Sutra Preached by Vimala-kīrti* (*Weimojie suoshuo jing;* Skt. *Vimalakīrtinirdeśa-sūtra*). Together with commentaries on the *Lotus Sutra* and the *Śrīmālādevī-sūtra,* it is known as one of the "Three Commentaries" (*Sangyōgisho*) of Shōtoku Taishi. The earliest accounts of this text date to the eighth century, and records indicate that a copy of the text was at Hōryūji in the mid-eighth century; the earliest manuscript extant today is from the thirteenth century. Scholars have long doubted the authenticity of the attribution of this text to Shōtoku because of the lack of early records or additional corroborating evidence, as well as the great similarity to other commentaries on the *Vimalakīrtinirdeśa* composed in China. Thus, while questions about Shōtoku's authorship still remain, it is not unreasonable to think that this *Commentary* (as well as the other two commentaries attributed to Shōtoku) was either originally a Chinese or Korean composition or a work written with a Chinese model in hand—or perhaps, it is more a transcription with interpolations than an original composition. Although the majority opinion today is that the *Commentary* was not composed by Shōtoku Taishi, this in no way diminishes the significant role this text has played in the history of Japanese Buddhism.

Given the *Vimalakīrti Sutra*'s dramatic narrative of an awakened merchant prince, it was long popular in China as presenting a model for the sage-ruler, which had obvious appeal to Japanese rulers in the sixth–seventh centuries as well. This era marks the beginning of the Japanese state, a time when the numerous clans that had ruled various localities on the islands were coming together for the first time under the rule of a single family. The course of state formation was both caused by and aided by the steady movement of immigrants, ideas, and technology from Korea and China, and the introduction of Buddhism was perhaps one of the most significant elements of this process. Adopting Buddhism as the state religion, initiating diplomatic relations with Korea and China, and integrating the superior technologies of the continent required great changes in the legitimization of rule and the structure of virtually every aspect of Japanese life.

Shōtoku Taishi and his family have long been seen as central pillars of this "internationalization," as well as the subsequent consolidation of the Japanese state, and hence as symbols of the very nation of Japan and the highest Japanese values. The connection between the *Commentary* and Shōtoku Taishi assured its importance and influence to this day. There are records of the *Yuimagyōgisho* being carried to China with diplomatic missions, and in the fourteenth century the famous scholar-monk Gyōnen wrote a forty-fascicle commentary on the *Commentary,* the *Yuimagyōsho anraki* (*Dai Nihon Bukkyō Zensho;* Tokyo: Suzuki Research Foundation, 1970, vol. 13). Even today the image of Shōtoku as a sage-ruler along the model of the *Vimalakīrti Sutra* is often found in scholarly writings, the popular press, and religious apologetics.

The commentary follows a fairly normal pattern for Chinese commentaries of the fifth and sixth centuries (the so-called *kepan* or *fenke* style, "analytic parsing"), breaking the text into an outline format using sections and subsections, going further and further into more and more detailed sections, subsections, sub-subsections, and so on—indeed, as many as thirteen levels deep in the case of the *Commentary.* Some of the divisions are fairly conventional, utilizing conceptual categories common to the Chinese Buddhist world of the time (such as preface, main teaching, and dissemination), while others are particular to the structure of the *Vimalakīrti Sutra.* In addition to breaking the text into analytically dense structural divisions, this type of "expository commentary" (*yishu*) also provides explanations of terminology, similes and metaphors, and conceptual frameworks found in the root text. For example, among the standard divisions in this sort of commentary is a discussion of the time and place that the teaching was given. Because the teaching of the *Vimalakīrti Sutra* goes back and forth between two different locations (at Vaiśālī, with Śākyamuni Buddha, then at Vimalakīrti's home, and then back to Vaiśālī) and some parts even take place in buddha lands in far-distant galaxies, the *Commentary* pays considerable attention to the question of exactly who the audience is in these various locales.

Another characteristic of this sort of commentary is that it does not actually include or embed the entirety of the text that it is analyzing, nor does it actually comment on the entire text. Indeed, the *Commentary* seems to slow down as it goes through the text. For example, approximately eighty percent of the *Commentary* is devoted to the first five chapters of the *Vimalakīrti Sutra* (these same five chapters only comprise about forty percent of the sutra itself), while the remaining twenty percent addresses the remaining nine chapters of the sutra. Indeed, while the first chapter of the root text receives eight hundred and forty-two lines of commentary, the final chapter of the sutra gets only twenty-one.

Although the lack of the entire *Vimalakīrti Sutra* together with exegesis of only selected passages (even seemingly randomly selected passages) means that such a commentary must be read together with the original text, scholars are also coming to appreciate the way that an individual author structures a commentary as significant in its own right. We can learn perhaps as much (or even more) about the author's point of view from their structural analysis as we can from their actual commentary. Given the importance of this text in the history of Japanese Buddhism, much contemporary scholarship has been devoted to this task. Although I have not been able to make extensive use of this work for the present translation, it is hoped that this scholarship will also move forward as translations of the other commentaries attributed to Shōtoku Taishi appear.

The present translation of the *Commentary* is from the *Taishō shinshū daizōkyō,* vol. 56, no. 2186. I also consulted Hanayama Shinshō's two Japanese transliterations of the *Commentary,* which are listed in the bibliography. The Chinese version of the *Vimalakīrtinirdeśa,* the root text addressed by this *Commentary,* was translated by Kumārajīva (ca. 350–409). As noted above, only short phrases and snippets of this root text are embedded in the *Commentary,* which will make following the overall narrative of both the root text and the *Commentary* translated here difficult for the reader. Nonetheless, I have consulted the root text extensively for my translation, using the original Chinese translation of the *Vimalakīrti Sutra* of Kumārajīva (Taishō no. 475), the other two Chinese translations of the text (Taishō no. 474, translated by Zhi Qian; and Taishō no. 476, translated by Xuanzang), and the various English translations listed in the bibliography. I have also made great use of the wonderful multilingual text published by Taishō University, which includes the recently discovered Potola Palace Sanskrit manuscript of the *Vimalakīrtinirdeśa* and the Sde dge and Peking editions of the Tibetan translation collated with the three Chinese translations.

While this has greatly helped my understanding of various nuances of the text, in the end my purpose was to translate the Chinese of the *Commentary* as closely as I could imagine it being understood at the time of its composition in a literary Chinese cultural milieu, rather than that of the Sanskrit original. So too, on occasion I consulted the numerous other Chinese commentaries on the *Vimalakīrti Sutra* included in the Taishō canon. Indeed, it was clear at numerous points that the author of the *Commentary* had a distinctly different understanding of the root text than the Sanskrit manuscript would allow, thus also forcing changes to the way that I rendered the embedded root text. The names of the famous buddhas, bodhisattvas, and disciples were as familiar to the Chinese Buddhist as they are to a modern English audience, and so I have generally rendered transliterated terms and well-known proper nouns in Sanskrit (e.g., *prajñā;* Maitreya), but have translated terms and proper names whose Chinese is likewise translated (e.g., the "elder's son Jewel Accumulation" for Ratnākara; "discerning awareness" when *prajñā* has been translated rather than transliterated). Some translated terms I have also rendered in Sanskrit because they have become so well known in English (e.g., samsara and nirvana).

In the translation itself, embedded passages from the root text of Kumārajīva's translation of the *Vimalakīrti Sutra* appear in quote marks. As indicated above, while I believe that the analytic division or outline of an "expository commentary" is important, because it is not explicitly part of the text itself I have not added outline section numbers to the translation, except as they regularly appear in the prose part of the text. In addition, in the interest of clarity and ease of reading, I have simplified the structure somewhat, retaining chapter divisions but omitting additional fascicle and part divisions that appear in the original work.

One aspect of this project that deserves mention is how completely the translation process has changed with the advent of the many sophisticated electronic and Internet tools available to translators. I early on received an electronic version of the *Commentary* that, in keeping with the theme of the sutra itself, had "miraculously appeared" on a colleague's hard drive (subsequently published in the *Saṃgaṇikīkṛtaṃ Taiśotripiṭakaṃ: The Taisho Tripitaka*, www.l.utokyo.ac.jp/~sat/), and electronic versions of virtually all of the other Chinese, Tibetan, and Sanskrit manuscripts of the root text have also been available to me as I worked. In particular, the electronic texts of the Chinese Buddhist Electronic Text Association (CBETA, www.cbeta.org) and Dr. Charles Muller's Digital Dictionary of Buddhism (www.buddhismdict.net/ddb/) were extremely useful in my research. The ability to instantly search the entire Taishō canon for a citation or immediately access innumerable specialized Buddhist dictionaries when searching for the proper nuance of a term has enhanced the work of researchers and translators immeasurably.

I wish to thank my very good friend and colleague Issho Fujita, who kindly read through the entire translation and made countless corrections and suggestions. His warm companionship was as invaluable as his expertise. Jundo Nagashima read the entire translation against the Chinese original for the Publication Committee of Bukkyō Dendō Kyōkai America; as he was part of the team at Taishō University that published the multilingual edition of the *Vimalakīrti Sutra,* his corrections were particularly welcome. Finally, kudos must be given to Marianne Dresser and the staff at BDK America in Berkeley, whose expert eyes and enthusiastic attention to detail in the copyediting phase caught many errors and helped a great deal to make my translation readable. This kind of effort is rare in today's world of academic publishing, and I am deeply grateful. Being part of the Bukkyō Dendō Kyōkai translation project is an honor, and having such a capable team to work with is a joy.

EXPOSITORY COMMENTARY
ON THE VIMALAKĪRTI SUTRA

[Preface]

Composed by Prince Jōgū
(Shōtoku Taishi)

Vimalakīrti was a great sage who had achieved true awakening. To speak of his essence, he was profoundly one with suchness; to discuss his manifestation, he was co-extensive with all things. His virtues crowned the appearance of the many sages and his path exhausted the limits of sentient beings. [For Vimalakīrti,] phenomena were phenomena because they were uncreated, and perceptual attributes were perceptual attributes because they were devoid of perceptual attribute.

How then can we describe [his] name and attributes? Affairs of state are troublesome, but with neverending great compassion he sought to benefit sentient beings. He appeared to be a worldly merchant and lived in the city of Vaiśālī. When his work of teaching was complete and he was about to return to the profound source, he manifested as though physically ill and took to his bed so as to be able to explain the underlying principle of the inconceivable to those who would therefore come to inquire about his illness. Thus Mañjuśrī, knowing that the time was right, accepted the charge to inquire about Vimalakīrti's illness. Manifesting all sorts of miracles, the Mahasattva encouraged the newly declared [bodhisattvas]. Because there is no question but that the essential nature of Vimalakīrti's illness was his great kindness and compassion, the main point of his teaching was to restrain the Small [Vehicle] and spread the Great [Vehicle].

"Vimalakīrti" is the Indian pronunciation; in Chinese it is [translated as] "Pure Reputation." Although his radiance is diffused and he mixes with the impurities [of this world], he is not defiled by his involvement with the world, hence he is called "Pure Reputation." Because of the sublime instructions that he gave, it is called his "teaching." A "scripture" (*jing*) is understood as the law and understood as constant. Although the teaching of the Sage may change with the time and conventions, neither the sages of yore nor the wise

3

ones of later years can change its certainty, and so it is called "constant." Because it is the "rule" of beings it is called "law" (*fa,* Dharma). Of course, "scripture" (*jing*) is a Chinese word; in the foreign language it is called "sutra." The five meanings of "sutra" are as usually explained, [among which the two meanings of "a constant wellspring" of truth and "a plumb line" that is straight like a "rule" are the most important]. Now, while the person [that teaches] and the Dharma [that is taught] are two [different categories], they are the same, and hence [the Chinese word] "scripture" (*jing*) has been used in place of [the foreign word] "sutra." The meaning of "two yet the same" is also as usually explained.

"Liberation," in "Another name is 'The Inconceivable Liberation,'" refers to the two knowledges of the conventional and the real of the eighth level and above. The two knowledges of the essence and manifestation are distinct and are called "inconceivable" because neither is taught within the two vehicles. Moreover, the two knowledges of the conventional and the real are not taught in the same way in the various scriptures. This scripture takes the elucidation of the underlying principle of the two truths to be the real, and the transformational appearance [in the world] in order to benefit [others] to be the conventional. Because both of these two knowledges destroy attachment, it is called "liberation."

This scripture has two names: the first, *Vimalakīrti,* uses a person's name for the title; the second, *Inconceivable Liberation,* uses the teaching as the title. It is on another level from the first title that uses a person's name, and so it is considered another [name for the sutra, that is, a name] according to the teaching.

20b

4

Chapter One

Buddha Realms

The elder's [son] Jewel Accumulation visited [the Buddha] and offered a canopy that, [when opened,] revealed the pure lands of the buddhas of the ten directions. In this way, the practices of the bodhisattvas' pure lands were also extensively revealed. Therefore it is called the chapter "Buddha Realms." If this were like other scriptures, this [chapter] would be called "Introduction." The introductory comments of this scripture, however, are made up of not one but four [chapters] in all, and so, according to the topics [that are discussed], they are given different names and not [grouped together and collectively titled] "Introduction."

As with numerous other scriptures, this scripture first unfolds in three sections: the introductory teaching, the main teaching, and the dissemination of the teachings. The Sage teaches the Dharma to save beings, and the reason for utilizing these three sections is that the underlying principle is very deep and subtle, but the faculties of beings are dull. If they suddenly hear of this deep underlying principle, not only will it be difficult to comprehend but a slanderous mind will arise. For this reason, extraordinary sights that give rise to aspiration in beings are first revealed. The revelations [described in] the introductory comments are thus necessary for the main teaching. If beings have already given rise to aspiration, then there will be no hesitation when the underlying principle [is revealed to them], and therefore the main teaching is given after that.

When both the introduction and main [teaching] have been given, all the sentient beings present will reap benefits. Because the kindness and compassion of the Sage is inexhaustible and [he would ensure that beings] into the far-distant latter ages acquire the same benefit as [those he teaches] now, there is the third part [of the scripture], the dissemination of the teaching.

As for the text, this scripture has fourteen chapters in all. The first four chapters comprise the introductory teaching; from the chapter "Mañjuśrī's Inquiring about the Illness" to where it says, "[the Wondrous Joy world returned to its original place] and all of the assembly saw it" in the chapter "Seeing Akṣobhya Buddha," not quite eight chapters, is the main teaching. From the place in the chapter "[Seeing] Akṣobhya Buddha" where it says, "The Buddha asked Śāriputra, 'Do you see the realm Abhirati and the Buddha Akṣobhya or not?'" [to the end of the scripture], not quite three chapters, comprises the dissemination of the teaching.

The first section, the introductory teaching, is divided into two parts. The first is from the beginning up to the part where [the Buddha, sitting on his lion throne,] "eclipsed the entire vast multitude assembled there," and this is called the common introduction. The second is from "At that time in the city of Vaiśālī there was an elder" to the end of the first fascicle, and this is called the specific introduction.

"Thus" and the rest of the five items [elaborated below] are common to the myriad scriptures, and because the meaning of the revelation is the same, [the first part of the introduction] is called the "common introduction." The various scriptures all have unique introductions as well: sometimes light rays are emitted or the ground shakes; sometimes [the scripture begins with] the sending of a letter or the seeking of alms; this scripture begins with the offering of canopies. Because these various [scenes] are not the same, it is called the specific introduction.

The common introduction is made up of five items. The first is "Thus," the second is "I have heard," the third is "at one time," the fourth is the place [where the scripture is taught], and the fifth is the audience. Although the common introduction is [interpreted as having] five sections, in terms of their inner meaning [these five sections] are divided into three. [The first is that] both "Thus" and "I have heard" are evidence of the fact that the scripture is based on the oral transmission of Ānanda [from the Buddha] and was not just made up by [Ānanda] himself.

The second meaning is that "at one time" discloses the significance of the oral transmission, in that the teaching is delivered in accordance with the spiritual capacity [of the audience at one particular time].

The third meaning is comprised of the dwelling place and the audience, both of which corroborate the above two meanings. Although we say, "[thus have] I heard," we of course "hear" in a [specific] place together with the

other people [in the audience]. Therefore, the dwelling place and the audi- 20c
ence are considered to be corroborations [of the first two meanings].

There are many ways to understand "thus." I rely solely on the tradition
as taught in a particular school. "Thus" refers to "faith," because the teachings of the sages are given so that sentient beings will be able to believe.
Therefore the first utterance is "thus." Hence the *Shilun* says, "The Buddha-
Dharma is like the ocean. Knowing enables one to cross over [to the other
shore of liberation] and faith is what enables one to enter [the vehicle to lib-
eration]; 'Thus' manifests that faith." Dharma Master Sengzhao also agrees
with this interpretation. However, he elaborates the meaning slightly by
adding, "'Thus' is an expression of concurring faith, a faith that agrees with
the truth of what is spoken. If there is agreement, then the path of the teacher
and the student will be fulfilled. The scriptures are neither expensive nor
cheap, but without faith they are not passed on. Therefore the expression
'thus' is used from the start."

"I have heard" shows that Ānanda has personally received [this teaching]
and its transmission is without error. It also aims to [differentiate it from] the
errors of the non-Buddhist paths [that are based upon] personal revelation.

"At one time" indicates that the teaching was given at a particular time
in sympathetic resonance [to the needs of the audience], in accord with each,
so that it was of great benefit to beings.

Next the the dwelling place and the audience are listed and corroborated.

[The text] says that when "The Buddha was staying in the Āmrapālī
grove in Vaiśālī," he taught this Dharma. Vaiśālī means "City of Excellent
Rice." *Āmra* is the name of a fruit, but it is not translated. Dharma Master
Sengzhao also says, "[The *āmra*] is like a peach, but it is not a peach. Previously in other scriptures 'pear' was also used." This scripture was actually
taught in Vimalakīrti's room, but it says "in the Āmrapālī [grove]" because
that is where it was entrusted [to the assembly].

Next the audience is listed and corroborated in order to illustrate "at
one time." It says that [the scripture] was spoken to people in accord with
their spiritual capacities; this also illustrates "I have heard." Because it says
that in this way a number of people listened to [the teaching] together, [we
know] that what they heard was not imagined. Some might wonder if all
the bodhisattvas in the audience were of the eighth level or above. If it has

already been said that it is not limited to those whose spiritual capacity is of the first level and above, how could the spiritual capacity of those of the eighth level and above be an issue for this scripture?

It seems to me that Ānanda enumerated the members of the audience simply because he wished to illustrate "I have heard," rather than precisely showing "at one time." Judging from this, the three assemblies in the audience are given as hearing [this teaching] together, but not in order to censure or praise the degree of their spiritual capacity.

This is explained in detail in two parts. The first is the listing of the retinue that [went to hear the teaching] in Vimalakīrti's room; the second is from "at that time the Buddha, [surrounded and venerated] by countless multitudes of hundreds of thousands," and is the concluding listing of the assembly at Āmrapālī.

As for the first, the listing of the retinue [that went to hear the Dharma] in Vimalakīrti's room, there are three. The *bhikṣu* community is listed first, the community of bodhisattvas is listed second, and the community of ordinary people is listed third. If [these groups] were listed in order of status from the exalted to the lowly, then the bodhisattvas would be listed first. If the order went from the lowly to the exalted then ordinary people would be listed first. Here, however, the *bhikṣu*s are listed first.

In short, this has two meanings. The first is presented according to the phenomenal appearances [of what they do]. The *śrāvaka*s' minds are set on their own salvation and not on transforming others. They are always in attendance at the Buddha's side and do not bestow the teachings [on others]. Hence they are listed first. The bodhisattva's mind is set on benefiting beings, bestowing the teachings on [others] without limit. Bodhisttavas do not always follow the Buddha, and their comings and goings are not fixed. Hence they are listed a bit further on. Ordinary people are ensnared by desire, far from the path, and rarely meet a buddha, and so they are further down in the listing.

The second meaning is presented according to the underlying principle. *Śrāvaka*s spurn samsara and seek nirvana. Ordinary people love samsara and fear nirvana. The two are both mistaken about the profound intention of the Buddha and so lose the Middle Way. Therefore they are listed at the two extremes of first and last. Because the bodhisattvas' minds are set on benefiting sentient beings, they do not scorn samsara [and so do not share the

21a

8

bias of the *śrāvaka*s]. Because they wish to realize the everlasting fruits of the manifold virtues, they do not fear nirvana and so differ from the bias of ordinary people. Marvelously they attain the middle path, and therefore they are listed between these two.

There is no fitting translation for "*bhikṣu*." Bodhisattva Nāgārjuna interpreted the word as having three meanings: 1) [one who] terrorizes Māra, 2) a destroyer of evil, and 3) a seeker of alms. Some say that the reason their virtues are not extolled and their names are not listed [in this scripture] is that surely the main point of this teaching was to restrain the Small [Vehicle] and spread the Great [Vehicle]. If the virtues [of the *bhikṣus*] were praised their attachments would grow stronger, and so they were omitted. [That the scripture] says "[assembly of] great [*bhikṣus*]," however, indicates that it is not a community of nuns (*bhikṣunīs*). In any case, at the time the Buddha taught this scripture, those who heard it together were not yet set up [in this way]. Later, when Ānanda gathered [the scriptures], he profoundly understood the Buddha's intent and so arranged it this way—how could we say that [their names] were omitted in order to censure or praise them?

Moreover, when Ānanda gathered the scriptures it was after [the Buddha had passed away under] the *śāla* trees. All of the *śrāvaka*s had become bodhisattvas. Who among them would still have attachments? Even if it were appropriate that their virtues were not praised [because it would lead to attachment], why aren't they even mentioned, since it would be no problem at all to determine their ranks and list their names? Moreover, I have never heard a thorough interpretation [of this] in the earlier commentaries. It seems to me that the Buddha gave his order to go to [Vimalakīrti] and ask about his illness to five hundred *śrāvaka*s and eight thousand bodhisattvas. Now, therefore, [their names and virtues] are all left out and only ten disciples and four bodhisattvas are mentioned. This being the case, it is also possible that when Maitreya (Ānanda?) gathered the scriptures he knew well the suitability of the physical area, and so omitted and left out [their names and virtues].

Within the listing of the second group, the bodhisattvas, there are five items. The first illustrates the category, which is "bodhisattva." The second gives the number, and this is "thirty-two thousand." The third, from "known to the many people" onward, is the praise of virtues. The fourth is from "The names [of the bodhisattvas] were. . ." and this is the listing of the names.

The fifth is from "[thirty-two thousand bodhisattvas] like this" and concludes the enumeration.

Some say that the main point of this scripture is none other than to praise the twin insights of the bodhisattva and criticize the biased practices of the two vehicles. In other words, the contemplative practice and eradication of the entanglements in the seventh level and below are the same as in the two vehicles. Hence, it is only those of the eighth level and above that are praised. We won't adopt that [view] here.

21b   The first two [of these five items, the category and the number,] can be understood. The third item, the praise of the virtues, is divided into three. The first is from the beginning up to "not lacking in the power of skillful means," and is the shared praise of the bodhisattvas of the three levels from the eighth and above. The second is from "arrived at non-attainment," and is the specific praise of the [bodhisattvas of the] three levels. The third is from "accomplished in all of the countless merits," and is the concluding shared praise of the three levels.

The reason that the shared praise [of the bodhisattvas of the eighth level and above] comes first is because once one enters the contemplation of emptiness in the eighth level and above, there is a prolonged experience of non-differentiation of leaving and entering [nirvana and samsara]. Although it is said that there is no differentiation of leaving and entering [nirvana and samsara], it is not the case that there is no distinction between deep and shallow, and thus the second part praises [each level] separately. Nonetheless, they are the same in the sense of equally surpassing the two vehicles in their benefiting of living beings, and thus the third, concluding part is also shared praise [of the three levels].

The first item, shared praise, also has two sections. The first is the praise of their past deeds; the second, from "in order to defend the fortress of the Dharma," is the praise of their present virtues.

"Known to many people." This means that when great beings (mahā-sattvas) appear in the world and kindly and compassionately transform living beings, they are known by all variety of sentient beings near and far. Dharma Master Sengzhao says, "If the sun and the moon are in the heavens, all those with eyes will see them; when a great being appears in the world, all sentient beings will know them." This line praises their reputation.

"All had entirely accomplished the great knowing and the essential practices." The "great knowing" is the knowing of the Buddha. The myriad practices of the eighth level and above are the "essential practices" [that lead to] the Buddha's knowing. The bodhisattvas of the eighth level and above have already thoroughly cultivated [these practices], and so it says that they "all had entirely accomplished." It is also said that the "great knowing" is the knowing of the eighth level and above; the "essential practices" are of the seventh level and below. However, as was already pointed out, only those bodhisattvas of the eighth level and above are being praised, and so if this referred to [those of] the seventh level [and below], the meaning would be garbled; we don't adopt this [interpretation] here. In fact, this line praises their past deeds.

"Sustained by the numinous authority of the Buddha" takes up the essence of the practice and concludes the praise, showing that the essence of the practice is already exalted—how could the practices born thereof not be profound? Dharma Master Sengzhao says, "Although the moisture of the heavens is impartial, it cannot make a withered tree lush; although the Buddha's authority is universal, it does not support those without the capacity. How vast the capacity for the path must be for those who are supported!"

From "in order to defend the fortress of the Dharma" is the second item [of shared praise], the praise of their present virtues; this item also has two divisions. The first is the diffuse praise; the second is from "minds constantly at peace," and is the praise according to the gate of the Dharma.

As for the first, the diffuse praise, this also has two items. The first is the abbreviated praise of their self-cultivation and their transformation of others. The second, from "able to roar the lion's roar," is the extensive praise of their self-cultivation and their transformation of others.

"In order to defend the fortress of the Dharma"—There are two functions of a "fortress" in this world: the first is that evil outsiders cannot invade; the second is the royal path that flows through it. The internal correspondence [of this simile] is that bodhisattvas above the eighth level subjugate the demon Deva-Māra and prevail over the those on non-Buddhist paths, and so have the same meaning as a worldly fortress that cannot be invaded by evil outsiders. Protecting the Buddha-Dharma and spreading the Mahayana has the same meaning as the royal path that goes through a worldly fortress;

21c   therefore it says "In order to defend." This line constitutes the abbreviated praise of the [bodhisattva's] transformation of others.

"Receiving and holding the true Dharma"—the teaching of the Sage is equivalent to the underlying principle and not false, therefore it is "true." Because it is a guideline for sentient beings, it is the "law" (Dharma). Because the bodhisattvas above the eighth level are steadfast in their acceptance [of the Dharma] and do not let it go, it says "receiving and holding."

From "able to roar the lion's roar" is the second item, the extensive praise of [the bodhisattvas'] self-cultivation and their transformation of others. Within this are six lines; the first four lines detail [the praise of] their transformation of others, and the last two lines detail [the praise of] their self-cultivation.

"Able to roar the lion's roar"—they are able to preach the Dharma to the multitudes without fear, which is the same as the roar of a lion that does not fear being hunted by a pack.

"Their names were heard in the ten directions"—because all under heaven is filled with [the bodhisattvas'] good works, all who have ears hear of them. This line is similar to the praise of their reputation but because it says that their "names were heard," it corroborates the virtue of the lion's roar, and illustrates how because of their superb virtue their names fill the ten directions. This line [illustrates] "Above, broaden the path of the Buddha."

"Without being asked they befriended people and comforted them"— because the bodhisattvas' kindness and compassion do not await the people's entreaties, it says, "without being asked." Teaching and transforming sentient beings, the same highest fruits are realized, and so it says "befriended and comforted them." Dharma Master Sengzhao says, "The true friend in direct contact with the underlying principle awaits no invitation. Their care is like a loving mother going to her child." This line illustrates "Below, transform myriad living beings."

"Transmitting and enriching the Three Jewels so that they will never die out." Because they widely spread the scriptures and teachings, the Dharma Jewel will never die out. Because there will always be those who receive and practice [the Dharma,] the Sangha Jewel will never die out. Cultivating virtue in accordance with the teachings, [beings] will ultimately attain omniscience and thus the Buddha Jewel will never die out. Building upon the above, "able to roar the lion's roar," this fully explains the earlier [phrase], "royal path that goes through it." This line illustrates "Above, broaden the path of the Buddha."

"Defeating Māra, prevailing over those on the many non-Buddhist paths." Bodhisattvas do not intentionally manifest their authority because they want to vanquish [Māra and heretics]. Rather, Māra is the master of heretical views, and when he sees the great beings (*mahāsattvas*) propagating the path, he is shamed of his own accord; because of this meaning, it says "defeating" and "prevailing." Māra is said to be "defeated" and those on non-Buddhist paths are described as [having been] "prevailed over." Because Māra well knows that he is wrong and gives rise to an evil mind desiring to destroy the Buddha-Dharma, he is said to be vanquished. Those on non-Buddhist paths, on the other hand, are in search of the true path but their understanding is grasping and contrary to the teaching; hence, they are said to be "prevailed over." This verse illustrates "Below, transform and nurture living beings." It also builds upon the earlier [phrase], "befriend without being asked," as well as detailing the above, "not invaded by evil outsiders."

"Completely pure and forever free from obstruction and afflictions." These two expressions detail the "self-cultivation" mentioned above. Because [bodhisattvas] skillfully receive and hold the true Dharma, the three activities [of body, speech, and mind] are entirely pure, and they are also able to be forever free from the five obstructions and the ten afflictions.

From "minds constantly at peace" is the second aspect of the praise of [the bodhisattvas'] present virtues—that is to say, praise according to the Dharma gates [through which they have passed]. There are seven types of Dharma gates. The first is unobstructed liberation; the second is that their thoughts are established in correct mindfulness; the third is their concentration that is a state of concentration devoid of perceptual attribute; the fourth is their total retention [of the Buddha's teachings, i.e., retention through the use of *dhāraṇīs*]; the fifth is their eloquence, which refers to the four perfect manners of speech and teaching; the sixth is [their mastery of] the six per- 22a fections; and the seventh is their skillful means. These can be understood by examining the text.

From "Arrived at the state of non-attainment" onward is the second aspect among the praises of the [bodhisattva's] virtues, the specific praise of the three levels; this has three topics. The first is from the beginning up to "like reverberating thunder," and is the specific praise of the eighth level. The second is from "without measure," and is the specific praise of the ninth level. The third is from "nearly equal with the unequaled [buddhas]," and is the specific praise of the tenth level. Each of these three [topics] has two aspects: One is establishing the rank and the other is the actual praise of the virtues.

"Arrived at the state of non-attainment and the serene acceptance of the non-arising of *dharma*s" is [establishing] the rank. From "They were able to be in accord [when turning the irreversible wheel]" is the actual praise of their virtue. In reaching the essence of the ultimate principle, there is no distinction between one who attains and that which is attained, hence it is called "non-attainment." "Arrived" means "to attain." Because their clear understanding attains to this underlying principle, it says "arrived at non-attainment."

"Serene acceptance" means [discerning] awareness. Because they are well at ease in the underlying principle of the non-arising of phenomena, it says "serene acceptance." Having attained this understanding, there is no more coursing in the two extremes of existence and nonexistence; therefore it says "non-arising."

The actual praise of the virtue is elaborated in three items. The first is the praise of the lower level of serene acceptance; the second, from "their deep faith is firm," is the praise of the middle level of serene acceptance; the third, from "deeply penetrated interdependent origination," is the praise of the superior degree of serene acceptance.

The lower level of serene acceptance also has three aspects. The first is the praise of the virtue; the second is from "merit and discerning awareness," and is the praise of the body; the third is from "their fame and honor towered above [Mount Sumeru]," and is the praise of their reputation.

"They were able to be in accord [with the needs of beings] when turning the irreversible wheel." In general, "reversible" has three aspects. The first is the level that is reversible; the second is the practice that is reversible; and the third is the thought that is reversible. Endowed with the profound Dharma of the three irreversible attainments, the Tathāgata widely teaches the three things that can be reversed. Here, in accordance with the Buddha, bodhisattvas of the eighth level also skillfully turn the wheel of the profound Dharma of the irreversible attainments. Within the world they widely proclaim the three things that can be reversed. A wheel is something that is able to turn and thereby deliver things; the Buddha-Dharma too is well able to turn sentient beings toward the fruits of buddhahood; hence it is called the "wheel of the Dharma." This line praises the virtue of tranforming others.

"Thoroughly understanding the attributes of *dharma*s and knowing the capacity of sentient beings." "Attributes of *dharma*s" refers to the underlying principle of the two truths and the phenomenal attributes of the Great and Small Vehicles. "Knowing the capacity" refers to knowing the sharp or dull faculties of beings and their aspirations. These two lines praise the bodhisattvas' ability to know the disease and identify the medicine. This also refers to their self-cultivation.

"Surpassing all in the great assembly, fearing nothing." This is a concluding summary of the praise of the bodhisattvas' self-cultivation and their transformation of others, and shows how both virtues surpass those of the multitudes. Because their profound understanding goes beyond the limits of the two vehicles, they surpass all in the great assembly and fear nothing.

From "Merit and discerning awareness" is the second item [of the actual praise of the lower level of serene acceptance], the praise of their bodies. "They cultivated their minds with merit and discerning awareness" is the praise of their minds.

"The attributes and marks adorned their bodies and their physical form was unsurpassed." The "attributes" are the thirty-two attributes of a great being; the "physical form" refers to the eighty marks of a great being. If we gloss "unsurpassed" with reference to things, there is nothing in the triple world that is superior; if we interpret it according to the underlying principle, they have cut off the bonds of karmic retribution; hence they are called "unsurpassed."

"Abandoned worldly beautification" raises some issues. There are three 22b interpretations. The first is that although the essence of the Dharma body is originally without physical attributes, confused beings see them; hence it means "abandoned the physical attributes seen by worldly beings." The second interpretation is that although the bodhisattvas have fundamentally abandoned worldly beautification, they posses only transcendent adornments; hence it means "abandoned worldly beautification." The third is that the word "abandon" means "different," and that because the physical attributes of the bodhisattvas of the eighth level are all produced from the profound source, this is different from worldly beautification.

"Their fame and honor towered above Mount Sumeru" is the third aspect [of the praise of the lower level of the bodhisattvas' serene acceptance], the praise of their fame. Because the inner and outer virtues of the bodhisattvas of the eighth level are naturally accomplished, their wonderful reputation is heard far and wide, and so it towers above Mount Sumeru.

From "their deep faith is firm" is the second aspect, the praise of the middle level of the bodhisattvas' serene acceptance. Within this are the two aspects of self-cultivation and transforming others.

Their faith in the unborn [nature of phenomena] is unshakable; it is like the strength of an adamantine thunderbolt (*vajra*); this line praises their self-cultivation.

"The jewel of their Dharma universally illuminated and rained down like nectar." Because their profound understanding gives guidelines to beings, it is called "law" (Dharma). Because it is valued by the myriad sages, it is called a "jewel." Because they completely illumine spiritual capacities in a single instant of thought, it says "universally illuminated." Nectar is a medicine that is able to increase the life of the gods; because the profound understanding of the eighth-level bodhisattvas is also capable of leading beings and maturing the wisdom-life of the Dharma body, nectar is used here as a metaphor.

"Within the assembly, the subtlety and delicacy of the sound of their words were unsurpassed." This clarifies the delicate resonances of the eight vocal qualities used to teach in accord with the spiritual capacity.

From "Deeply enter interdependent origination" is the third aspect, that is, the praise of the superior level of the [bodhisattvas'] serene acceptance. Within this aspect there are, again, the two aspects of self-cultivation and transformation of others. "Deeply enter interdependent origination" indicates that they have realized the nonexistence of defiled sense objects of material form. This line praises their knowledge. "Abandoning myriad false views" refers to the confusion of the ten defilements, none of which are true; hence, they are collectively labeled "false views."

"No vestigial influence of the two extreme [views] of existence and nonexistence remained." The two views of annihilation and permanent existence are not in accord with the middle path, and therefore they are called extreme views. These two lines deal with abandoning; hence, up to this point is the praise of their self-cultivation.

"Their proclamation of the Dharma is as fearless as the roar of a lion." Their teaching of the Dharma is in accord with the spiritual capacity [of the audience] and without the slightest error of fear. This line clarifies "Above, broaden the path of the Buddha."

"Their sermons and lectures resounded like thunder" indicates that their kind and compassionate teaching of the Dharma benefits beings, just as spring thunderstorms nurture the hundred grasses. These two lines praise their transformation of others. The middle and upper levels of serene acceptance also should be specifically praised in terms of the reputation and the body, but they have already been lauded within the praise of the lower level of serene acceptance.

From "Immeasurable" is the second aspect of specific praise, the praise of the ninth level. Within this there are again two aspects. The first establishes the rank, and the second, from "accumulated the myriad jewels of the Dharma," is the actual praise of their virtuous qualities.

"Immeasurable." Material *dharma*s have measurable form. Mental *dharma*s do not have measurable form. The bodhisattvas of the ninth level thoroughly penetrate the realm of mental function, and so it says that they are "immeasurable."

They have passed beyond the limits of material form, and therefore it says "passed beyond measure." Dharma Master Sengzhao has a slightly different interpretation: "Having already attained the Dharma body, the bodhi-   22c
sattvas have entered the realm of the unconditioned. Their minds cannot be sought by means of knowledge; their form cannot be grasped by their shape. Therefore, it says 'immeasurable.' The sixth level and below is called 'measurable.'" Therefore it says "passed beyond measure."

From "accumulated the myriad jewels of the Dharma" is the second aspect of the praise, the actual praise of [the bodhisattvas'] virtuous qualities. Within this, too, there is praise of their self-cultivation as well as praise of their transformation of others.

"Accumulated the myriad jewels of the Dharma and were like guides on an ocean." This means that [the bodhisattvas] lead myriad living beings and together embark upon the ocean of the Dharma, encouraging and exhorting them to cultivate virtue, ultimately attaining the treasure of merit and discerning awareness. The meaning is the same as a guide taking a group of merchants and together embarking on the great ocean, skillfully teaching them how to get jewels and enabling them to reap great profit. This line is praise of their transformation of others.

"Completely understood the profound meaning of the myriad *dharma*s." This means that [the bodhisattvas] completely understood the emptiness of the provisionally real. This line explains that [the bodhisattvas] are skilled at identifying the medicine [appropriate for various maladies].

"They well know the prior and potential tendencies of all beings [and the workings of their minds]." "Prior" means past and "potential" refers to the future; "tendencies" refers to the reasons for the arising of the disease; "workings of their minds" means good and evil. These two lines clarify that the [bodhisattvas] are able to know the cause of the arising of disease. This all praises their self-cultivation. Although understanding the medicine and knowing the disease seem to refer to transforming others, it does not yet include others, so this refers to self-cultivation. In my opinion, [if one's goal is to] lead [sentient beings] and gather treasure, how could it be that one would be able to benefit others if one doesn't personally understand the disease and discern the medicine? If that is the case, we can say that "self-cultivation" goes together with "transformation of others." The difference is that the former line praises the kind mind of arousing aspiration in "Above, broaden the path of the Buddha," and the latter line praises the compassionate mind that eliminates the sufferings [of others] in "Below, transform and nurture living beings." That the praise of their fame and bodies are not distinguished can be inferred from the above example of the praise of the [fame and bodies of bodhisattvas of the] eighth level; hence, they are not praised. We can also say that because [bodhisattvas of] the ninth level have passed beyond the limits of material form, it is in accordance with their accomplishments that their fame and bodies are not praised [separately].

From "nearly equal with the unequaled [buddhas]" is the third aspect of the specific praise, the praise of the tenth level. Within this there are again two aspects: first, establishing the level; and second, from "barricaded all [the gates to the various evil destinies]," the actual praise of the virtue. "Equal with the unequaled" means that although the buddha path cannot be equaled, the many buddhas attain it equally; hence, it is said to be "equal with the unequaled." Bodhisattvas of the tenth level are very near to the fruit of buddhahood, and therefore it says "nearly equal with the unequaled [buddhas]." From "the unhindered [discerning] awareness of a buddha" lists the virtues of the unequaled abode. In describing these sorts of virtues, it therefore says "unequaled." Although bodhisattvas of the tenth level have not yet completely perfected the [discerning] awareness of a buddha, they have drawn near.

From "barricaded all [the gates to the various evil destinies]" is the second aspect, the actual praise of the virtue; this also has [the two aspects] of self-cultivation and the transformation of others.

"Barricaded all the gates to the various evil destinies." The fruits of the five paths of existence are in principle unwholesome. Therefore, they are collectively called the evil destinies. Bodhisattvas of the tenth level have already 23a gone beyond the retribution of these five paths, and therefore it says "barricaded." Not being born within the five paths is not limited to [bodhisattvas of] the tenth level—those of the first [level] are also [not born within the five paths]. However, it is in the tenth level that all causes for birth [in the five paths] are thoroughly eradicated, and therefore what is praised about the tenth level is not being born [within the five paths]. This line praises their self-cultivation.

From "nonetheless were born into the five paths" is the praise of [the bodhisattvas'] transformation of others. "Nonetheless were born into the five paths and manifested their bodies" clarifies that although the Dharma body is unborn, [bodhisattvas] appear to undergo birth only because they wish to transform beings.

From "As great physician kings" interprets the meaning of bodhisattvas' appearance [in the world]. It clarifies how, due to their simple wish to benefit beings, their [real nature] is unborn, yet they appear to undergo birth.

From "countless merits" is the third aspect of the praise of [the bodhisattvas'] virtues, the concluding shared praise of the three levels. Within this there are three parts. The first is the shared praise of their self-cultivation and transformation of others. The second, from "Those who saw or heard them," is the shared praise of their lack of error with regard to the spiritual capacities of those whom they convert to the path. The third part, from "In this way," is the concluding praise.

"Accomplished all the countless merits" is the shared praise of their self-cultivation. "Adorned and purified all the countless buddha lands" is the shared praise of the [bodhisattvas'] transformation of others. "Of those who saw or heard them, there were none that did not benefit, and none of their countless deeds were done in vain" is the praise of their lack of error with regard to the spiritual capacities of those whom they convert to the path. Because it shows how their conversion of beings to the path is without mistake in accordance with the spiritual capacities of those beings, all those who saw or heard them benefited. This also shows how none of their deeds were in vain. "In this way they were fully endowed with all merits" is the third, concluding praise.

From "Their names were. . ." is the fourth feature [of the bodhisattvas], the listing of their names. In all, there are thirty-two thousand bodhisattvas, but here only the names of fifty-two are listed. "There were thirty-two thousand bodhisattvas like this" is the fifth feature, the conclusion of the enumeration.

From "There were also ten thousand *brahmadevas*, Śikhin, and others" is the third group among the audience, the listing of ordinary people. Within this [group] there are four types. The first is the listing of the Brahmā kings of the world of form; the second is from "There were also twelve thousand [Indras]," and is the listing of Indras in the world of desire; the third, from "and there were also other great and powerful [heavenly beings]," is the listing of the eightfold assembly. The fourth is from "many *bhikṣus*," and is the listing of the assembly of human beings.

"Śikhin" is the name of a Brahmā king. In Chinese he is called "[Flaming] Tuft of Hair." He does not live here, and so it says that he came "came [down] from the other [worlds]." "Indra," the Emperor of Heaven, dwells at the summit of Mount Sumeru in the heaven of the thirty-three deities; this is a listing of the deities of the desire realm.

The third is the listing of the eightfold assembly. There are two types of "*nāga*s." The first is the *nāga* of the earth and the second is the *nāga* of the skies; there are four different ways that *nāga*s are born. "Spirits" experience the fruits of good and evil; in form they are superior to a human being but inferior to the gods; their bodies are light and subtle and difficult to know.

"*Yakṣa*s" are called *qingjian* in Chinese. There are three kinds. The first dwells and flies about in the sky; the second dwells on earth; the third dwells

23b

20

in heaven and constantly guards the gates of the heavens. "*Gandharva*s" are celestial musicians. They dwell above the earth in the Jewel Mountains. When the *deva*s wish music, they create diverse forms, appear, and then quickly leave. "*Asura*s" are also rendered in Chinese as "spirits without wings." The male spirits are ugly, while the females are vivacious. They are very strong and fight with the *deva*s. "*Garuḍa*s" are golden-winged bird spirits. "*Kiṃnara*s" are also celestial musicians. They are more lowly than the *gandharva*s and resemble human beings, though they have a single horn on their heads. "*Mahoraga*s" are snakes of the earth; legless, they go about on their bellies. This eightfold assembly of spirits uses spiritual powers to transform into human shape and they sit together to listen to the Dharma.

From "many *bhikṣu*s" is the fourth listing, the listing of the assembly of human beings. The reason that they are listed after the spirits is that the spirits are envoys of the heavenly [realms], and thus human beings are listed after [all residents of the] heavens. These *bhikṣu*s are of the category of home-departed ones among ordinary people, and so they are listed last.

From "at that time the Buddha, [surrounded and venerated by countless multitudes of hundreds of thousands]" is the second aspect of the listing of the audience, completing the listing of those at the Buddha's side. Those at the Buddha's side refers to the assembly at Āmrapālī. Although this scripture was actually taught in Vimalakīrti's room, the reason that the listing of those at the Buddha's side [at Āmrapālī] is given last is because at the end both assemblies came together as one in order for [the teaching to be] entrusted to the [entire] assembly. Thus the complete listing of the two assemblies fully explains "I heard." Still, the assembly that gathered in Vimalakīrti's room was not as large as that at Āmrapālī, and so only the Āmrapālī assembly was given to conclude [the listing].

"At that time the Buddha, surrounded and venerated by countless [multitudes of hundreds of thousands], taught the Dharma for them." "That time" is from the point of view of Ānanda's later recounting in the council this earlier teaching of the Dharma, therefore it says "that time." It could also refer to "that time" when the assembly from Vimalakīrti's room was about to come.

"Taught the Dharma for the countless multitudes" means that the Buddha taught the Dharma for the assembly at Āmrapālī before the assembly from Vimalakīrti's room arrived.

From "Like Mount Sumeru, king of mountains" further illustrates the appearance of the assembly at that time. "Eclipsed the entire vast multitude assembled there" refers to the assembly that went to visit Vimalakīrti. However, if we consider the above with the fact that at the beginning of the specific introduction it also says "at that time," then this could mean "at that time" when the assembly from Vimalakīrti's house had arrived at the gathering and the elder's [son] Jewel Accumulation arrived and offered the canopy. However, the elder's [son] Jewel Accumulation offered the canopy before Vimalakīrti's assembly had arrived, and so it cannot be so.

Therefore one commentator says that because the teaching of the Dharma at Āmrapālī continued without a break, the Buddha was preaching the Dharma for the assembly at Āmrapālī even before the arrival of Vimalakīrti's retinue; that was when the elder's [son] Jewel Accumulation arrived and offered the canopy. If, however, it refers to the time when Vimalakīrti's assembly had already gathered, then the elder's [son] Jewel Accumulation joined the Āmrapālī [assembly] to make one assembly. Hence, we should know that when it says "countless multitudes" it includes Jewel Accumulation. From this, we can infer that when Ānanda recounted the preaching of the Dharma at Āmrapālī he simply wished to clarify the initial appearance of the arrival of Vimalakīrti's entourage.

The reason we know that this preaching of the Dharma must have been taught for the assembly at Āmrapālī prior to the arrival of Vimalakīrti's assembly—and that "the vast multitude assembled there" also refers to Vimalakīrti's entourage—is that at the beginning of the "Practices of the Bodhisattva" chapter in the third fascicle, it says that when the Buddha was preaching the Dharma at Āmrapālī, Vimalakīrti and Mañjuśrī led the assembly from Vimalakīrti's room to pay their respects to the Buddha.

Another understanding is that from "that time" belongs to the specific introduction. In interpreting "that time," it is because it is from the point of view of Ānanda's later recounting in the council this earlier teaching of the Dharma that it says, "that time." As before, "taught the Dharma for the countless multitudes" is understood as referring to [the Dharma] taught [for the assembly] at Āmrapālī. "The vast multitude assembled there" refers to the time of the preaching the Dharma for the assembly at Āmrapālī before [the two groups] had come together; the other assembly [from Vimalakīrti's house]

23c

had yet to arrive. This school [of interpretation] takes it that, in general, Ānanda describes the teaching of the Dharma at Āmrapālī because he wishes to depict it as beginning with Jewel Accumulation's arrival [with his retinue] and offering their canopies. However, there is then the matter of the specific introduction also having "at that time," which would naturally be unnecessary.

Another interpretation takes it that there are two groups within the listing of the audience. The first is the listing of the actual audience. The second, from "at that time the Buddha, [surrounded and venerated by countless multitudes of hundreds of thousands]," is the condensed description [of how the Buddha] appeared when teaching the Dharma to the assembly for the sake of the entrustment. "The vast multitude assembled there" is either referring to [the assembly gathered] at the time of the preaching of the Dharma for the sake of the entrustment, or to the other assembly that came [from Vimalakīrti's house]. This school takes Ānanda's description of this teaching of the Dharma to be simply an abbreviated description of the time of the preaching of the Dharma for the sake of the entrustment, not a description beginning with Jewel Accumulation's offering of the canopy nor a description of the arrival of the entourage from Vimalakīrti's room. The subsequent "at that time" simply refers to the time when the Tathāgata had Vimalakīrti expound the inconceivable and the elder's [son] Jewel Accumulation arrived to offer the canopy.

From "At that time in the city of Vaiśālī" is the second part of the introductory teaching, the specific introduction. It is divided into three parts: 1) The "Buddha Realms" chapter is called the starting point of the introduction; 2) the "Skillful Means" chapter is called the introduction that describes the virtues; 3) the two chapters on "The Disciples" and "The Bodhisattvas" are called the part of the introduction that reveals [Vimalakīrti's] virtues.

The reason [that this is called the starting point of the specific introduction] is that Vimalakīrti and Jewel Accumulation are both great beings of the Dharma body, companions forever protecting the fortress of the Dharma. Enjoying their travels together and their dwellings, they always eat and rest together. This time, however, Jewel Accumulation has come by himself and Vimalakīrti has not come. Knowing that Vimalakīrti has not come because of his illness, [the Buddha] sent Mañjuśrī to inquire of his illness. This leads to [Vimalakīrti's] disclosure of the underlying principle of the inconceivable; hence this part of the introduction is called the starting point.

This part [of the introduction] is unpacked in five items. The first explains the offering of the canopies by Jewel Accumulation and the others. The second, from "the Buddha's numinous authority," explains Buddha receiving the canopies; the third, from "at that time everybody in the great assembly," explains how the great assembly praised the unprecedented display and reverenced him with the three actions [of body, speech, and mind]. The fourth aspect [of this part of the introduction] is from "the elder's son Jewel Accumulation," and describes Jewel Accumulation's vision of the pure lands of the ten directions manifested within the canopy and his subsequent inquiry as to the cause and results of the pure lands. The fifth aspect is from "The Buddha said 'Excellent, Jewel Accumulation!'", and is the Tathāgata's extensive explanation of the causes and results of the pure lands, whereby the question is answered.

"That time" refers to "that time" when the Tathāgata had Vimalakīrti teach the inconceivable. It also refers to "that time" when the Buddha was in Āmrapālī and taught the Dharma for the assembly.

Within the second aspect, the Tathāgata's receiving of the canopies, there are four items. The first is when the five hundred canopies become one. The second is from "spread over the three thousand [worlds]," and explains how the canopy spread over [the universe]. The third is from "also [covered] the three thousand realms," and describes the various things that appeared because of the canopy. The fourth is from "and the ten directions," and describes the appearance of the pure lands of the ten directions and the many buddhas preaching the Dharma [therein].

The five hundred canopies fusing together as one has, in short, three meanings. The first is that the main point of this sutra is none other than the teaching of the inconceivable. Because the Tathāgata is already the master of this teaching, he also is the first to manifest an aspect of the inconceivable; this, then, is a foretaste of Vimalakīrti's teaching of the inconceivable. The second meaning is the wish to demonstrate that although the causal practices differ, the fruit that is obtained is the one fruit of the Dharma body. The third meaning is that [the Buddha] wished to dispel the discriminating minds of the five hundred elders' [sons], and therefore he fused the [canopies] into one.

The second aspect [of the Buddha's receiving the canopies, after making them one,] is when [the single canopy] "spread over the three thousand worlds." This seeks to show that the Tathāgata's kindness and compassion is universal and covers the six realms. The third aspect, manifesting the various things [within the canopy], intends to show that the Tathāgata's illumination reaches everywhere in the *dharmadhātu*. The fourth aspect, making visible the pure lands of the ten directions, is because the Buddha wishes to cause sentient beings to pursue the pure, discard the polluted, and earnestly cultivate virtue.

The third item, reverencing [the Buddha] with the three activities [of body, speech, and mind], can be understood.

The fourth item, [Jewel Accumulation's inquiry about the practices that created the pure lands,] has two aspects. The first is the praise of the Tathāgata's miraculous powers. The second is from "at that time the elder's son," and is the actual inquiry.

The first aspect of praise has thirty-six verses of praise in total; they are divided into nine categories.

The first [category] is the two verses that praise the Buddha's three activities [of body, speech, and mind]. The second is the two verses from "we have seen the Great Sage perform a miraculous transformation," and is the praise of his fusing the canopies into one and thereby causing the pure lands of the ten directions to appear. The third is the five verses from "the Dharma King's power of Dharma surpasses all beings," and is the praise of the Buddha's possessing the virtues of a Dharma King. The fourth [category of praise] is the six verses from "first subduing Māra beneath the *bodhi* tree with your power," and is the praise of the virtue of the Buddha's entire lifetime spent transforming [sentient beings]. The fifth is the two verses from "like Mount Sumeru, unmoved by insult or honor," and is the praise of the Buddha's impartial kindness. The sixth is the four verses from "now we offer these humble canopies to the World-honored One," and is the praise of the Buddha's joining the canopies, spreading them to cover the three thousand worlds, and manifesting therein the myriad phenomena. The seventh is the eight verses from "Great Sage and Dharma King, refuge of the multitude," and is the praise of the two mysteries of the Buddha's body and speech. The eighth is the four verses from "we bow to the unflagging vigor of your ten powers," and is the praise of the two virtues of the Buddha's knowing and his eradication [of entanglements.] The ninth is the three verses from "completely knows the

24b

nature of the comings and goings of all sentient beings" and is the praise of the Buddha's twin knowledge of the true and the conventional.

"Eyes pure and broad as a blue lotus." Within the body the eyes are higher and so the praise begins there; this line praises [the Buddha's] physical actions.

"Mind purified, already perfected in myriad meditative concentrations." This is the praise of [the Buddha's] mental actions.

"Long accumulating pure karma, immeasurably praiseworthy." This corroborates the above two actions [of body and mind], and shows that [the Buddha] has obtained this excellent reward because of long cultivating pure actions.

"Guiding the assembly with quiescence—we bow to you!" This is praise of the [Buddha's] action of speech.

The second [category] is the praise of his fusing the canopies [into one] and thereby causing the pure lands of the ten directions to appear, and can be understood.

The third, the praise of the Buddha's possessing the virtues of the Dharma King, is spread over three [aspects of his virtue]. The first is the initial line, which is the actual praise of the virtue of the Dharma King, who is called "Dharma King" because he has obtained mastery of all *dharmas*. Because he subdues Deva-Māra and prevails over the many non-Buddhist paths, it speaks of his "power of Dharma." These two virtues transcend the multitudes, and so it says, "surpasses all beings." The second is the following single line that interprets "Dharma King." This explains that because he is "constantly bestowing the treasure of the Dharma to all," he is called the "Dharma King."

From "skillfully discriminating" is the third, giving the attributes of the treasure of the Dharma. This is further divided into two. First, the initial two verses are the common teaching that shows how [the Buddha] teaches existence without contradicting [the teaching of] nonexistence; second, the latter two verses are the distinct teaching that shows how [the Buddha] teaches nonexistence without contradicting [the teaching of] existence. Not distinguishing the conventional and real is called the common teaching; distinguishing the conventional and real is called the distinct teaching. "Skillfully discriminating the many attributes of *dharmas*" means to illuminate and penetrate the meaning of the causes and conditions of provisional existence.

"Unwavering in the ultimate meaning." The word "waver" is contrary [to the truth of nonexistence]. Although penetrating the underlying principle of conventional existence, there is yet no contradiction with the underlying principle of true nonexistence. These two lines truly clarify how he teaches existence without contradicting [the teaching of] nonexistence.

"Already obtained mastery of all *dharma*s" explains how [the Buddha] is able to teach existence without contradicting [the teaching of] nonexistence. This shows that he has such an attainment because he has already obtained mastery of all *dharma*s.

"Therefore we bow to this Dharma King" is the conclusion.

From "teaching that *dharma*s do not exist [nor are they nonexistent]" is the second [of the third level of praise of the Tathāgata's miraculous powers], the distinct teaching that explains how the [Buddha's] teaching of nonexistence does not contradict [the teaching of] existence. "Teaching that 24c *dharma*s do not exist nor are they nonexistent" means that real *dharma*s are entirely empty; hence it says that they "do not exist." If existence is nonexistent, how can nonexistence be nonexistent? Hence it says "nor are they nonexistent." One interpretation takes it that "nor are they nonexistent" means that the conventional truth is not nonexistent.

"*Dharma*s arise due to causes and conditions" means that existence and nonexistence are without a fixed existence but come into being solely due to causes and conditions. These two lines clarify the teaching that the nonexistence of real *dharma*s does not contradict the existence of real *dharma*s.

"No self, no doing, no one who receives [the fruits of doing]" shows that the self, the doer [of actions], and the one who receives [the fruits of actions] are all entirely empty; hence it says that they "do not exist."

"Yet good and evil karma is not lost." This shows that although the ultimate truth is nonexistence, the conventional truth is not nonexistent; hence, it says that "[good and evil karma] is not lost." These two lines clarify that the teaching of the nonexistence of the provisional designation does not contradict the existence of the provisional designation.

The fourth category [of verses of praise] is the praise of the Buddha's entire lifetime spent transforming [sentient beings]; the six verses are further divided into three. The first two verses praise the Buddha's initial awakening and *samādhi*. The next three verses praise his preaching of the Dharma after obtaining buddhahood. The third is the final single verse that is the concluding homage.

"First subduing Māra beneath the *bodhi* tree with your power." This shows that the Buddha first subdued Māra beneath the *bodhi* tree.

"Attaining the nectar of extinction and awakening to the path" shows that [the Buddha] obtained the sweet nectar of extinction (nirvana) and attained omniscience.

"Without intention or action you have already vanquished all the non-Buddhist paths." This explains that the Buddha did not intentionally assert his authority, wishing to vanquish [non-Buddhists] and make them accept the true path; rather, he established the truth and the false was thereby naturally vanquished. One interpretation takes it that this line praises the [Buddha's] actions before his attainment [of awakening]. "Without intention or action" refers to when the Buddha followed non-Buddhist paths, without the slightest mind to follow those practices but solely desiring to overcome them and turn away from the false to enter the true.

The second [of the three categories of the praise of the Buddha's lifetime of transforming sentient beings,] the three verses that praise his preaching the Dharma after obtaining buddhahood, is divided into two. The first two verses praise his twelve years of teaching concerning the [conditioned] perceptual attributes, and the third verse praises his thirty-year–long preaching of the *prajñā*[*pāramitā*] within the five periods [of his teaching career].

"Three turnings of the wheel of the Dharma in the great chiliocosm" refers to the teaching of the four truths. "Three turnings" refers to 1) the affirmation [of the Four Noble Truths]; 2) the teaching [that the Four Noble Truths should be followed]; and 3) the benefits [that are obtained, that is, direct knowledge of the Four Noble Truths]. This means that through the turnings [of the wheel of the Dharma,] multitudes of beings give rise to the three kinds of knowing.

"The wheel, primordially and forever pure." This means that the underlying principle of the four truths that extinguishes obstacles and gives rise to understanding is primordial and unchanging.

"The heavenly beings and people who attained the path are its proof." This refers to Kauṇḍinya and the others of the original five disciples obtaining the fruits of arhatship and eighty-thousand heavenly beings obtaining the stage of stream-enterer (*śrota-āpanna*).

"The Three Jewels appeared in this world." Having attained awakening to the way, he is the Buddha Jewel; [the wheel] of the four truths that was turned became the Dharma Jewel on its own; Kauṇḍinya and the five disciples by themselves became the Sangha Jewel.

"By this profound Dharma saving myriad living beings" means that [the teaching of] the *prajñā[pāramitā]* within the five periods [of his teaching career] is more profound than the teaching of perceptual attributes.

"Once receiving [this Dharma] there is no regression, only eternal quiescence" means that some sentient beings among the three vehicles that only hear of the four truths of the existence of perceptual attributes regress; those, however, who hear of the nonexistence of perceptual attributes attain the undefiled true understanding and will never again revert to the world of samsara.

The verse beginning with "Putting an end to old age, sickness, and death" is the concluding homage. Some say that all three verses praise the twelve years [during which the Buddha] preached the teaching of perceptual attributes; if so desired, this [interpretation] can also be used.

The two verses from "[Like Mount Sumeru,] unmoved by insult or honor" are the fifth category of praise: praise of the Buddha's virtue of impartiality. Unmoved by the eight winds [that fan the emotions, the Buddha] is likened to Mount Sumeru. The eight winds are praise and censure, suffering and joy, profit and loss, and defamation and commendation.

"With equal kindness for the virtuous and nonvirtuous" clarifies that the Tathāgata is equally kind to sentient beings without discrimination, whether they commit evil [deeds] or cultivate virtue.

"Impartial in mental acts, like empty space" explains [the Buddha's] proficient impartiality. That is to say, completely penetrating the underlying principle of impartiality, he cultivates his mind as empty space and therefore he is proficient [in impartiality] like this.

"Hearing of this treasure of a person, who does not respect him?" On hearing of his impartial kindness, who would not turn to him in respect? Dharma Master Sengzhao says, "In heaven a treasure for the heavens, among humankind a treasure for people. A treasure for heaven and humankind, how wonderful for humanity and heaven! Thus there are none that do not respect him."

25a

The four verses from "Now we offer [these humble canopies] to the World-honored One" is the sixth category [of praise], praise of the Buddha's [joining the canopies into one,] universally covering the three thousand worlds, and manifesting therein the myriad phenomena; they can be understood.

"With ten powers he lovingly reveals these transformations." "Ten powers" is an honorific for [the Buddha's] discerning awareness. "Lovingly reveals" is another way to say "great compassion." With his ten powers he is able to discern the spiritual capacity [of sentient beings], and because of his great compassion he removes their suffering. The underlying principle has great benefits such as this, and therefore these transformations are revealed.

The eight verses from "Great Sage and Dharma King" is the seventh category, the praise of the two mysteries of the Buddha's body and speech. This has three parts. The first is the initial verse that wishes to praise the two mysteries and first points to the master of the two mysteries. The second part is the next line that briefly praises the mystery of the body. The third is the six lines that praise the [Buddha's] mystery of speech.

All those born by the four methods in the six realms each see the World-honored One and think that he is of the same kind as themselves, hence it is called the mystery of the body; because this is only attained by buddhas, it says "unique."

The third part, the praise of the mystery of speech, itself has three mysteries. The first is "The Buddha proclaims the Dharma with a single sound, and sentient beings each understand it according to their own type, all of them believing the World-honored One to be speaking their own language." The Buddha preaches the Dharma with a single voice yet two people, one from the east and the other from the west, each hear it in their own language.

The second is "The Buddha proclaims the Dharma with a single sound, and sentient beings universally receive and practice it and thereby attain benefit, each and every one according to their own understanding." This means that that which [beings] hear is not the same—some, for example, hear [the truth of] the origin of suffering [and others hear different teachings].

The third is "The Buddha proclaims the Dharma with a single sound, and some are afraid, some are joyous, some give rise to feelings of aversion, while others eradicate doubt." This means that the understandings born of [the Buddha's preaching] are not the same. Some hear the truth of suffering

25b

as harsh words, and so give rise to fear and then aversion. Others hear the truth of suffering as gentle and nurturing words, and so give rise to joy and eradicate doubt. Although it is simply like this, there are some problems with [the interpretation of] "single sound."

Let me first give Dharma Master Fakong's interpretation: the profound essence is absolute and without a single sound; it is only in the world of the manifested transformations that there are the ten thousand distinctions [among sounds]. This single sound is discussed just in terms of those who have heard it. Imagine if two people, one from the east and one from the west, heard the Buddha preaching the Dharma. The person from the east thinks that he taught [the truth of] suffering, while the person from the west thinks that he taught [the truth of] the origin of suffering. They would then argue with each other, one saying, "The Tathāgata taught [the truth of] suffering, but you say he taught the [truth of the] origin of suffering—you are wrong." [The other would say,] "The Tathāgata taught [the truth of] the origin of suffering, but you say that he taught [the truth of] suffering—you are wrong."

Now because each of these two people is taken by their own particular interpretation, they hear only a single sound. But this [interpretation] isn't so neat. If you say that there is one sound for each of the people involved, then if there are two other people and there is the simultaneous teaching of suffering and the origin of suffering for one, and the simultaneous teaching of the extinction of suffering and the path that leads to the extinction of suffering for the other—there would then be two sounds for each. In the end, how is this different from the ten thousand sounds in [the world of] manifestation?

My interpretation is a bit different. That is, because hearing two [different things] does not constitute two, the Buddha himself only speaks with one sound. But this [interpretation] too is not so neat. Wouldn't this mean that everything that these two people heard was without cause? Isn't there a cause? If all of it was without cause, then what they were hearing would be false and arbitrary and there would be no praising of the Buddha. If there was a cause, then these two people are both right; how then could you say that there are not two [different things that are] heard?

If both are right, then why is "single sound" a problem? To comment, the power of the Buddha's knowing is never without reason, and so it makes no sense to say that there is no cause. However it is not of a fixed perceptual attribute, and so it doesn't make sense to expect it to be of a fixed expression either. Therefore, hearing two different things is not a problem because the perceptual attribute of that which is lacking a fixed existence means that there is not a single perceptual attribute [that applies to it].

Again, Zhonggong's analysis says that the profound essence is without language and there is but one ultimate. But those who experience it are each different and do not receive it as one. To speak of a "single sound" is to enfold the manifestation in the explanation of the essence, and thus it says "single." But there are some questions about this—if the distinctions of the ten thousand virtues exist within the essence, how can the essence be called "single"? In any case, I have yet to find a definitive interpretation [of these matters]. My own thought is that although the ten thousand virtues are distinguished, the essential nature is single and complete.

Dharma Master Sengzhao understands this to say that a "single sound" is a mystery [of the Buddha's speech] but the meaning is difficult to understand. Another understanding has it that the first instance of "single sound" [in the sutra] refers to a single language and means that when preaching to a person from the eastern regions the Buddha preached the Dharma using the single language of the eastern regions, yet the ten thousand different kinds [of beings] all [hear the teaching] in their own language.

The next use of "single sound" refers to the "one" within the Dharma that was taught. In order to accommodate those who [needed to hear the teaching of] suffering, the Buddha thus taught the single [sermon] on suffering, though some heard a sermon on suffering and some heard a sermon on the cause of suffering. The next use of "single sound" also refers [to the one teaching] about suffering that gives rise to different understandings; this is similar to the above interpretation. This understanding has the virtue of agreeing with the text, but doesn't solve all the problems.

That is to say, the distinguishing of suffering, the cause of suffering, and the two languages of east and west is entirely a distinction that comes from the person who receives [the teaching]. How could it be that in the Way of the Tathāgata there is only the language of a single region? Or that [the Buddha] would only teach a fixed, single sermon on suffering? Again, I have yet to hear a definitive explanation. However, my own thought is that these

25c

are all just provisional explanations. If you don't push the analysis further, it will stop here. If you work at it, nothing is impossible.

The four verses from "We bow to [the unflagging vigor of your] ten powers" are the eighth [category of praise], praise of the twin virtues of the Buddha's knowing and his eradication [of entanglements]. There are two aspects to this [praise], the first of which is the two verses that praise the Buddha's knowing, and the second of which is the two verses that praise his eradication [of entanglements]. The praise of his knowing can be understood. Within the praise of his eradication [of entanglements], the first verse praises his eradication of the causality of limited, ordinary [samsara] and the latter verse [praises his eradication of even] the causality of miraculous transformations [in the samsara experienced by bodhisattvas]; these can be understood.

The three verses from "knows [the nature of the comings and goings of] all sentient beings" is the ninth [praise], the praise of the Buddha's two knowledges of truth and convention.

This has two divisions: the first is the initial one-and-a half lines that praise the Buddha's knowledge of the world. The one-and-a half lines from "Constantly within [the cultivation of emptiness and tranquility]" is the praise of the Buddha's knowledge of truth; this can all be understood.

From "At that time the elder's [son]" is the second aspect of [Jewel Accumulation's] inquiry, the actual question. This has two aspects. The first gives the objective of the inquiry, showing that the inquiry is not just for himself but indeed for all five hundred elders' [sons]. The second aspect, from "wish to hear," is the actual inquiry. Within this there are the two questions about cause and effect. "We wish to hear how to obtain the purity of a buddha realm" is asking about the effect. "We only ask that the World-honored One explain for the bodhisattvas the practices by which those lands are purified" is asking about the cause.

Now, because the reason for these two questions is the revelation of the pure lands within the combined canopies, some issues arise. That is, because this was manifested by the Buddha's miraculous powers, in principle they must be real lands; hence, the inquiries about the ultimately pure land obtained upon buddhahood and the bodhisattva practices that purify the lands.

From "The Buddha said, 'Excellent, excellent!'" is the fifth item [of the beginning of the specific introduction], the Tathāgata's extensive explanation of the cause and result of the pure land in answer to [Jewel Accumulation's] inquiry. This unfolds in three levels. The first is the assent to give the teaching; the second, from "The Buddha said, 'Jewel Accumulation, the types of sentient beings,'" is the actual answer to the question. The third is from "Śāriputra had the thought" and explains [Śāriputra's] doubt.

The first, the assent to the teaching, is further divided into two items. The first is the Tathāgata's assent to give the teaching. The second is Jewel Accumulation's respectfully listening as instructed. These can be understood.

The second aspect, the actual answer, has two parts. The first is the answer to the inquiry regarding the results, the aforementioned "We wish to hear how to obtain the purity of a buddha realm." The second is from "Jewel
26a   Accumulation, you should know that a sincere mind is the pure land of a bodhisattva," and is the answer to the inquiry regarding the cause, the aforementioned, "We [only] ask [that the World-honored One] explain for the bodhisattvas the practices by which those lands are purified."

The first, the answer to the inquiry about the result, has three parts. The first is the actual answer. The second is from "Why is this?" and is the explanation of the answer. The third is from the next "Why is this?" and is an additional explanation.

The first is the actual answer. "The types of sentient beings are the buddha lands of the bodhisattvas." The difference between the pure and the defiled with regard to the realm [in which beings dwell] is all experienced due to the virtue and evil of sentient beings. Therefore this means that sentient beings necessarily determine their own realms.

The knowledge of the Sage, however, is perfectly unified with the underlying principle of suchness and has long since exhausted the limits of name and perceptual attribute (nāma-rūpa), having neither this nor that, neither attachment nor aversion. They already have vast space as their physical form and the illumination of the ten thousand dharmas as their mind. How can name and perceptual attribute measure him? So too, how can [a land] be determined as "his land"?

Nonetheless their compassion is neverending and they bestow the teaching according to spiritual capacity; thus, there is no place where there are sentient beings to which they do not go, and so it says that "the types of sentient beings are the buddha lands of the bodhisattvas." However, Jewel Accumulation's question above was really about how to achieve the Buddha's pure land, and so what does it mean that this answer only mentions the buddha lands?

I interpret this as meaning that although the Tathāgata is primordially without his own land, he makes sentient beings that are to be transformed become the buddha lands. Sentient beings are all in either a pure land or a defiled land, and so the Tathāgata similarly accords with this in order to bestow the teachings. Now, if only the pure lands were mentioned in the answer or [the answer] only considered the buddha lands of those sentient beings in the pure lands, then the sentient beings of the defiled lands would be left out. Therefore "buddha land" is given as the common answer [for both], and it does not speak of the Buddha's pure land.

However, if the many buddhas and bodhisattvas are essentially without [their own] lands and the types of sentient beings that are to be transformed become the buddha lands, then shouldn't the direct reply be that all the worlds of the ten directions are the buddha lands of the bodhisattvas? What is the point of being so circuitous and saying, "The types of sentient beings are the buddha lands of the bodhisattvas"?

I interpret this to mean that this reply also intends to make generally clear that the buddhas and bodhisattvas do not fix lands as their own. If it were directly stated that the worlds of the ten directions are the buddha lands of the bodhisattvas, then it wouldn't make clear that the buddhas and bodhisattvas do not fix realms as their own. Thus it uses a roundabout answer in order to make clear that the buddhas do not establish lands [as their own].

Another question: Jewel Accumulation only asked about achieving the Buddha's pure land and did not ask about the bodhisattvas' lands. Why then does the answer include the bodhisattvas?

I interpret this as follows: if you want to show that [the buddhas] do not fix lands as their own, then all [bodhisattvas] above the seventh level are the same as buddhas in not having [their own] lands. If you only said "buddha lands" in your answer, then beings would think that the determination of "not having [their own] lands" only applies to buddhas and not to bodhisattvas. Then it wouldn't be clear that [bodhisattvas] above the seventh level   26b are the same as the many buddhas in terms of not having [their own] lands. Therefore, bodhisattvas are also included in the answer.

From "Why is this?" is the second [aspect of the answer to Jewel Accumulation,] the explanation of the answer. This has two parts: the first is the explanation of the reward [lands] of sentient beings; the second, from "Because of the many sentient beings," is the explanation and clarification of the Buddha's response land.

There are two kinds of realms: 1) the reward lands of sentient beings, and 2) the response lands of the Tathāgata. The Tathāgata enters both lands equally to bestow the teachings; this indicates that the meaning is related to the master of the teachings, and so all are taken as buddha lands. This is why it says that "the types of sentient beings are the buddha lands of the bodhisattvas." If, however, we differentiate the two lands, that is, the reward [land of sentient beings] and the response [land of the Buddha], even though the [reward land of sentient beings] is fundamentally a result of the teachings of the Sage, it is actually experienced according to the virtue and evil of sentient beings. Therefore we discern it as related to sentient beings. Although the response land [of the Buddha] is fundamentally a result of the spiritual capacity of beings, it actually appears because of the Tathāgata's supernatural powers; therefore we discern it as related to the Tathāgata.

There might be a question about this, namely, if the buddhas are without [their own] lands, shouldn't we simply say that they are without [their own] lands? What is the reason for going to all the trouble to say that "The types of sentient beings" are the buddha lands?

"According to their transformation of sentient beings, bodhisattvas acquire buddha lands." This clarifies that, in their time as bodhisattvas and in accordance with transforming sentient beings according to their abilities and natures, they teach and cause [beings] to cultivate virtue and experience the two realms of purity and defilement. When the bodhisattvas' practices are complete and they become buddhas, they return to enter into [the world] and bestow the teachings. Thus the meaning is related to the master of the teachings, and so it says "buddha lands."

If the point was just to explain about the teachings of the present time, then it should say "the bodhisattvas, according to their transformation of sentient beings." However, in order to clarify the teaching activities [of the bodhisattvas] during their period of training, it says, "According to their transformation of sentient beings, bodhisattvas acquire buddha lands."

"According to their discipline of sentient beings, bodhisattvas acquire buddha lands." This also has the same meaning. Between these two verses, the former verse is explained in terms of the sentient beings of the five vehicles (humans, deities, *śrāvaka*s, *pratyekabuddha*s, and buddhas and bodhisattvas); the latter verse is distinct and is explained in terms of the sentient beings of the three vehicles. Why? Because the first verse simply says "transformation." "Transformation" is a term common to the five vehicles. The latter verse says "discipline." "Discipline" is understanding the underlying principle. Understanding the underlying principle is not possible for the vehicles of humans and deities, and hence the certainty of this [distinction between the five vehicles and the three vehicles] is known.

"They obtain buddha lands according to whatever realm sentient beings need to enter into the Buddha's discerning awareness." This is interpreted as referring to the [Buddha's] response land. It also illustrates that the various attributes of the response lands are manifested according to the spiritual capacities and aspirations of sentient beings, causing them to enter into the Buddha's awareness. Therein they bestow the teachings, which means that it is related to the master of the teachings; hence it says, "buddha lands."

"They obtain buddha lands according to whatever realm sentient beings need to arouse the faculties of the bodhisattvas." This has the same meaning, except that the previous line about "enter into the Buddha's discerning awareness" is interpreted to refer to the first [bodhisattva] level and above, while this line, "arouse the faculties of the bodhisattvas," refers to the abodes below [the bodhisattva ranks].

A question about entering [the world and] bestowing the teachings: 26c Although there are differences of broad or narrow, the bodhisattavas are able to respond skillfully to all kinds. What does it mean that in the actual answer [to Jewel Accumulation's question] given above, the bodhisattvas are also mentioned in the answer, but here, in the explanation of the answer, it only deals with the Tathāgata entering [the world] and bestowing the teachings, and thus it refers to buddha lands? Why doesn't it deal with the bodhisattvas' bestowal of the teachings as bodhisattva lands?

Answer: That bodhisattvas are also mentioned in the actual answer above is as previously explained. That in the explanation of the answer only the Tathāgata's entering the world and bestowing the teachings is given has, in short, two meanings. The first is that Jewel Accumulation's question above is primarily about the buddha lands and not about the bodhisattva lands. The second is that the purification of another land and making it their own [buddha] land occurs only above the seventh level. Below this are actual lands. That the ultimate purity is without [buddha] lands shows that it is only said about the buddhas. These are the two meanings. Hence, here in the explanation of the answer, it only mentions the Tathāgata entering the world and bestowing the teaching, thereby illustrating the attributes of the land.

Another question: In the reward lands there actually are sentient beings to be transformed, and therefore truly [those lands] ought to be entered and [the teachings] given to them. Therefore, the meaning of this is related to the master of the teachings, and so they are referred to as buddha lands. Response lands, however, are only manifestations and not real; so for which sentient beings are the teachings given such that they are referred to as buddha lands?

This is interpreted to mean that although there are no real sentient beings, it is not that they are nonexistent in the response [land]. For sentient beings in the response [land] the teachings should be given. Because the teachings are bestowed within the response [land], the meaning is related to the master of the teachings and so it is referred to as a buddha land. To pass on a more remote meaning, although there are no real sentient beings within the response [land], there really are those that benefit because of the response [of the buddhas]; for this reason, it is a buddha land. Now, within the reward land the causal period is also present, but in the response land only the result is seen.

Another interpretation takes these three things as above. However, "According to their transformation of sentient beings bodhisattvas acquire the buddha lands" does not separately mean the teaching and transformation as the causal period [of their obtaining the buddha land], but says only that because of the place in which sentient beings are being transformed, it is taken as a buddha land. Therefore, it says that "The types of sentient beings are the buddha lands of the bodhisattvas."

Put more thoroughly, [it would read], "Why is this? According to their transformation of sentient beings, the many buddhas and bodhisattvas obtain the buddha lands and bodhisattva [lands]." This reading gives both [buddhas and bodhisattvas]. The response land is also thus. Accordingly, because of the response land, the place where sentient beings enter the path is taken as a buddha land.

From "Why is this" is the third level clarifying the above explanation. Within this is the explanation of the teaching and an illustration with a metaphor.

There might be a question about this. If upon becoming a buddha there is no fixed existence of lands, then during the period as a bodhisattva they should transform sentient beings by means of the teaching devoid of perceptual attribute, and thereby cause them to obtain omniscience. What is the reason that they [obtain] a buddha land by encouraging [sentient beings to strive] for a pure land, returning and entering [the world] in order to give the teachings?

Interpretation: During their days in the causal stage, bodhisattvas encourage obtaining the pure land, but this is not actually for their own sake. Rather it is certainly because they wish to richly benefit myriads of living beings.   27a
The explanation of the response land is also like this.

To explain the question [further]: if there are no [buddha] lands, then one should say straightaway that there are no [buddha] lands. Why go to the bother of making up the response land and taking it as their land?

Explanation: Again, it is because they wish to transform beings.

Second, an explanation by way of an example is given. [In the example,] "person" refers to the body of the bodhisattva who wishes to obtain the pure land. "Building a house" is a metaphor for the mind that wishes to obtain the land. This illustrates that if a person wishes to build a house he must use the land as well as [the empty space in] the sky.

The internal correspondence [of this simile] is that because the bodhisattvas broaden the path of the Buddha above and transform and nurture living beings below, they arouse the mind to achieve the two lands, the reward land and the response land. They do not use only [the empty space in the] sky, [that is, the teaching of emptiness]. "If they try to build it in the empty space in the sky they will never be successful." This means that if a person tries to build a house in the [empty space of the] sky alone and not on land, [that is, not making use of the reward lands and the response lands in order to transform and nurture living beings,] he will be unsuccessful. It should also say that if a person tries to build only on the land and does not make use of [the empty space in] the sky, he will likewise not be successful, but the text is abbreviated. The internal correspondence [of this simile] is also like this—if both of these two things are not complete, then the bodhisattva's mind for obtaining the [buddha] land likewise will be incomplete.

Another way of interpreting this is that a house must be built [both] on land and in the [empty space of the] sky. The internal correspondence [of this simile] is that because bodhisattvas wish to perfect both the practices of emptiness and the practices of existence, they arouse a mind to achieve the [buddha] land. "If they try to build it in the empty sky they will never be successful." This says that if they only understand emptiness but do not transform beings within existence, they will likewise be unsuccessful in arousing the mind to achieve the [buddha] land. This is how Zhonggong understands it. The internal correspondence [of this simile] should be thus understood.

Yet another understanding is that if buddhas are without lands, then we should straightaway say there are no lands; what then is the reason that [their] entering another land and bestowing the teachings is taken as [achieving] their own buddha land?

Interpretation: Entering [the lands], bestowing the teachings, and taking another land as one's own land is not without purpose—it is because they certainly wish to richly benefit sentient beings.

The interpretation of the example is also like this. Taking another land as one's own land is certainly because they wish to perfect sentient beings— it is "not in the [empty space of the] sky." Where it should read, "Buddhas and bodhisattvas vow to obtain the buddha realms," it is abbreviated and only lists one, [the bodhisattvas]. Seeking the meaning of this text, it also seems to illustrate the causal period.

From "Jewel Accumulation, you should know" is the second [level of the fifth item of the beginning of the specific introduction], the answer to the question about the cause [of obtaining the pure buddha lands]. This unfolds in three aspects: 1) the first is the actual explanation of the ten thousand virtues that are the real cause of the pure lands; 2) the second is from "Like this, Jewel Accumulation," and illustrates that the many practices are all accomplished together and not isolated from each other; 3) the third is from "Therefore, [Jewel Accumulation,] if a bodhisattva . . . ," and is the exhortation to [cultivate] the cause of purity.

The first aspect, the actual explanation of the ten thousand virtues that are the cause of the pure lands, has seventeen aspects in all. It is not necessary to enumerate them all; it is acceptable to interpret them following the text. "A sincere mind is the bodhisattva's pure land." This means that when bodhisattvas are cultivating the cause [of the pure land], their self-cultivation is to develop a sincere mind devoid of perceptual attribute with which to teach sentient beings and cause them to develop a sincere mind. The bodhi- 27b sattva's sincere mind, devoid of perceptual attribute, thus experiences the fruits of buddhahood.

The sincere mind of sentient beings marked by perceptual attribute is their own experience of the pure land. While the sincere mind of sentient beings is taken as the actual cause, for bodhisattvas the sincere mind is only taken as an indirect condition. Here we are using "condition" in response [to the question of] cause. Therefore we say that the bodhisattva's sincere mind is the cause of the pure land.

"Sentient beings who do not flatter will be born in their realm" means that bodhisattvas skillfully teach sentient beings and cause them to cultivate a sincere mind that, in return, does not flatter; this enables them to be born in that bodhisattva's realm. If sentient beings do not cultivate a sincere mind, then that land will not be accomplished. It says "sentient beings who do not flatter will be born in their realm" in order to disclose this meaning.

Therefore, because it is evidently the sincere mind of sentient beings that brings about their experience [of the pure land], then in fact it is the sentient beings' pure land. Nonetheless, the fact is that the original condition is the bodhisattvas' perfected practice, achieving buddhahood, then returning and entering [the world] to bestow the teachings, thus it actually is related to the master of the teachings; therefore it is called "their (the bodhisattvas') realm."

The following sixteen items can be understood by this example. There are, however, two kinds of virtues. One is the virtue of the practice and the other is the virtue of the reward.

It first says, "sincere mind"—this is the virtue of the practice; afterward it says, "do not flatter"—this is the virtue of the reward. There are four types of causes. The first is that similar attributes give rise to each other; this is called the consistency cause. This means things such as first cultivating the sincere mind that later returns [with the result that one] does not flatter. The second is that different kinds give rise to each other; this is called the retribution cause. This is like good and evil giving rise to suffering and joy. The third is the mutually aiding cause. This is like the practice of generosity that is the cause that gives rise to being moral. The fourth is the similarity cause. Among the causes of the reward there is one cause that is foremost—such as not taking life, which leads to a long life.

Among these seventeen virtues some have all four causes, some have two or three of the causes, and some simply have one cause. This can be judged by looking at the text. We will abridge this and just give ten questions and answers in order to show what we mean.

The first question is that Jewel Accumulation's inquiry was only about the actual cause of the many bodhisattvas' [purification of the buddha lands]. He did not ask about the actual cause of the sentient beings' [attainment]. Now, however, you say that the bodhisattva's sincere mind is the indirect cause and only the sincere mind of the sentient being is the actual cause. Then, following your words, if the bodhisattvas are devoid of the actual cause, doesn't your answer make the condition into the cause, and so aren't you not really answering the question?

Answer: The bodhisattvas are in fact the true cause, but this is concealed and not answered. It is also said that the question is not really answered. However, the bodhisattvas do not essentially have the intention to themselves be the actual cause. They only wish to liberate sentient beings from their manifold sufferings. Therefore they teach them to cultivate a sincere mind and cause them to experience the pure land. Hence, the fact of the actual cause is surely the sincere minds of sentient beings. It is simply that when speaking of the bodhisattvas in the answer, it refers to the condition as the cause.

The second question is that you say the bodhisattvas are fundamentally 27c not the actual cause. The fact of the actual cause is necessarily sentient beings. Now they cultivate a sincere mind and experience their pure land—what kind of sentient beings must they be?

Answer: In all, there are three kinds [of beings] that are born in the pure land. The first is those above the seventh stage up to the diamond [stage].

This can be inferred without discussion. Although there is only birth in response [to the needs of sentient beings], there is no real birth. The second is from the [stage of the] initial resolve up to the sixth stage. These beings are born [in the pure land] because of their past karma and the strength of their vows; it is not that they are experiencing joy now and so arouse the mind, producing the cause of birth. The third is ordinary worldlings among those outside the path; there is nothing to discuss about them—they receive the bodhisattvas' transformative teachings, arouse the will to cultivate a sincere mind, and experience birth in the pure land. They are without doubt within the shared ranks of ordinary people.

The third question: In the above answers about the result, both the pure and the defiled are given as the buddha lands. Taking this as an example, even if there is purity and defilement in the cause, the answer is given based on the Tathāgata. In this example it is surely the case that in the previously given answer about the result, only the sentient beings of the pure land are given as the buddha land.

Answer: The Tathāgata is essentially without his own land. It is only for the sake of the sentient beings that are to be transformed that he makes buddha lands, and so [buddha lands] are within both purity and defilement. The Tathāgata accords identically with both in order to bestow the teachings, and both pure and defiled become the buddha land.

In the [Buddha's] answer [to Jewel Accumulation's question,] only the pure [land] is mentioned. In brief, this has two meanings. The first is that, in the question above, Jewel Accumulation only asked about the cause of the pure [lands] and did not ask about the cause of [obtaining] a defiled [land]. The second is that the compassionate nature of the Sage only wishes to bestow purity and not defilement. Sentient beings' desires and aspirations, however, are not the same and do not accord with the mind of the Sage. Thus he is in accord with that which will support every practice, and so too he encourages the cause of defilement and liberates them from the many sufferings of the three evil destinies. If you inquire as to the real intention of the Sage, it is only [to encourage] purity; this is why the answer only mentions the cause of purity.

The fourth question: Because the land is ruled by fetters, the buddhas are primordially without their own land; likewise the bodhisattvas don't seek [their own land]. Only through the nonexistence of perceptual attribute do they teach and transform sentient beings, causing them to enter the path of the Buddha. Why, then, do they encourage the cause of [attaining] purity and thereby make them obtain this land of fetters? Non-Buddhist texts say that you should not give to people that which you do not yourself want. The differences between Buddhists and non-Buddhists aside, surely this is not at odds [with a Buddhist position]?

Answer: It is not at odds [with a Buddhist point of view]. However, the spiritual roots of each sentient being differ and their desires and aspirations are not the same. Hence it is not possible simply to transform them by means of the [teaching] devoid of perceptual attribute. Some in the defiled world have deep obstacles of the five degenerations and are not easy to transform. Because birth in the pure land is free of these obstacles of the five degenerations, transformation is easy. Thus they are first encouraged to [cultivate] the cause of purity and made to experience the pure land, but in the end their intent is [to obtain] the same equality of being without [their own] land.

28a   The fifth question: As previously said, birth in the pure land is free of the obstacles of the five degenerations and is a basis for studying the path, and therefore the pure land is encouraged. Is it the case, then, that somebody who is once born in the pure land will never again return to the three evil destinies, or will they return? If there are those who return, then isn't birth in the pure land without benefit?

Answer: If a person of superior pure karma is born in the superior level of the pure land, they might, due to their vow of wishing to transform sentient beings, take birth in the three evil destinies; but there is actually no returning and experiencing the evil [destinies]. If a person of inferior pure karma is born into the inferior level of the pure land, it is simply not fixed, and some may meet with virtuous conditions, increasingly cultivate that which is devoid of perceptual attribute, and not return. [On the other hand,] if it is not like this, [that is, those of inferior pure karma do not meet with virtuous conditions nor cultivate that which is devoid of perceptual attribute,] why don't they return? Whether one returns or doesn't return, once born in the pure land, the rewards are greatly superior to that of the defiled lands. Therefore the sages warmly and sincerely encourage [beings] to cultivate purity.

The sixth question: It is always said that prior to the sixth mind are the ranks from which one can regress. Therefore some interpretations say that one regresses to a *śrāvaka,* and other interpretations say that one will commit the four types of grave offenses and the five heinous crimes if one regresses. You have already said that if one arouses the will to cultivate the sincere [mind] and experiences the pure land, he or she is certainly within the shared ranks of ordinary people. This is the way in which it is below the sixth level of mind. How is it, then, that those who are within the shared ranks of ordinary people, and due to the superior level of their pure karma are born into the superior level of the pure land, do not retrogress?

Answer: In brief, there are two types of ordinary people in the outer ranks who enter the initial mind: the first is the one who cultivates the superior level of pure karma and enters the pure land from the superior level; they do not retrogress. The other is those for whom it is simply not fixed, even though they have entered [the stage of the intitial mind].

The seventh question: If ordinary people of the outer ranks first produce the [cause of] the three evil destinies, they will then experience evil retribution. But if they are taught and transformed by the bodhisattvas and according to the teachings cultivate the pure karma of the superior level, which retribution will they receive first? If the evil retribution is experienced first, then what use is the pure karma? If the pure karma is experienced first, is the evil karma extinguished and they then go [to the pure land]? If it is extinguished and they go [to the pure land,] we can say then that those who enter the initial mind from the superior level of the pure land will never again retrogress into evil. If [the evil retribution] is not extinguished, then, even though they are within the pure land they still have evil karma. How can you say that birth in the superior level of the pure land will never return to evil?

Answer: If the strength of the pure karma is stronger, then the pure retribution is received first; if the evil karma is superior, then the evil retribution is received first—it can be reckoned according to the weight [of the karma]. The *Sutra of Immeasurable Life* (*Wuliangshou jing*) says, "Only excluding those who commit the five heinous crimes and slander the Dharma." But this refers to [having a believing mind] for even a single thought. It does not speak of those who practice their entire lives until they die. If the two kinds of karma are equal, then the first to ripen will be experienced first. But if the two kinds of karma are equal, then what makes one ripen sooner or later?

The answer is that it is difficult to comprehend the power of sentient beings' karma, whereby they receive retribution. If the pure karma is stronger than the evil karma, and the evil karma is not extinguished, how is it possi-

28b   ble that evil karma remains even in the pure land and thus evil is never ended? On the other hand, suppose it is not extinguished and you go [to the pure land]. However, previously you said that, having been born in the pure land, wherever you turn all teach the true path and benefit is gradually [acquired] through [the reality] that is devoid of perceptual attribute—how can it be that evil karma exists and has not been extinguished? In any case, it is clear that once born into the superior level of the pure land, there is no returning to the three evil destinies.

The eighth question: You said that although one might have the karma [to obtain] the pure land, if one's evil karma is stronger then they will first receive the evil retribution; if it is equal, then whichever ripens [first] is experienced first. Achieving pure karma is encouraged but the benefit is not yet clear.

Answer: What was said is that those who cultivate a sincere mind and thereby obtain the pure land—this is surely talking about those who culti- vate the practice according to the teaching and obtain benefits according to their practice, and not those who do not obtain [the benefit]. And even those who first receive evil retribution—after the evil retribution is exhausted they may encounter virtuous conditions and again arouse the mind of aspiration; adding to their original virtue they obtain birth in the pure land. How can you say that the cultivation of [pure] karma is encouraged but the benefits have not yet been clarified?

The ninth question: Is it the case that the pure land experienced through the same pure karma has three [different] realms? If not, then it is the same as the great void—why is that? If it is the case [that there are three different realms that can be experienced within the pure land], why is it that the place that is obtained is different, even though the karma is the same?

Answer: Why wouldn't there be three realms? The place that is obtained is not the same because the state of concentration is different. This is because when in the desire realm a person cultivates pure karma [and so experiences its fruits here in this desire realm, while] those who study concentration in the form realm will experience [those states of concentration] in the site of the form realm. If they study concentration in the formless realm, so too what they experience will be in the site of the formless. So the question is: are there differences in the kinds of pleasure in the three worlds?

Answer: In just that one world there are the distinctions of superior, middle, and lower. But these are not the distinctions of the three realms. Now, the state of concentration surely has [distinctions of] depth. However, because concentration is only the condition for [discerning] awareness and not the condition for concentration, the kinds of pleasure in the three worlds are likewise without distinction.

Another question: If this is so, then, because of this pure karma, does one experience solely the reward of the pleasure, [that is, the joys of the pure land,] and not knowledge and understanding?

Answer: How could this not be a supporting condition [for experiencing knowledge and understanding]? But the actual experience is only like this[—that is, the pure land].

The tenth question: At the time when they are cultivating the cause, bodhisattvas teach sentient beings; perfecting their practice they achieve buddhahood and return to the world to bestow the teachings, and so this means that it is related to the master of the teachings. Moreover, because of this indirect condition it is acceptable to call it "their realm." But there remains a doubt. You have already said that for people in the semblance stage to obtain true discernment will certainly require the cultivation of the practice for immeasurable eons.

Needless to say, achieving buddhahood is not simply a matter of several eons. Even being born with an immeasurable life span in the pure land—now, while a bodhisattva completes the practices and obtains buddhahood, surely some sentient beings in the pure lands, conditioned by that which is devoid of perceptual attribute, will eradicate their entanglements and the ordinary [person] will become a sage. Again, others will cultivate myriad actions and for ten thousand million lives experience immeasurable worlds.   28c Why do they not guard the sincere mind and only live in one place? Still, the term "buddha realm" is actually a matter of the master of the teachings and is not discussed in terms of the indirect conditions.

Answer: As you said, it is a fact that they are not constantly in one place. Further, this indirect condition is certainly found at the outset of the sincere mind. Still, when those bodhisattvas' practices are perfected and they obtain buddhahood, they see the import of the conditions that were created in the distant past. Therefore, although they experience innumerable worlds through countless births, they always respond and bestow the teachings in accordance with those places. Further, even if there are other actions that are cultivated, they all arise at the outset of [arousing] the sincere mind, and thus the significance of the distant conditions is not lost. Moreover, there are also those who experience innumerable births in a single place.

The "ten virtuous actions" are the bodhisattva precepts. The precepts are innumerable but here they are abridged and listed as ten. They are complete and there is no vow unaccomplished, and so it says "entirely fulfilled." With "serene acceptance" the bodhisattvas cultivate accommodation, and so the auspicious attributes [of those born in their land] are entirely complete. It is shown that it is because of "discerning awareness" that beings are transformed, and so among the three groups it is "those who have right concentration" who are born in their land. At first it is because of the four methods of approaching people that [bodhisattvas] are embraced. Now they themselves cultivate embracing [beings] and are free of the embrace of others; therefore it says, "embraced by liberation."

Among the "eight difficult situations," the three evil destinies, the northern continent where all is pleasant, and the long-life heavens, are the five difficulties of place. The difficult situation of being born as a worldly philosopher is a mental difficulty. Being born before or after a buddha is a difficulty of time. Being born deaf, blind, or mute is a physical difficulty. People and deities within the four [fortunate] wheels[—that is, virtuous places, virtuous friends, correct aspiration, and prior virtue—]can avoid these eight difficult situations.

From "Like this, Jewel Accumulation" is the second aspect [of the inquiry regarding the cause of the pure land], the explanation of the mutual support of the many practices perfected together. The above "sincere mind" illustrates how the pure land is experienced. Hence it now further illustrates that the many practices are all mutually supporting and cannot be perfected individually.

"In accordance with their sincere mind, [the bodhisattva] is aroused to act" means that because their minds are sincere bodhisattvas are aroused to myriad acts. Consequently, the sincere mind is the origin of the ten thousand acts. The meaning of this shows that the practices are gradually, subtly, and mutually related.

"In accordance with [the bodhisattva] being aroused to act, he gains a profound mind" shows that when the myriad acts have accumulated, then the mind of the Way becomes very profound. "In accordance with [the bodhisattva's] profound mind, his thoughts are disciplined" shows that because the [bodhisattva's] mind of the Way is profound, he abandons evil and accords with virtue, and his mind is not rough and crude. "In accordance with the discipline of his thoughts, his actions are in conformity with the teachings" means that because the [bodhisattva's] mind is flexible and adaptable, having heard [the teachings] he is able to act in accord with the teachings. "In accordance with his actions in conformity to the teachings, he is able to dedicate his merits" means that because his actions are in conformity with the teachings he has heard, he is able to bestow [the teachings and] turn the masses together toward the fruits of buddhahood.

"In accordance with his dedication of merits, he has skillful means" shows that [the bodhisattva's] dedicating his merits without attachment is the source of skillful means in the Mahayana. Up to here [the text] clarifies the bodhisattva as the primary condition.

"In accordance with his skillful means, he brings sentient beings to perfection" establishes the practices that, endowed with the skillful means of the Mahayana, bring beings to perfection. "In accordance with his bringing   29a sentient beings to perfection, his buddha land is pure" shows that because sentient beings have established pure practice, he is able to attain the pure land. These two lines clarify that sentient beings are the actual cause.

"In accordance with the purity of his buddha land, his teaching of the Dharma is pure" clarifies that the land is pure and without defilement, and so there is purity of the teaching. "In accordance with the purity of his teaching of the Dharma, his discerning awareness is pure." With purity of teaching, those followers who receive the teachings are able to attain pure [discerning] awareness. "In accordance with the purity of his discerning awareness, his mind is pure." Having aroused pure knowing, the mind is also clarified. "In accordance with the purity of mind, all of the merits are pure." Because the mind is the source of the ten thousand merits, how could any impure merits arise once the mind is purified? Hence it says "therefore all of the merits are pure."

All of this clarifies the benefits of the pure land. From "Therefore, Jewel Accumulation" is the third [aspect of the inquiry regarding the cause, namely] the exhortation to cultivate the cause of purity. As already noted, the pure land is actually experienced because of the virtuous actions of sentient beings. So why is it that now only bodhisattvas are exhorted [to cultivate the cause of purity], but not ordinary people? In brief, this has two meanings. The first is that, for the most part, only bodhisattvas are mentioned in the question and answer, not ordinary people. Therefore, here only bodhisattvas are exhorted [to cultivate the cause of purity]. The second meaning is that if the teachers advance, then the disciples will follow of their own accord, and so they are not encouraged separately.

From "At that time, Śāriputra" is the third part of the Tathāgata's answer to the inquiry [regarding the cause of the pure lands], namely the explanation of [Śāriputra's] doubt, which corresponds to the text and is self-explanatory. This is first unpacked in two parts. In the first the narrator describes the nature of the doubts of Śāriputra, the person being addressed in the sutra. The second, from "The Buddha knew his thoughts," is the actual explanation of the doubt. Now, the reason that Śāriputra gives rise to this doubt is that right before this, in exhorting the cultivation of purity, it says that "[if] the bodhisattva wishes to obtain the pure land then they should purify their minds."

The second item, the actual explanation of the doubt, has three aspects. The first is the Tathāgata's own interpretation. The second, from "at that time Conch Crested Hair Brahmā King," is the directly witnessed account of Conch Crested Hair Brahmā King. The third is from "at that, the Buddha touched the earth with his foot," when the Tathāgata again manifested his supernatural powers and eliminated the doubt.

The main point of these three is the three kinds of doubts. The first is light and can be removed by being instructed [to abandon it]; the second is medium and is removed by using language [to explain the matter]; the third is heavy and requires miraculous events to be eliminated. Therefore these three levels are used in the explanation.

The first, the Tathāgata's own interpretation, also has three aspects. The first aspect is the Tathāgata's posing a metaphorical question to Śāriputra. The second is from "[Śāriputra] replied" and is his respectful reply. The third is from "Śāriputra" and returns to the Tathāgata and his giving the actual interpretation.

The "sun and the moon" are comparable to the Tathāgata, and the myriad forms that are illuminated are comparable to the Tathāgata's pure land. The "blind person who does not see" is comparable to [followers of] the two vehicles. One interpretation takes it that the "sun and moon" are heavenly   29b
palaces, and [that the Tathāgata], in the palaces of the sun and moon, is forever illuminating the myriad forms of the world below. The heavenly beings in the sun and moon [palaces] are like the Tathāgata. The sun and moon are like the practices in the Tathāgata's pure land. The five colors that shine on [the world below] are like the rewards of the Tathāgata's pure land. The blind person who does not see has the same meaning as before, [namely, the practitioners of the two vehicles].

From "at that time, Conch Crested Hair [Brahmā King]" is the second aspect, the directly witnessed account [of the Brahmā king]. If the Buddha had simply said that it was the fault of sentient beings [that they do not see the purity of his land] and did not let them actually see it, then sentient beings would still doubt this [type of explanation] as mere words without reality. Therefore, [the second explanation] gives the directly witnessed account of what is seen by the faultless Conch Crested Hair [Brahmā King].

Within this too there are three things. The first is when Conch Crested Hair Brahmā King initially relates what he sees and asks Śāriputra a question. The second is from "Śāriputra" and is Śāriputra's answer relating what he sees. The third is from "Conch Crested Hair Brahmā King" and explains the reasons given by Conch Crested Hair Brahmā King for why you can or cannot see [the pure land].

From "at that the Buddha" is the third aspect [of the Tathāgata's own explanation], the removal of doubt by the manifestation of the [Buddha's] supernatural feat. There are two parts to this: the first is the transformation of the polluted into the pure and eliminating the doubts of those with sharp faculties. The second is from "The Buddha withdrew the supernatural power of his foot" and is the elimination of the doubts of those with dull faculties by taking away the supernatural feat.

Within the first aspect of transforming the polluted into the pure, there are four parts. The first is when the Tathāgata asks Śāriputra about the transformation; the second details Śāriputra's reply about what he has seen; the third, from "The Buddha said," is the Tathāgata's reply; the fourth is from

"When the Buddha manifested this [purity of the land]," and is the actual details of the elimination of the doubts of those with sharp faculties.

Because a pure land had never been seen or heard of in the corrupt world in which we live, [Śāriputra] says "originally not seen nor heard."

In "My buddha realm is always pure like this," the "like" means "such as." This shows that the reward land that he obtains is always as pure as this response land.

"It is like heavenly beings that eat, sharing a jeweled bowl, but in accordance with their virtues and merits the color of the food is different for each." There are three ways of understanding this sameness and difference. The first is "different place, different characteristics." In other words the pure and the defiled are distinct and separate—the boundaries of the land are not the same. The second is "same place but different characteristics." This is like our own corrupt world, which has both purity and defilement mixed together without obstructing each other. The third is "same characteristics but seen differently." This is like water of the Ganges River, which appears as water to the virtuous but as fire to the hungry ghosts (*pretas*). Dharma Master Sengzhao concurs with this opinion.

Inferring from the text, the latter two understandings are possible, but the first is a bit difficult—how? If we say that both the place and the characteristics are different, how can we say that "[heavenly beings that] eat, sharing a jeweled eating bowl, but in accordance with their virtues and merits the color of the food is different for each"?

From "When the Buddha manifested this [purity of the land]" is the fourth, the actual details of the elimination of the doubts of those with sharp faculties.

"Obtained the serene acceptance of non-arising" shows that the Buddha's awareness is entered at the first level. It may also be entered at the eighth level. This also corroborates the above "[Because they bring sentient beings] into the Buddha's discerning awareness according to whatever realm they are in, they obtain the buddha lands."

"Aroused the mind for supreme [awakening]" shows that people below this abode [of the eighth level] entered the first level. This also completes the above "[Because they cause sentient beings to] arouse the faculties of the bodhisattvas according to whatever realms they are in, they obtain the buddha lands."

29c

From "The Buddha withdrew the supernatural power of his foot" is the second aspect, eliminating the doubts of those with dull faculties by taking away the supernatural [feat]. When those of dull faculties in the two vehicles saw the purity change back to impurity, they awakened to impermanence and obtained the benefit. The "Dharma eye" means that they obtained the first fruits. "[Achieved the] elimination of all outflows and [liberation] of mind" means that they achieved the fruits of arhatship.

Chapter Two

Skillful Means

Because this chapter explains the many and various skillful means that Vimala-kīrti uses to transform beings, it has this title. This is the second part of the specific introduction; that is, the introduction that describes [Vimalakīrti's] virtues. Why wasn't this introduction [given by the Buddha] at the time this scripture was taught? Because afterward Ānanda had a deep understanding of the Buddha's intention; desiring to enable sentient beings of later ages hear of these lofty virtues and deeply respect the teachings, he gave this one chapter that entirely praises Vimalakīrti's virtuous conduct—hence, this is called the introduction that describes [Vimalakīrti's] virtues.

In fact, however, Vimalakīrti was already Golden Grain Tathāgata in the past. However, he obscured his radiance in order to transform beings and therefore became a disciple. Advancing but not perfectly awakened, holding back but not ranked with the lowest. Thus we here take his manifestation to be of the eighth level or above.

This is unpacked in two parts. The first is the wish to relate his virtues as a householder, and so he is initially described as a virtuous person. The second, from "in the past he made offerings," is the actual account of his householder virtues. The first can be understood. The second, the actual explanation, is divided into two parts. The first is from the beginning up to "respected by the Lords of the world" and relates the profound essence; the second is the rest of the chapter from "desiring to save people [he] therefore [used his skillful means]," and relates the manifestation of his skillful means.

The point of these two praises [of Vimalakīrti's] virtues is that without the essence, the traces will not be left behind; without the traces, there will be no revelation of the essence. Therefore both the essence and the traces are related, the true and the response are both praised. Describing the essence leads beings to arouse a mind of deep respect; praising the traces leads beings to dispel confusion about things.

With regard to the first aspect, describing the essence is further divided into three parts. The first begins with the essential practice. The six lines together make three couplets that comprise the actual praise, ending with the conventional and the real. The second aspect, from "accomplished his great vow," begins with his primary vow. The four lines together make two couplets that are the actual praise, ending with the virtues of both body and mind. The third is from "The many buddhas sighed," and gives the concluding, shared praise by others.

"In the past he made offerings to innumerable buddhas." This gives the essence of the practice, and shows that the resulting actions are wondrous because the essence of the practice was lofty.

30a · "Deeply planted virtuous roots." The mind that aspires to *bodhi* is the root of the myriad virtues. Therefore it says "virtuous roots." Because these have been cultivated for eons it says "deeply planted." We could also say that the practices of the seventh level are the cause for the eighth level. and thus they are called "virtuous roots." These two lines are called the beginning of the root practice.

The six lines from "Obtained the serene acceptance of non-arising" together make three couplets that are the actual praise. "Obtained the serene acceptance of non-arising" shows that the knowing of the eighth level and above is consistent with the underlying principle of non-arising. This line praises [Vimalakīrti's] understanding of emptiness.

"His eloquence unobstructed" means that in traversing existence and transforming beings, his use of the four perfect manners of speech is unhindered. This line praises his understanding of existence. These two lines make a pair of emptiness and the existence of perceptual attribute in relation to each other.

"He sported freely in the supernatural powers" shows that outside he sported about freely in accordance with his wishes. This line praises his external virtues.

"Attained total retention [of the Buddha's teachings, i.e., *dhāraṇīs*]." One [aspect of "total retention"] is to have complete retention of the texts, and the other is to have complete retention of the meanings; neither is ever forgotten. This line praises his internal virtue. These two lines make a pair of the inner and outer [virtues] in relation to each other.

"Obtained fearlessness" refers to the four kinds of fearlessness.

"Overcame the annoyance and resentment of Māras" refers to the four demons that harass beings. These two lines praise his strong role.

"Entered the profound Dharma gates" means that [Vimalakīrti] completely illuminated and penetrated the myriad Buddhist teachings. This line praises his gentle role. These three lines make a pair of gentleness and strength in relation to each other.

"Well versed in the perfection of knowing (*prajñāpāramitā*)" praises his knowing reality. "Mastered skillful means" praises his knowledge of the conventional. These two lines bring together the two knowledges of the conventional and the real.

From "Accomplished his great vow" clarifies the second [aspect of Vimalakīrti's essence], beginning with the primal vow. Four lines constitute two couplets that are the actual praise, ending with the two virtues of body and mind. "Accomplished his great vow" refers to his vow: "Above, broaden the path of the Buddha; below, transform and nurture living beings." This vow is called "great" because it is essential among his vows. This line is said to begin the primal vow.

"He clearly knew the mental inclinations of sentient beings" shows that [Vimalakīrti] was able to illuminate the mental aspirations of sentient beings.

"Further, he was able to discriminate whether their faculties were sharp or dull" means that he was able to illumine and penetrate the nature of the faculties of sentient beings. This line praises his [ability] to illumine confused things.

"Long within the Buddha's way, his mind was pure and clear." The word "clear" means "virtuous." This shows that he was pure and virtuous within the Buddha-Dharma and directed toward the Buddha without confusion. This line praises his accomplished purity. These two lines pair purity and confusion in relation to each other.

"Certain in the Mahayana" shows that he had skillfully penetrated the underlying principle of the conveyance and his seeking mind was certain. This line praises his self-cultivation.

"All of his actions are well and skillfully conceived." [Vimalakīrti] graciously responds to the six paths and teaches the Dharma for the sake of sentient beings without any error in regard to their spiritual capacity. This verse praises his transformation of others. These two lines pair self-cultivation and transformation of others in relation to each other.

"He dwelled within the Buddha's majesty" shows that he was no different than the Buddha with respect to the four majestic postures. This line praises his bodily actions.

30b   "His mind was like the vast ocean" shows that he penetrated the ten thousand spiritual capacities and there were none to which his illumination did not extend. This line praises his mental functions. These two lines conclude [the praise of] both of [Vimalakīrti's] virtues of body and mind.

From "The many buddhas sighed in approval" is the third [aspect clarifying Vimalakīrti's essence], and gives the concluding, shared [praise] by others. "The many buddhas sighed in approval and the disciples, Indra, Brahmā, and the Lords of the world respected him" shows that because he was possessed of these meritorious practices, the many buddhas above sighed their approval and the many deities below honored him.

From "Wishing to save people" is the second aspect of the actual explanation of [Vimalakīrti's] virtues as a householder, the relating of his manifestation [of skillful means]. This unfolds in two items: the first begins from here and goes to "[Vimalakīrti] used innumerable skillful means in order to richly benefit sentient beings," and praises the manifestation of his skillful means before his illness. The second is from "And with his skillful means he made his body appear as though ill" to the end of the chapter, and relates the manifestation of his skillful means after he appeared ill.

The first aspect is further divided into three. The first briefly explains that [Vimalakīrti] appeared to dwell in Vaiśālī because he wished to save people, but it was not a real birth. The second, from "Immeasurable wealth," is the individual telling of his many and varied manifestations. The third is from "The elder Vimalakīrti" and finishes telling how his skillful means benefited beings.

The first aspect can be understood. The second, the individual descriptions [of Vimalakīrti's various skillful means], has two parts. The first is from "immeasurable wealth" up to "his mind was steadfast when he went into saloons," and praises the manifestation of his teaching beings just in the city of Vaiśālī. The second is from "If he was among the elders," and praises the manifestation of his transformation of beings everywhere throughout the three worlds.

The first, the appearance of his manifestations within Vaiśālī, is further divided into two. The first, "But he [preferred] the taste of meditation," praises the serenity of his conduct when at home; the second, from "if he went to a gambling place," praises his manifestations when he left his house and roamed about.

The first, [the praise of his conduct while at home,] is divided into two parts. The first gives the six perfections and praises the way in which his virtuous conduct benefited beings, and explains eliminating the evils of the six impediments for the sake of sentient beings. The second is the six lines from "Although wearing the white robes [of a layman]," and praises how [Vimala-kīrti] was able to dwell in evil situations without harming himself; all of this can be understood.

The second part, the praise of his conduct when roaming about away from home, also has two aspects. The first praises his going about near town, preaching the Dharma and saving people. The second, from "Walked the crossroads," is praise of his many acts of transforming beings when he traveled far from his hometown; these can be understood.

A question: It has already been said that the profound essence is without shape but appears with a shape in response to beings. Here, however, in praising the essence there is praise of [Vimalakīrti's] body and mind. Further, in praising the manifestation there is [praise of Vimalakīrti's] perfection of *prajñā*. Isn't this the "existence" of the profound essence? In other words, aren't the essence and its manifestation beyond distinction? How is that you now praise them individually?

Answer: The profound essence is truly without shape or form. In the above praise of [Vimalakīrti's] body and mind, the body means the Dharma body and the mind means discerning awareness. But it is not that the essence has a physical body and mind. We can also say that because the true body is the essence of the form that appears in response [to the needs of sentient beings], a body and mind is given even for the essence. Still, the essence does not truly have a body and mind. Moreover, each and every item in the above praise is real, and thereby we can know that the essence is praised separately. The profound form exists above the eighth level and so the text is appropriate.

30c

Within the praise of the manifestation it says, "Desiring to save people, he therefore used his skillful means and lived in Vaiśālī." This means that although [Vimalakīrti] was not actually born [in Vaiśālī] he appeared to be born there; although he did not actually dwell [in Vaiśālī] he appeared to dwell there. How could this not be his manifestation? Thus we can know that the essence and the manifestation can be separated. Further, although the sixth perfection [of *prajñā*] is the function of the profound essence, it does not [function] for itself but for saving beings. How could the goal of saving beings not be the manifestation? So too, none of the things like "gambling," "fond of alcohol and sex," and such are real—it is clear that they are just the workings of the manifestation in response [to the needs of sentient beings].

From "If he was among the elders" is the second of the individual descriptions [of Vimalakīrti's skillful means], praise of the manifestation of his transforming beings everywhere throughout the three worlds.

An "elder" is a virtuous person in a town. Many teach the ways of the world through conventional laws, and so for them [Vimalakīrti] taught the superior transcendental law. "Laypeople" accumulate wealth and possess virtue, and so he enabled them to eliminate greed and attachment, to disperse their wealth and seek happiness. *"Kṣatriya"* are those of royal lineage; they are self-dependent and they are often angry. Thus he made them patient. "Brahmans" cultivate purity, are smart and quite arrogant, [but through the example of his own honor he taught them humility]. "Ministers" aid the realm, and so he taught and established them in the true Dharma. "Princes" covet the realm and are rebellious, and so he taught them loyalty and filial piety. The well-thought-of women of the "inner chambers" engage in much devious conduct, and so he taught them and made them upright. The "common people" are lowly and of shallow happiness; he taught them to cultivate happiness. Those of the "Brahmā heavens" are greatly attached to their pleasures, and so he taught them a superior [discerning] awareness. "Indra" is indulgent with the five objects of desire, and so he taught him insight into impermanence. The "world-protectors" are the four heavenly kings. They rule the demons and spirits and keep them from harming people; therefore he took birth among the four heavenly kings and taught many demons and spirits and protected the people.

From "The elder Vimalakīrti" is the third aspect, the concluding description of his path of benefiting beings through skillful means [before manifesting his illness].

From "With these skillful means he made it appear that he was physically ill" is the second [part of relating the manifestation of Vimalakīrti's skillful means], describing the manifestation of skillful means after he appeared to be ill. This is further revealed in three sections. The first shows [Vimalakīrti] manifesting as ill and describing the arrival of the visitors. The second is from "these guests" and shows [Vimalakīrti] using the occasion of his illness to preach the Dharma for his guests. The third is from "Like this, the elder Vimalakīrti," and shows the many guests arousing their minds and attaining benefits.

The first can be understood. The second, using the occasion of his illness to preach the Dharma for his guests, is further divided into three. The first is the admonishment to abandon evil. The second, from "Good people, you should abhor this [body]," is [Vimalakīrti's] exhorting them to cultivate virtue. The third, from "good people, if you wish to attain the buddha body," concludes the previous exhortation and admonishment.   31a

The first, the admonishment to abandon evil, lists the five teachings (literally, "five gates") as the admonishment. The first, up to "cannot be trusted," gives the teaching on impermanence. From "it is suffering, it is afflicted" gives the teaching on suffering. Internally it is called "suffering" because our minds are unreliable. Externally [the body] is oppressed, and so it is called "afflicted." Because nothing goes the way that one wants either internally or externally, it is called "a coming together of a mass of ills."

From "This body is like a mass of foam" is a teaching on emptiness in ten similes. This is further divided in two: the first five similes illustrate the internal emptiness of self, and the five similes from "This body is like a dream" illustrate the external emptiness of self. It is also said that the first five similes separately illustrate the internal emptiness of the five *skandhas* and the latter five similes collectively illustrate the internal emptiness of the five *skandhas*. The scripture says, "Form is like a mass of foam, feeling is like bubbles, perception is like a flame, impulse is [insubstantial] like a banana tree, and consciousness is like an illusion." This clarifies that the reality of this body cannot be grasped even by the hand of knowing.

From "This body is without a master" gives the teaching on no-self in two parts. The first lists each of the four elements in a simile to illustrate no-self. The second, from "This body is without reality," uses all four elements together with other things to illustrate no-self.

In "Like earth," "earth" is provisionally formed by the four minute atoms and is without a self (literally, "without a master"). Now this body is likewise provisionally formed by the five *skandhas* and is without a self, and so it is "like earth." "Like fire" is provisional. Fire arises from burning wood but there is no self. This body is provisionally designated "easterner" or "westerner" but, "like fire," it is without self. The wind, in "like the wind," is continuously moving, without self, showing that our many thoughts are continuous and without self, and so it is "like the wind." "Like water" means that just as water will fill a square or a round form and is without a real [shape of its own], the body bows and kowtows according to the rituals and is without self, "like water."

"This body is without reality but takes the four elements as its dwelling" is to say that the body is but a composite of the four elements—how could it be real? "This body is empty, separate from self and properties of the self" means that internally the body is without self, and so how then could the external properties of the self not be empty? "This body is without knowledge, like the grasses and trees" is to say that it is without a soul. "This body is without volitional action, moved about by the power of the wind." Movement is what is called volitional action, but that which is moved by the power of the wind in fact does not act [on its own].

From "This body is impure" clarifies the teaching of [the body's] impurity in two parts. The first explains the thirty-six kinds of impurity. The second is from "unreal and false"; both clarify that in principle all is impure. Knowledgeable ones know that all unreal and false things are impure, and so we say that in principle they are impure. Some say that this is out of order and that the above has already explained the four teachings, and from this point further clarifies impurity, impermanence, suffering, and no-self. Another [interpretation] says that from "unreal and false" concludes the above five verses. "Unreal and false" concludes the teaching on emptiness; "although we temporarily bathe [the body]" concludes the teaching on impurity; "certainly will be destroyed and disappear in the end" concludes the teaching on impermanence; from "as a disaster" concludes the teaching on suffering; "[a coming together of] the five *skandhas* and eighteen realms" concludes the teaching on no-self. This can all be understood and taken as you wish.

From "Good people" is the second aspect of [Vimalakīrti's] using his illness to preach the Dharma to his guests, the exhortation to cultivate virtue.

31b

This is divided into three. The first is the immediate exhortation to seek the Dharma body. The second is from "Why?" and explains [Vimalakīrti's] exhortation. The third is from "immeasurable merits" and explains the cause of the Dharma body.

"Good people, you should abhor this [body]." Because [Vimalakīrti] wished to exhort [people to cultivate] the buddha body, he first encouraged them to detest [their physical bodies] through the above five teachings. The second aspect explains this counsel. Because the "buddha body" is the Dharma body, it should be sought. The third aspect, explaining the cause of the Dharma body, also has three parts. The first is the summary that the ten thousand virtues are the cause of the Dharma body. The second, from "[it is born] from morality (*śīla*), concentration (*samādhi*), and [discerning] awareness (*prajñā*)," individually clarifies the essential nature of the practice. The third, from "like this," is the summary conclusion that the ten thousand virtues are the cause of the Dharma body.

From "Good people" is the third aspect of [Vimalakīrti's] using the occasion of his illness to explain the Dharma for his guests, the summary conclusion of his exhortation and admonishment. This can all be understood.

However, what kind of body is this Dharma body? There are two understandings. The first is that it is the seven hundred incalculable [number of] bodies [produced by the Buddha in order to save sentient beings]. The second is that it is the eternally abiding body. The reason is that, although this scripture comes before [those scriptures that] explain "eternally abiding," the central part of this scripture comes after Mañjuśrī raises the main point and asks about [Vimalakīrti's] illness. Now, this chapter is from when Ānanda gave the scripture at the later assembly because he profoundly understood the Buddha's intention to enable sentient beings of later times to hear of these great virtues and revere the teachings. Thus this one chapter entirely praises the virtues of Vimalakīrti's boundless transformation of beings. Therefore it is known that there is no reason that it might not be explaining the eternally [abiding body, even though that is not explicitly discussed in this scripture].

If it refers to the seven hundred incalculable [number] of bodies [produced by the Buddha in order to save sentient beings], then there would be an admonition by another teaching within the admonition by means of the five teachings [given above]; the admonition could not be just within the teaching of impermanence. This is because if it does refer to the seven hundred incalculable bodies, it would not avoid impermanence (i.e., it would be impermanent). The question is this: how could we say that they should aspire to the body of the Tathāgata? If this problem comes up only in regard to Ānanda, it makes sense. But this chapter also contains Vimalakīrti's teachings. If Ānanda simply followed the Buddha's intention and preserved it (i.e., this teaching), then what is Vimalakīrti's intention? Moreover, does this chapter necessarily only preserve the things from the question about the illness? If so, then we could say that [interpreting the Dharma body as] the eternally abiding body would likewise not be correct. Interpretation: it is not only one thing that is clarified by this manifestation of [Vimalakīrti's] illness. Those receiving [these teachings] are also innumerable—why must it be like this? Moreover, Vimalakīrti's intention is also like this. If Mañjuśrī was not in the multitude when inquiring about the illness, then there would likewise be no problem with teaching the eternal [buddha body].

31c

The schools that say that this scripture has already clarified "eternally abiding" naturally give up.

From "Like this elder" is the third aspect within the manifestation of [Vimalakīrti's] skillful means after appearing as though ill, describing the guests who have inquired about his illness and, on hearing the Dharma, arouse the mind [for perfect enlightenment] and obtain benefits.

Chapter Three

The Disciples

[This chapter] describes how the Tathāgata heard of Vimalakīrti's illness and asked five hundred disciples to go and inquire about his illness; this is the reason for the title of the chapter. This chapter and the chapter "The Bodhisattvas" comprise the third part of the specific introduction, the introduction that reveals Vimalakīrti's virtues. Because the Tathāgata's three penetrating insights naturally illuminate the ten thousand spiritual capacities [of sentient beings] equally, why didn't he know that he should only send Mañjuśrī to inquire about [Vimalakīrti's] illness? The five hundred śrāvakas were not up to the task, nor were the eight thousand bodhisattvas able to do it. He asked all of them to go because he wished each to relate how they had been shamed in the past [by Vimalakīrti] and thereby reveal that there is no equal to Vimalakīrti's eloquent arguments and virtuous practices. Hence this [part of the introduction] is called "the introduction that reveals his virtues."

This is unpacked in two parts. The first shows the narrator describing Vimalakīrti's thought that [the Buddha should] send [somebody to visit him]; the second is from "the Buddha knew his thoughts," and is the actual requesting [the disciples and bodhisattvas] to go [and inquire about Vimalakīrti's illness]. The first can be understood. The second, actually requesting [the disciples and bodhisattvas] to go, has two sections. The first is initially sending the śrāvakas, and the second is sending the bodhisattvas. As for sending the śrāvakas first and afterward asking the bodhisattvas [to go]—if the bodhisattvas [were asked first and they] declined because they were not capable, there wouldn't be any point in [considering] sending the śrāvakas. In principle, however, there is no reason that the bodhisattvas would decline if they were asked after the śrāvakas had declined because they were not up to the task—they should accept [the Buddha's request] and go. Therefore the śrāvakas were first [asked to] go, and the bodhisattvas were asked afterward.

The first section, dispatching the śrāvakas, also has two parts. The first is the individual directives to the five hundred disciples; the second is the general summary [of all five hundred disciples declining] as not suitable to the task.

The first [disciple] directed [to visit Vimalakīrti] was Śāriputra, foremost among the ten [chief] disciples in discerning awareness, and so [he was the] first to be asked. There are two aspects to this: the first is the Buddha's request and the second is [Śāriputra's] refusal as not being up to the task. This also has three aspects: the first is just the declining; the second is the explanation for declining; and the third concludes by [stating that he] is not up to the task.

32a

The first, the simple refusal, can be understood. The second aspect, the explanation for declining, has two parts. The first gives the situation leading to [Vimalakīrti's] criticism of [Śāriputra]; the second, from "At that time Vimalakīrti," is the actual criticism. The first, the background situation, can be understood. The second part, the actual criticism, is unpacked in three items. The first gives the general criticism that what Śāriputra takes to be tranquil [sitting] (śamatha) is not, in actuality, adequate. The second item, from "Tranquil sitting is. . . ," gives specific criticisms about different aspects of [tranquil sitting]; the third, from "If you are able to do this [kind of sitting]," is the summary conclusion of the criticism.

"Śāriputra, this sitting is not necessarily [true] tranquil sitting." If we speak of tranquil [sitting] from the point of view of the underlying principle, it is not necessarily like Śāriputra's [sitting]. Śāriputra was trained in the Hinayana and so, vexed by the distractions and disturbances of the world, he wanted to retreat to the mountains and forests in order to control his body and mind. However, Vimalakīrti criticized this because if you understand that the ten thousand realms are empty and do not believe in [the duality of] here and there, how then can there be a body and mind and the arising of distraction and disturbance? If you think that the ten thousand things [actually] exist and are not able to let go of them, then how will you be able to abandon [things like] distractions and disturbances even if you retreat to mountains and forests?

The second item is the specific criticisms. "Tranquil sitting is not manifesting the body or mind within the three worlds—this is tranquil sitting." This says that if you let go of [the duality of] both here and there, there is no mountain to run to, no world to flee. This is not manifesting body or mind within the three worlds, and is called "tranquil." Śāriputra believes in the [real existence of] here and there, and so rejects the ordinary world and runs off to the mountains—this manifests body and mind within the three worlds. How can this be called superb tranquility? This line criticizes his inability to control his body and mind.

"Not arising from your *samādhi* of cessation, yet manifesting authority and decorum [in the world]—this is tranquil sitting." "Arising" means to "come out of." Although one's knowing is one with emptiness, within the world of existence one still manifests all manner of authority and decorum and transforms beings everywhere—this is called "tranquil [sitting]." Śāriputra only thinks to save himself and that benefiting beings is bothersome— how can he obtain superb tranquility? This line criticizes his inability to be equanimous with regard to the two realms of emptiness and existence.

"Not abandoning the qualities of the Way, yet manifesting the concerns of ordinary people—this is tranquil sitting." The "qualities of the Way" are the saintly qualities. This is to say that while one is proficient in the saintly qualities, one nonetheless manifests the concerns of ordinary people within the qualities of the ordinary world and transforms beings in accordance with their spiritual capacity—this is called truly tranquil. It is discriminatory for Śāriputra to think that ordinary people should be abandoned in favor of obtaining the saintly Way—how can he obtain superb tranquility? This line criticizes his inability to be equanimous with regard to the two realms of the ordinary and the sage.

"The mind dwelling neither internally nor existing externally—this is tranquil sitting." The underlying principle of the two truths is "internal" and the six sense objects are "external." This says that one should neither be attached to the two truths nor attached to the six sense objects. When the internal and the external are both abandoned, it is called superbly tranquil. It is a dualism of positive and negative for Śāriputra to believe that the six sense objects should be abandoned and the two truths should be cultivated— how can he obtain superb tranquility? This line criticizes his inability to eliminate the duality of positive and negative.

Dharma Master Sengzhao says, "The body is an illusory dwelling— why would you dwell in the internal? The ten thousand things are unreal— why would you live in the external? The [followers of the] Hinayana guard their thoughts and thus their minds are attached to the internal. Because of their numerous desires, ordinary people chase after the external in their

32b   thoughts. Because of their even-minded contemplation, the great ones are dependent upon neither internal nor external."

"Unmoved by sundry views yet practicing the thirty-seven factors of enlightenment—this is tranquil sitting." "Moved" means "aroused." If one is able to understand that the many views are empty and do not need to be abandoned, and if one also practices the thirty-seven factors of enlightenment, then this is called truly tranquil. If Śāriputra believes that the many views should be rejected and the factors of the Way should be practiced, then he is grasping at phenomenal attributes—how can this be called superb tranquility? This line criticizes his inability to be impartial with regard to the true and the conventional.

"Not eradicating mental afflictions yet entering nirvana—this is tranquil sitting." If you can understand that mental afflictions are empty and do not need to be eradicated, there is the natural realization of nirvana. If Śāriputra believes that only after one's mental afflictions have been eradicated can one enter nirvana, then this is discriminatory—how can it be called tranquil? This line criticizes his inability to realize the skillful method of [entering] nirvana. Dharma Master Sengzhao says, "The true nature of mental afflictions is nirvana. Those whose power of [discerning] awareness is strong see that the mental afflictions are empty and they enter nirvana—they do not wait until they have eradicated [the afflictions] in order to then enter [nirvana]."

The general meaning of all of these is the same, though the text varies according to the item—a positive is raised and a negative is clarified.

From "If you are able to do this [kind of sitting]" is the third item [of the actual criticism], the summary conclusion of the criticism. From "At that time, World-honored One, I [listened to his teaching in silence and could not reply]. . ." is the third aspect of the [disciple's] declining [Śākyamuni's request], the conclusion that he is not up to the task.

The second [disciple] asked [to go and visit Vimalakīrti] was Maudgalyāyana. He was foremost among the ten [chief] disciples in supernatural powers. Within this there is both the request and the refusal. As with [Śāriputra's refusal], [Maudgalyāyana's] refusal has three aspects. The second aspect, the explanation of his declining [to visit Vimalakīrti], also unfolds in three parts. The first describes the situation leading to Vimalakīrti's criticism; the second, from "At that time, Vimalakīrti . . . ," gives the actual criticism;

the third, from "When Vimalakīrti explained this Dharma," describes how the bystanders benefited from his critique.

There are two mistakes for which Maudgalyāyana was criticized. The first is erroneously expounding the existence of perceptual attribute to those with the spiritual capacity for [understanding] the absence of perceptual attribute; the second is erroneously expounding the Hinayana to those with the capacity for the Mahayana. It is for these two mistakes that Vimalakīrti criticized him.

The second part, the actual criticism, also has two items. The first is the general criticism and the second, from "the Dharma is without sentient beings," gives specific criticism of [different] things. "Mahāmaudgalyāyana, in teaching the Dharma for the white-robed laity you should not teach as you do." This means that one should not be mistaken about [people's] spiritual capacity when teaching. "The Dharma should be taught in accordance with the Dharma" means that the Dharma must only be taught after ascertaining the spiritual capacity of the audience.

The second part, the specific criticisms, is divided into two sections. The first is from here up to "It is with this understanding that you should teach the Dharma," and criticizes the mistaken teaching of the existence of perceptual attribute to those with the spiritual capacity for [understanding] the absence of perceptual attribute. The second is from "[You] should know the sharp and dull abilities of sentient beings," and criticizes mistakenly 32c teaching the Hinayana to those with the spiritual capacity for the Mahayana. The first, the criticism of the mistaken [teaching of existence of perceptual attribute to those with the capacity for understanding the] absence of perceptual attribute, has two aspects. The first aspect is straightaway giving the absence of perceptual attribute and critiquing the existence of perceptual attribute. The second is from "Mahāmaudgalyāyana," and through the conclusion of his criticism instructs Maudgalyāyana in how to give a Dharma talk devoid of perceptual attribute.

The thirty lines of the first part (sic), the actual criticism, are divided into two aspects. The first is the initial ten lines that make the critique through the emptiness of provisional designation. The second, the twenty lines from "the Dharma is without the properties of the self," make the criticism by giving the emptiness of real *dharma*s. The first aspect, the critique via the emptiness of provisional designation, has two parts. The first is the initial four lines that explain the emptiness of sentient beings. The second, the latter six lines, gives the proof by explaining the emptiness of the underlying principle.

"The Dharma is without sentient beings" indicates that within the ultimate meaning there are no sentient beings to be found. "Because it is removed from the defiled [notion] of sentient beings." How can you know that [the Dharma] is without sentient beings? When you contemplate the nonexistence of sentient beings, tally this with the underlying principle of things and then you are able to eliminate the defilement of that which reckons sentient beings; therefore you can know that the [the Dharma] is without sentient beings. The following three examples are explained in the same way.

Further, one interpretation takes this to mean that this refers to one who [falsely] reckons and refutes that which is reckoned. That which is reckoned is sentient beings; that which reckons is the deluded mind. "The Dharma is without sentient beings" means that the Dharma that is devoid of perceptual attribute is without sentient beings that are reckoned to possess a soul. "Because it is removed from the defiled [notion] of sentient beings." "Removed" means "empty of." This means that the deluded mind that [falsely] reckons is empty, let alone [the soul that is falsely] reckoned; hence it says that "[the Dharma] is without sentient beings." "The Dharma is without self because it is removed from the defiled [notion of] self" is also like this. One interpretation says that because the defilement that [falsely] reckons the self is empty, the one who does that [reckoning] is also empty.

"The Dharma is without life span because it is removed from birth and death." Consciousness is continuous, without break—this is what is meant by "life span." The explanation is also as above. One interpretation says that "birth" is the beginning, "death" is the end, and the "life span" is what happens in between. This shows that because both the beginning and end are empty, how could the life span in between not be empty?

"The Dharma is without personhood because it is cut off from boundaries of front and back." "Front and back" refer to the two boundaries of birth and death; the explanation is as above. One interpretation says that the front boundary refers to the past and the back boundary refers to the future. Personhood is in the present; because the two boundaries of past and future are empty, how could the present personhood not be empty?

From "The Dharma is forever quiescent" is the second aspect, giving the proof by explaining the emptiness of the underlying principle. This clarifies that the underlying principle is itself empty and thereby shows that sentient beings are empty.

"The Dharma is forever quiescent because it has extinguished all perceptual attributes" shows that the ultimate truth is just as it is. "The Dharma is removed from perceptual attribute because it is without objective factor." Within the worldly truth, the mind is taken as the subjective factor and perceptual objects are taken as the objective factor. In ultimate truth, however, the subjective factor—the mind—is removed from perceptual attribute. This is because the objective factor—perceptual objects—are empty; therefore how could a subjective factor [arise]? One interpretation says that it should read, "The Dharma is without objective factor because it is removed from perceptual attribute." Either way is fine. These two lines explain that mental functions are completely extinguished.

"The Dharma is without name or words because it eradicates language." Names are born from language. Because language is already eradicated, [the Dharma] is without name or words.

"The Dharma is without explanation because it is removed from supposition and analysis." Explanations arise because of supposition and analysis; within the underlying principle there is no supposition or analysis, and so there are no explanations. These two lines clarify that the path of language is eradicated.

"The Dharma is without perceptual attributes of shape because it is like the empty sky." This concludes [the aforementioned] "mental functions are completely extinguished." This means that phenomenal attributes are born of existence; because the underlying principle is one with the void there is no perceptual attribute of shape. It is one with emptiness and so what could be the perceptual object even if you wanted it? Therefore, we say that it concludes the above [statement] "mental functions are completely extinguished."

"The Dharma is without frivolous arguments because it is ultimately empty." This concludes the [earlier statement that the] "path of language is eradicated." This means that frivolous arguments arise because of existence; because the underlying principle is ultimately empty, how could there be frivolous arguments? The underlying principle is ultimately empty, so even

33a

if you wanted to speak, what could be said? Hence we say that this concludes the [earlier statement, the] "path of language is eradicated."

From "the Dharma is without the properties of the self" is the second aspect of the actual criticism of [Maudgalyāyana] by giving [a teaching on] the absence of perceptual attribute. The critique by way of the emptiness of real *dharma*s has twenty lines that are divided into four parts. The first line generally clarifies the emptiness of real *dharma*s. The six lines from "The Dharma is without discrimination" clarify the emptiness of the six sense objects. The five lines from "The Dharma is immovable" show that the six sense consciousnesses are empty. The eight lines from "The Dharma is without beauty or ugliness" clarify the emptiness of the six sense organs.

"The Dharma is without the properties of the self." The sense organs, sense consciousnesses, and sense objects are all the "properties of the self," and therefore we say that none of them are to be attained within the ultimate meaning. "Because it is removed from the properties of the self" is as explained above. One interpretation says that "removed" means empty. In the underlying principle, the sense organs, sense consciousnesses, and sense objects are entirely empty, therefore we know that they are "without the properties of the self."

The second part, the six lines that separately teach the emptiness of the six sense objects, is divided into two parts. The first is the initial three lines that actually clarify the emptiness of the six sense objects; the second is the three lines from "The Dharma is the same as the Dharma-nature," which concludes that [the six sense objects] are devoid of perceptual attribute.

"The Dharma is without discrimination because it is removed from any of the consciousnesses." Within the worldly truth the six sense objects are discriminated, but within the ultimate meaning they are entirely empty. Because they are removed from the sense consciousnesses, there is no discrimination. One interpretation says that discrimination of the six sense objects is only the function of consciousness. Since the six sense consciousnesses that are the subjective factors are already shown to be empty, how could the six sense objects that are the objective factors not be empty?

"The Dharma is without compare because it is without anything to which it can be related." "Comparison" arises because of relationship. Because the underlying principle is originally without relationship, it is "without compare."

"The Dharma is not within the causal realm because it is without condition." The causal realm arises due to conditions. Because conditions themselves are empty, [the Dharma] is not within the causal realm.

From "The Dharma is the same as the Dharma-nature" is the second part, concluding that [the six sense objects] are devoid of perceptual attribute. "The Dharma is the same as the Dharma-nature because it permeates all things" shows that the phenomena (*dharmas*) of the six sense objects are devoid of perceptual attribute in their essential nature; thus it says that the Dharma is the same as the Dharma-nature. "Permeates all things" means that the ulti-   33b
mate truth permeates all things. If ultimate truth was different from all phe-nomena, then how could the things of the six sense objects be the same as ultimate truth? Ultimate truth pervades all things, and thus the phenomena of the six sense objects are also the same as the Dharma-nature.

"The Dharma follows suchness because there is nothing to follow." This means that the phenomena of the six sense objects follow suchness. "There-fore, there is nothing to follow." Beings think that the essential nature of suchness and phenomena are different, one following after the other; hence they say "follow." This shows that suchness and phenomena have the same one attribute that is devoid of attribute—there is neither following nor non-following. Thus the phenomena of the six sense objects are able to follow suchness. If the essential nature of [suchness and phenomena] were differ-ent, how could we say that [the six sense objects] follow suchness?

"The Dharma dwells at the apex of true reality because it is unmoved by peripheral extremes." "Dharma" means the six sense objects. "Apex of true reality" means the ultimate truth. This shows that the six sense objects are entirely empty, [and so the Dharma] is unable to be moved by the two extremes of existence and nonexistence. Thus it says, "dwells at the apex of true reality." We could also say that, as above, "Dharma" means ultimate truth. Whereas above "things" were used to clarify ultimate truth, here ulti-mate truth is used to explain ultimate truth—the ultimacy of the underlying principle is just this. But if we look at the text this interpretation will natu-rally be discarded.

From "The Dharma is immovable" is the third aspect, clarifying the emptiness of the six sense consciousnesses. There are five lines divided into two parts; the first two lines explicitly describe the emptiness of the six sense consciousnesses, and the three lines from "The Dharma conforms with emptiness" conclude that [sense consciousness] is devoid of perceptual attribute.

"The Dharma is immovable because it is not dependent upon the six sense objects." This means that in the worldly truth the six sense consciousnesses chase around after the six sense organs, discriminating the six sense objects. In ultimate truth, however, the essential nature of consciousness is empty and not dependent upon the six sense objects; hence it is immovable. One interpretation says that the six sense objects are entirely empty; having already shown that the six sense objects that are the objective factors are empty, how could the six sense consciousnesses that are the subjective factors not be empty?

"The Dharma has no going or coming because it is non-abiding." This too means that in the worldly truth also the six sense consciousnesses come and go with the six sense organs, but within ultimate truth the six sense consciousnesses do not abide for even a single moment, and so it has "no coming or going."

"The Dharma conforms with emptiness, accords with the absence of perceptual attribute, and responds to the wishless." These three lines, the second aspect [of the emptiness of the six sense consciousnesses], conclude that they are devoid of perceptual attribute. This means that the six sense consciousnesses are no different than the three emptinesses.

From "The Dharma is removed from beauty and ugliness" is the fourth aspect, illustrating the emptiness of the six sense organs. There are eight lines that are divided into two parts: the first is the initial four lines that actually describe the emptiness of the six sense organs, and the second is the following four lines that give the emptiness of the underlying principle as proof.

"The Dharma is removed from beauty and ugliness." Although in the worldly truth the six sense organs distinguish between what is beautiful and what is ugly, in ultimate truth there can be no such distinction. "The Dharma is without increase or decrease." In the worldly truth the six sense organs have growth and decline, but in the ultimate truth there is neither growth nor decline. "The Dharma is without birth or extinction." In the worldly truth the six sense organs have birth in the beginning and extinction afterward, but ultimate truth is primordially without birth or extinction. "The Dharma returns nowhere" means that in the worldly truth the six sense organs produce good

33c

and evil that necessarily will return [in the form of karmic retribution], but in the ultimate truth there is no producing goodness that will return to one [as birth among] humans or deities, nor is there the producing of evil that will return to one [as birth] in the three evil destinies. Therefore it says that "[the Dharma] returns nowhere." One interpretation might be that non-Buddhists reckon that the five elements give rise to the five sense organs and at death the five sense organs return to the five elements—but ultimate truth is utterly unlike this.

The four lines from "The Dharma transcends eyes and ears" is the second part that gives the proof by [explaining] the emptiness of the underlying principle. This shows that the underlying principle is, in and of itself, already empty. How, then, could the six sense organs not be empty? "The Dharma transcends eyes, ear, nose, tongue, body, and mind." This means that the six sense organs do not extend to the underlying principle. Some say that because emptiness transcends the various sense organs, it does not see them. "The Dharma is without highs and lows, forever abiding, immovable." "High" means the Sage, "low" refers to the worthy ones. This means that the ultimate underlying principle cannot be swayed by different kinds of knowledge. Some say that "high" refers to deities and "low" refers to human beings; in other words, the underlying principle is without highs and lows. "The Dharma is removed from all contemplative practices." This also means that the various contemplations do not reach to the ultimate underlying principle.

Some say that from "The Dharma is without the properties of the self" up to "unmoved by peripheral extremes" gives the overall explanation of the three emptinessess (of sense objects, organs, and consciousnesses); from "The Dharma is immovable" up to "responds to the wishless" shows the emptiness of the six sense consciousnesses; from "The Dharma is removed from beauty and ugliness" up to "The Dharma returns nowhere" illustrates the emptiness of the six sense objects; and from "The Dharma transcends eyes and ears" up to "removed from all contemplative practices" clarifies the emptiness of the six sense organs. In any case, for the most part the meaning is the same and you may take it as you wish.

From "Mahāmaudgalyāyana" is the second aspect within the criticism of his mistaken understanding of the absence of perceptual attribute that, through the conclusion of the criticism, instructs him in how to give a Dharma talk devoid of perceptual attribute.

"If the attributes of the Dharma are like this, how can it be taught?" This is the conclusion of the criticism. Because the underlying principle has already been shown to be [devoid of perceptual attribute] like this, why was it taught—thoughtlessly and in disregard for the spiritual capacity [of the audience]—as though the perceptual attributes exist?

From "To teach the Dharma" is the instruction in how to teach a Dharma talk that is devoid of perceptual attribute. This has two parts. The first gives the teaching of the Dharma and shows that neither the teacher nor the disciples exist. The second gives an example to show that neither the teacher nor the disciples exist. These can be understood.

From "You should know [the sharp and dull abilities of] sentient beings" is the second section within the specific criticism, the critique of [Maudgalyāyana's] mistaken teaching of the Hinayana to those with the spiritual capacity for the Mahayana.

"You should know the sharp and dull abilities of sentient beings." This criticizes not knowing the nature of sentient beings' disease. "With unhindered skillful insight." This criticizes his not knowing what medicine will remove [the disease]. These two lines show that [Maudgalyāyana] was not skilled in implementing "below, transform and nurture living beings."

"With a mind of great compassion praise the Mahayana." If the spiritual capacity is great then you should teach the Mahayana. "You should remember to repay the Buddha's kindness and never let the Three Jewels become extinct." This means that if you are able to teach in accordance with the capacity, then it is called the source of "remembering to repay the Buddha's kindness and never letting the Three Jewels become extinct." If, however, at odds with the capacity of the audience Maudgalyāyana teaches the Hinayana, then this is contrary to the Buddha's intention, and so how could it be called "remembering to repay the Buddha's kindness"? How can 34a it cause the seed of the Three Jewels to live long? These two lines show that [Maudgalyāyana] was not skilled in "above, broaden the path of the Buddha." "After this you should preach the Dharma." This means that the Dharma should be taught [as described by Vimalakīrti] above.

From "[When] Vimalakīrti [gave this teaching]" is the third part of the explanation of [Maudgalyāyana's] refusal, illustrating the benefits obtained by the bystanders because of the criticism. From [Maudgalyāyana's] declining as unworthy, "I am [not] eloquent like this," concludes the third part with [Maudgalyāyana's] unworthiness.

The third disciple asked [to visit Vimalakīrti] was Kāśyapa. He was the foremost among the ten disciples in austerities (*dhūta*s). This also has both the [Buddha's] request [that Kāśyapa visit Vimalakīrti] and [Kāśyapa's] declining. As above, [Kāśyapa's] declining also has three aspects. The second aspect, the explanation of his declining, is further divided into three parts. The first gives the situation that led to his being criticized; the second, from "At that time Vimalakīrti," gives the actual criticism; the third, from "World-honored One, when I [heard him speak these words]," describes how because of [Vimalakīrti's] criticism Kāśyapa obtained that which he had never had before.

The second part, actually giving the criticism, also has two items. The first is the actual criticism. The second, from "Kāśyapa, if you are able to eat like this," concludes the criticism. There are four mistakes for which Kāśyapa is criticized. The first is Kāśyapa's calculating in his mind that rich people, in the past, were afraid of committing offenses and cultivated virtue and that is why they had now attained wealth and pleasure. Poor people in the past did not cultivate virtue and so they now experience poverty and difficulty. [He further thought that] if in the present they did not cultivate goodness, then in the future they would again be poor. Therefore [he thought to help the impoverished, saying to himself that] he would now only beg food from the homes of poor people. Vimalakīrti criticized [Kāśyapa's] kindness and compassion as not even-minded, saying that poverty and wealth are not permanent conditions, which is all the more reason that he should instruct all impartially, with no distinctions.

The second error is [Kāśyapa's] reckoning only the inferior karmic rewards of [rebirth among] humans and deities as benefiting the donors and not considering the fruits of buddhahood. Therefore, Vimalakīrti further criticizes the shortsightedness of his concern.

The third error [for which Kāśyapa is criticized] is his fearful calculation that the dust and allure of prosperous towns will give rise to mental attachment; [thus, he thinks that] he should abandon wealthy villages and [beg alms] only from impoverished villages. Vimalakīrti's criticism says that if you understand that the objects of the six senses are empty and beauty and ugliness do not exist, why would you run away from the objects of the six senses? If you believe that the objects of the six senses should be avoided, then one will never be apart from them all day long. However, Kāśyapa isn't the only one who thought like this. The non-Buddhist *Laozi* also wrote, "The five colors make people blind; the five sounds make people deaf; the five tastes confuse people's palate; hard-to-get goods hobble people's behavior."

[Kāśyapa's] fourth mistake [was to think that] "I possess the merits of both knowing and eradication [of entanglements], and thus have the merit of the field of excellence. Those who make offerings to me truly will receive great benefit and so I truly should seek alms from them." But Vimalakīrti scolded him, saying that if he is able to do away with true and false and not believe in noble and inferior, then that truly can be called the merit of the field of excellence. But [Kāśyapa] believes in noble and inferior. It is discrimination to elevate yourself and dislike people—how can that be called a field of excellence? If a field of excellence is established by means of discrimination, because everybody has a mind of discrimination all would possess the merit of a field of excellence, not just Kāśyapa.

[Kāśyapa] was criticized for these four mistakes. Naturally, there are four parts to the actual criticism. The first is from the beginning up to "[and in this way] go about begging food in an orderly fashion," and criticizes the error of partiality in kindness and compassion. The second is from "Because there is no eating," and criticizes the error of [Kāśyapa's] shortsighted concern. The third is from "By considering the village to be empty," and criticizes the error of [Kāśyapa's] inability to eliminate [his reified understanding of] the objects of the six senses. The fourth is from "Kāśyapa, if without discarding the eight fallacies," and criticizes the error of [Kāśyapa's] calculations about the merit of a field of excellence.

"Mahākāśyapa, you have the mind of kindness and compassion but you are not impartial—you avoid the rich and powerful and beg alms from the poor." These two lines are the actual criticism of his mistake of not being impartial in his kindness and compassion.

"Kāśyapa, you should dwell in the equality of the Dharma and beg alms in an orderly fashion." This is [Vimalakīrti's] instruction.

From "Because there is no eating" is the second, the criticism of the error of [Kāśyapa's] shortsighted concern. "Because there is no eating you should go about begging food in an orderly fashion." This is to say that [Kāśyapa] should go about seeking alms in order to lead the almsgiver to attain the reward of nirvana, a state in which there is no eating. But Kāśyapa reckons only to wish for the almsgivers to attain the fruits of the [realms of] humans and deities that experience eating—this is not [the proper attitude]. This line illustrates the intention that should be established when first starting out to seek alms.

"You should take the morsels of food in order to destroy the perceptual attributes of the compounded." One should take the morsels of food in order to lead the almsgivers to destroy the samsaric body that is compounded of the five *skandha*s and attain the Dharma body that is devoid of perceptual attribute. But [Kāśyapa] plans to have them attain the body of humans and deities that is made up of the five *skandhas*—this is not [the proper goal]. This line shows the attitude to have when actually receiving food.

"Because there is no receiving you should receive that food." This means that [Kāśyapa] should receive the food because he wishes the almsgiver to attain the Dharma body that receives nothing. But Kāśyapa thinks to enable them to receive the pleasures of the five desires of humans and deities—this is not [the proper goal]. This shows the attitude to have when eating.

From "By considering the village to be empty" is the third criticism, the criticism of [Kāśyapa's] inability to eliminate the objects of the six senses. This also has three parts. The first is the general criticism. The second, from "the forms that you see," is the specific criticism of each of the six sense objects. The third, from "without self-nature," explains the emptiness of the underlying principle and corroborates the above two lines that give the general and specific criticisms.

"By considering the village to be empty you should enter the village." This is to say that if you are able to see the village as empty, then how could a beautiful object give rise to delusion? One interpretation says that if you see that the objects of the six senses are empty, just like an empty village with no people, then how could delusions arise?

From "The forms that you see" is the second part, the specific criticism of each of the six sense objects. "The forms that you see should be as seen by a blind person." This means that the "forms that you see" are empty, the same as [those seen by] a blind person—how, then, could "forms" give rise to attachment? "The sounds that you hear should be heard as an echo."

34c   Although the sound of an echo can be either pleasing or distasteful, the person who knows that the sound is not real neither likes nor dislikes it. If you see that auditory objects are empty and the same as echoes, then how could auditory objects give rise to delusion? One interpretation says that this is making an analogy because echoes arise from sounds but there is no delusion within the sound.

"The aromas that you smell should be as the wind." Although we smell aromas in the air, the air does not differentiate likes and dislikes. If we can see that the odors are empty and the same as the wind, then how can they give rise to delusion? One interpretation says that although [we say that] odorless air makes contact with the nose, no sense consciousness is aroused. The lack of a cause that would give rise to delusion is also like this.

"Not discriminating the flavors that you taste." If you see that flavors are empty and do not discriminate them, how could flavors give rise to attachment? "Experience touch as the realization of knowing." If you see that [the objects of] touch are empty in the way that the knowledge of non-arising realizes the many *dharma*s, then, again, how could they possibly give rise to attachment? "Know that *dharma*s are like an illusion." This refers to the objects of the mind, which is to say that if you see that the myriad *dharma*s are empty, how then could they give rise to attachment?

From "Without self-nature" is the third part of the criticism of [Kāśyapa's] inability to destroy the objects of the six senses. This explains the realization of the emptiness of the underlying principle, and brings together the general and specific criticisms given above.

"Without self-nature" means without the five *skandha*s of one's own; "without other-nature" means without the five *skandha*s of the other. One interpretation says that "without self-nature" means that the six sense objects belonging to oneself are entirely empty, and "without other-nature" means that the six sense objects of others are also nonexistent.

"Originally never burning and so now without extinguishing." If the Dharma was originally born, then in the end it would be extinguished. But because it is originally without birth, so too it is without extinguishing. This clarifies that beginnings and endings are both empty.

One interpretation says that "Originally never burning and so now without extinguishing" explains how the six sense objects of self and other are empty—if the Dharma has no beginning or end and all things are empty, how could the six sense objects of self or other be real?

From "Kāśyapa, without discarding the eight wrongs" is the fourth of the specific [errors for which Kāśyapa] was criticized, the criticism of [his thinking] that he had the virtues of a field of excellence. This has two parts: the first is criticizing him for thinking that he has the essential nature of a field of merit; the second, from "this almsgiver," criticizes him for thinking that he functions as a field of merit. There are two aspects to the first critique of his thinking that he has the essential nature of a field of merit: the first criticizes his thinking that he is a field of knowing; the second, from "One who eats like this," criticizes his thinking that he is a field of eradication [of entanglements].

"Without discarding the eight wrongs enter into the eight liberations." This says that to see the eight wrongs as empty and that there is nothing to be discarded within emptiness, whereby enter the eight liberations—this is called correct practice. But Kāśyapa believes that one must discard the eight wrongs and strive to cultivate the eight correct [practices]—this is discrimination, and so how can he attain correct practice? This line criticizes [Kāśyapa's] achievement of correct practice. One interpretation says that if you are able to be one with the eight wrongs while yet not being other than the eight liberations, this is not the same as the one-sided approach of *śrāvaka*s and ordinary people, and so can be called correct practice. The eight wrongs are: 1) wrong view, 2) wrong thought, 3) wrong speech, 4) wrong action, 5) wrong livelihood, 6) wrong mindfulness, 7) wrong effort, and 8) wrong concentration. There are three schemas of the eight liberations: 1) the eight meditative concentrations, 2) the [eight emancipations] described in the various texts related to such [emancipations] as [that achieved] when there is no subjective desire, etc., and 3) the eightfold correct path. Here I take the eightfold correct path as the eight liberations.

35a

"Enter the true Dharma by means of false attributes." Being able to see that false objects are empty and that nothing needs to be abandoned and thereby entering the true Dharma—this can truly be called seeing the true object. But if Kāśyapa believes that he can discriminate false and true [objects], how can he see the true object? This line criticizes his [inability to] see the true object.

"If you are able to give to all with one meal, making offerings to the many buddhas and myriad holy sages, then after that you may eat." If you are able to see the ordinary and the sage as equally extinguished in the one emptiness, then when you give a single meal it is an offering to all, since emptiness is nondual. One who is able to put an end [to discrimination] in this way is justly called a person [whose understanding] is correct. But Kāśyapa denigrates the ordinary and elevates the holy and thinks himself to be a field of merit—this is attachment to phenomenal attributes, and so how can he be a person [whose understanding] is correct? One interpretation says that somebody like Vimalakīrti, who is able to distribute a single meal to all without end, should be called a person [whose understanding] is correct. Kāśyapa is not able to do this, and so how can he be called a person [whose understanding] is correct? This line criticizes his thinking that he is a person [whose understanding] is correct.

From "Eat like this" is the criticism of the second aspect of Kāśyapa's thinking that he possesses the essential nature of a field of merit, the criticism of [his thinking that he] is a field of eradication [of entanglements]. "Eating in this way, with neither mental affliction nor removed from mental affliction." This means that within the underlying principle you cannot distinguish eradicating [affliction] and not eradicating [affliction]. One who is able to put an end to both eradicating and not eradicating can be said to possess the essential nature of a field of eradication. But Kāśyapa thinks that he can distinguish eradicating and not eradicating—how can he be said to possess the essential nature of a field of eradication? One interpretation says if you are able to give like this to all with a single meal, then it is the meal of a great being of the middle path. It is neither the offering of an ordinary person with mental afflictions, nor is it the meal offering of [disciples] of the two vehicles [who seek to] abandon mental affliction.

"Neither entering into a state of concentration nor arising from a state of concentration." "Entering a state of concentration" refers to knowing, and "arising from a state of concentration" refers to stupidity. Within the underlying principle there are no distinctions. One interpretation says that "not entering a state of concentration" means that the great being is continually in a state of concentration and yet at the same time is able to be one with mental distractions. "Not arising from a state of concentration" means that [great beings] are able to appear the same as [a person] with mental distractions, without contradicting their serenity.

"Neither dwelling in the world nor dwelling in nirvana." This means that the ultimate truth is just so. One who is able to put an end to thinking in terms of "worthy" and "unworthy" in this way can be said to possess the essential nature of a field of eradication—but not Kāśyapa. How can he be said to possess the essential nature of a field of eradication? This line criticizes him for his reckoning that he possessed the essential nature of a field of eradication. One interpretation says that ordinary people desire to live in the world but [disciples] of the two vehicles wish to leave the world. Great beings, however, hold the salvation of living beings in their minds, and so it is not the same as the *śrāvaka*s who seek to leave the world. At the same time, [great beings] do not forget buddhahood, and so they are not the same as ordinary people who wish to live in the world.

From "This almsgiver" is the second aspect, the critique of [Kāśyapa's thinking] that he possessed the function of a field of merit. "This almsgiver has neither great merit nor small merit." This means that within ultimate truth there is no obtaining great merit for giving to a sage or small merit for giving to an ordinary person. The one who in this way can put an end to [discrimination] can be said to possess the function of a field of merit. But Kāśyapa cannot do this, so how can he possess the function of a field of merit? This line explains [Kāśyapa's] lack of functioning as [a field of merit] based on [his misunderstanding] about the first step [of the practice of giving (*dāna*)].

"Neither for profit nor loss." This means that it is not the case that in ultimate truth you give to a sage and later attain merit, or you give to an ordinary person and later suffer loss. One who in this way is able to put an end [to discrimination] can truly be said to possess the function of a field of merit.

35b

But Kāśyapa discriminates and thinks about profit and loss—how can he possess the function of a field of merit? This line explains [Kāśyapa's] lack of functioning [as a field of merit] based [on his misunderstanding] of the final outcome [of the process of giving]. "This is the correct way to enter the buddha way, not relying on the [way of] the *śrāvaka*." This is to say that, as above, one should not think [in a discriminating fashion as does the *śrāvaka*].

"Kāśyapa, if you can eat like this, then the food given to you by others will not be eaten in vain." This is the second item of the actual criticism, the conclusion of the criticism. From "World-honored One, when I [heard him speak these words]" is the third part within the explanation of why [Kāśyapa] declined [the Buddha's request to visit Vimalakīrti], and describes how, because of [Vimalakīrti's] criticism, Kāśyapa obtained an unprecedented [teaching]. Within this there are five levels. The first is the praise of the unprecedented Dharma obtained [by Kāśyapa]; the second, from "[I aroused a deep respect] for all bodhisattvas," praises the people [now revered by Kāśyapa] whom previously he had not [held in high esteem]; the third, from "Again, I had the thought that. . . ," praises the unprecedented virtue [of Vimalakīrti]; the fourth, from "Who [could listen] to this and not arouse [the aspiration to seek highest awakening]," is the arousal of the unprecedented aspiration; the fifth, starting with "from that point onward I [will never exhort anybody to take up the practices of the *śrāvaka* or *pratyekabuddha*"], is [Kāśyapa's] establishment of an unprecedented resolve. These can all be understood. From "Because of this" is the third level of [Kāśyapa's] declining, the conclusion that he is unworthy.

The fourth [disciple asked to visit Vimalakīrti] was Subhūti, foremost among the [Buddha's] ten disciples in his understanding of emptiness. Within this section there is again the request and the declining. As above, there are three aspects to the declining. The second, the explanation of the declining, also has three parts. The first describes the situation that led to Vimalakīrti's criticism of Subhūti; the second, from "At that time Vimalakīrti [took my almsbowl]," is the actual clarification [of Subhūti] incurring the criticism; the third, from "When [Vimalakīrti] expounded this Dharma," describes the benefits attained by the audience at that time because of [Vimalakīrti's] criticism [of Subhūti].

The second part, the actual clarification [of Subhūti] incurring the criticism, also has four items. The first states the situation that led to his being criticized; the second, from "Ah, Subhūti," is the actual criticism; the third, from "At that time, World-honored One, when I [heard these words]," explains how [Subhūti] felt because of [Vimalakīrti's] criticism; the fourth, from "Vimalakīrti said, ['Ah, Subhūti']," is Vimalakīrti's encouragement in response [to Subhūti's doubts].

"[Vimalakīrti] took my almsbowl and filled it entirely with food." This shows that he was not stingy. [Vimalakīrti] was concerned that if he did not give [Subhūti enough food] he would leave and not hear the entire lecture. 35c Again, there are four mistakes for which Subhūti was criticized. The first is for reckoning that poor people disliked their poverty and regretted their lack of giving in the past, and that if he approached them and acted as an example they would not be stingy. Thus, although they are poor in this world, in the future they would surely be wealthy.

Wealthy people trust their wealth and happiness and are not afraid of not giving alms. Because they themselves are free of difficulties, they are unaware of others' needs. For this reason, although they are wealthy in this world, in the future world they will surely be poor. And it is for this reason [that Subhūti thought that] he should only beg alms from the wealthy. Vimalakīrti criticized him, telling him that regardless of whether one is rich or poor, one benefits because of the teachings. Because Subhūti abandons the poor, his kindness and compassion is not impartial.

The second [mistake for which Subhūti was criticized] was for reckoning that his understanding of emptiness was the best. Even though he went into prosperous villages he was not afraid that he would become attached to material objects, and he therefore thought that he should only preach in such villages. Vimalakīrti's criticism was that within the ultimate meaning there is neither understanding nor non-understanding [of emptiness], but Subhūti thinks that he understands—how, then, can his understanding of emptiness be foremost?

The third [mistake for which Subhūti was criticized] was for reckoning that because he had avoided non-Buddhist paths and followed the Buddha's teachings, he should be considered one of true learning. Vimalakīrti criticized him, saying that within the ultimate meaning there is no difference between true and false, and that only one who has this understanding can be said to have true learning. But Subhūti believed in true and false, constituting [the duality] of right and wrong—how could he be said to be one of "true learning"?

The fourth [mistake for which Subhūti was criticized] was for reckoning that because he had perfected both the virtues of knowing and the eradication [of entanglements], he surely possessed the virtue of a field of excellence. For this reason, he thought that it was up to him to beg alms and thereby bring benefit to the almsgiver. Vimalakīrti's criticism was that the ultimate meaning is primordially free of knowing and the eradication of entanglements, and only a person with that kind of understanding can be said to possess the virtues of a field of excellence. But Subhūti believed in the accomplishment and non-accomplishment of knowing and the eradication [of entanglements]—how could he be said to possess the essential nature of a field of excellence? It was for these four errors that Subhūti was criticized.

As for the second aspect, the actual criticism, it too has four parts. The first is the criticism of his biased mind. The second, from "If, Subhūti, you do not put an end to desire, anger, and ignorance," criticizes him for thinking that his understanding of emptiness is the greatest. The third, from "If, Subhūti, you do not see the Buddha," criticizes his running away from the false and clinging to the true. The fourth, from "If, Subhūti, you can adhere to false views," criticizes him for thinking that he possesses the virtue of a field of excellence.

The first part, the criticism of his biased mind, has two aspects. The first is the actual criticism and the second is the conclusion of the criticism. "Ah, Subhūti, if you are able to be equal about [all] food, then the myriad *dharmas* will also be equal." This means that for the person who is able [to understand that] within existence [all] the food that one receives from almsbegging is equal, then [one will be able to see that] the myriad *dharmas* are empty and likewise equal and without differentiation. This line gives the branch in order to reveal the root. "If [one understands that] the myriad *dharmas* are equal, then [all] food will also be equal." This means that if one can understand that the myriad *dharmas* are empty, equal, and without differentiation, then the many conditioned things within existence will also be seen as equal. This line gives the root in order to reveal the branch.

"If you can go about and beg [alms] in this way, then you can take the food." This is the second aspect, the conclusion [of the criticism of Subhūti's biased mind]. It means that one who is able to see the root and the branch as equal is able to take almsfood.

36a

The second part, the criticism of [Subhūti's thinking] that he is foremost in understanding emptiness, is further divided into three parts. The first criticizes [Subhūti] for being unable to put an end to [the dualism of] right and wrong. The second, from "neither free nor bound," criticizes him for not being able to put an end to [the dualism of] knowledge and stupidity. The third, from "If you can master all *dharma*s," is the conclusion of the prior two parts.

The first part, the criticism of his inability to put an end to [the dualism of] right and wrong, is made up of four lines. "If, Subhūti, you do not eradicate desire, anger, and ignorance, do not associate with them either." In the ultimate meaning, the three poisons are entirely empty; because there is nothing that can be ended, it says "do not put an end to." This is "wrong." But if the three poisons are entirely empty, what could the practitioner "associate with"? Hence it says "not associate with them either." This is "right." The next three lines are the same.

But Subhūti believes that he has eradicated the three poisons and is no longer associated with them—how can he be called foremost in his understanding of emptiness? One interpretation says that [this means] that the *śrāvaka* puts an end [to the three poisons] and so is not associated with them. Ordinary people do not put an end [to the three poisons] and therefore are associated with them. The great beings thoroughly penetrate the impartiality of emptiness, and so they are not the same as the *śrāvaka* who puts an end [to the three poisons] and is not associated with them. They are also not the same as ordinary people who do not put an end [to the three poisons] and so are associated with them. One who is able to be like this can be called foremost in their understanding of emptiness. The following lines are the same. One interpretation takes this to mean that if you are able to see that the three poisons are empty and lacking anything that can be cut off, then this understanding is one with the underlying principle and the three poisons are ended of themselves—with what, then, could the practitioner associate?

"Without destroying this body, nonetheless accord with the one attribute." If you argue that the underlying principle is empty then there is no need to wait until the body is destroyed to pursue emptiness—this body right now is itself empty. The person who understands this can be called foremost in the understanding of emptiness. But Subhūti reckons that after the body is destroyed one will be in accord with the one attribute—how can he be called foremost in the understanding of emptiness?

"Without extinguishing ignorance and attachment, giving rise to illumination and liberation." Understanding that ignorance and attachment are themselves empty and there is nothing that can be destroyed—this is itself illumination and liberation. But Subhūti believes that he has already destroyed ignorance and attachment and obtained liberation—how can he be called foremost in the understanding of emptiness? This line shows that he is not able to do away with entanglements. "Using the attributes of the five heinous offenses to obtain liberation" is interpreted in the same way.

From "neither liberated nor bound" is the second part [of the criticism of Subhūti's thinking that he is foremost in understanding emptiness] and criticizes him for not being able to put an end to [the dualism of] knowledge and stupidity. This has five lines. In "Neither liberated nor bound," "liberated" refers to knowing; "bound" refers to stupidity. In ultimate truth, however, no distinctions are possible.

"Neither seeing the four truths nor not seeing those truths." Seeing the [four] truths is to know; not seeing them is stupidity. In the ultimate meaning, however, there are no distinctions. If there is "no attaining the fruits" there of course must also be "no non-attaining the fruits," but this is simply missing in the text. This shows that in the ultimate meaning there is neither the attaining of the fruits by [followers of] the two vehicles because of their seeing the four truths, nor is there the non-obtaining of the fruits by ordinary people who do not see [the four truths].

"Lacking the nature of ordinary people." The nature of ordinary people is defiled—it is not the nature of ordinary people to be undefiled. Of course, it should also say "not removed from the nature of ordinary people," but this too is missing in the text. In the ultimate truth, however, there are no distinctions.

"Neither a sage nor not a sage." This is to say that ultimate truth is literally just as it is, and the one who, as taught above, can put an end to the opposition of knowledge and stupidity is the one who can be called foremost

36b

in the understanding of emptiness. Subhūti, however, is not able to let things be as they are, and so how can he be called foremost in the understanding of emptiness? "If you can master all *dharmas* yet be removed from the perceptual attributes of all *dharmas*, then you can take the food" is the third part, the conclusion of the prior two levels. This means that if you can master all of the virtuous *dharmas* and yet put an end to the opposition of right and wrong as well as of knowledge and stupidity, then you can take the food [offered to you while almsbegging].

From "If, Subhūti, [you do not see the Buddha]" is the third criticism, [the criticism of Subhūti's belief that because] he has avoided the false and followed the true [he should be considered one who has followed the true path]. This has two parts: the first criticizes his belief that he has followed the true [path]; the second, from "the non-Buddhist path," criticizes his avoiding the false [paths].

"If, Subhūti, you do not see the Buddha and do not hear the Dharma" means that within the ultimate meaning there is no buddha to be seen and there is no Dharma that can be heard. To [see and hear] like this is to really follow the true [path]. But Subhūti believed in seeing the Buddha and hearing the Dharma—how can this be the true [path]? One interpretation says that this means that it is precisely because Subhūti is not able to be like this and put an end [to duality] that he also does not see the Buddha or hear the Dharma.

From "The six teachers of the non-Buddhist paths" is the second criticism of [Subhūti's] avoiding the false. "Pūraṇa Kāśyapa" has the first name of Pūraṇa and the family name of Kāśyapa. His non-Buddhist path was the belief in false views. "Maskarin Gośālīputra" has the first name of Maskarin and his mother's name of Gośālī. His non-Buddhist path was to believe in fatalism. "Sañjaya Vairaṭīputra" has the first name of Sañjaya and his mother's name of Vairaṭī. His non-Buddhist path was extreme skepticism. "Ajita Keśakambala" has the first name of Ajita and the name "Keśakambala" because of the coarse [hair-fiber clothing that he wore]. His non-Buddhist path was to burn the body with the five fires. "Kakuda Katyāyana" has the first name of Kakuda and the family name of Katyāyana. His non-Buddhist practice was to hold the two views of annihilation and eternalism. In [the name] "Nirgrantha Jñātiputra" "Nirgrantha" is the common name for renunciants on non-Buddhist paths and has a meaning similar to that of the Buddhist *śramaṇa*. "Jñāti" is his mother's name. His non-Buddhist practice was the same as those [ascetics] who believed in plucking out one's hair.

"Take these as your teachers and under them leave home" means that in the ultimate meaning there is no difference between false and true. Subhūti believes that his teacher is the Buddha, but if [the teachings of the] Buddha and those of the non-Buddhist paths are equally empty, then there is but one nature, not two. Therefore, those on non-Buddhist paths should also be his teachers. Because emptiness is nondual, if those on non-Buddhist paths are not his teachers, then neither is the Buddha his teacher. One interpretation says that in the ultimate meaning there is essentially no difference between the Tathāgata and those on non-Buddhist paths, and one who can understand this can truly be said to be the Buddha's disciple. Because Subhūti has left home under the Buddha, he believes that the Buddha is different from those on non-Buddhist paths—this is the false view of grasping at perceptual attributes. Therefore it says to take the six non-Buddhist paths "as your teachers and under them leave home." This is a criticism based on the beginning [of Subhūti's spiritual path]. "Follow those [non-Buddhist] teachers and fall [into the same mistakes] as they have fallen into," because emptiness is nondual. One interpretation says that it is precisely because Subhūti believes in falling and not falling [into error] that he has false views. Hence if non-Buddhists fall [into error], he too falls. This is a criticism based on the end [of Subhūti's spiritual path]. "Then you may take the food." If [Subhūti] is able to follow what he has been taught above then he may take the almsfood [that is offered to him].

From "If, Subhūti [you can enter into the erroneous views]" is the fourth of the actual critiques, the criticism of Subhūti's belief that he has the virtue of a field of excellence; this has four parts. The first criticizes Subhūti's belief that he possesses the essential nature of a field of excellence. The second, from "If those who give you alms," criticizes Subhūti's belief that he possesses the function of a field of merit. The third, from "If you join hands with the legions of Māra," concludes the first [criticism that Subhūti] is lacking the essential nature of a field of merit. The fourth, from "[If you can have a hostile mind] to all sentient beings," concludes [the second criticism that Subhūti] is lacking the function of a field a merit.

The first, the criticism of Subhūti's belief that he possesses the essential nature of a field of merit, has four lines divided into two parts. The first two lines show that he is not a field of eradication [of entanglements]; the latter two lines show that he is not a field of knowing.

"[If,] Subhūti, you can enter into the many false views and not reach the other shore [of enlightenment]." "Enter into" means to understand. If he can understand that the false views are empty and without anything to be abandoned, and that the other shore is empty and without any place to be reached, he can truly be said to possess the essential nature of a field of eradication. But Subhūti believes that false views should be abandoned and that nirvana within this world should be reached. This is the discriminating [mind] that grasps at perceptual attributes, still carrying the seeds of bondage. How can he have attained the essential nature of a field of eradication?

One interpretation says that within the ultimate meaning there is no difference between false views and the other shore [of enlightenment], but Subhūti reckons that he has already abandoned false views and arrived at the other shore. [He also believes that] ordinary people enter into false views and so do not reach the other shore. In other words, this is a discriminating [mind] attached to perceptual attributes, all the more entering into false views and not reaching the other shore. My interpretation is that within emptiness there is no discrimination; if you wish to reach the other shore you should not abandon the many views. Thus it says "enter into false views." If you wish to abandon the many views, you will certainly not reach the other shore. Hence it says, "not reach the other shore." Because emptiness is nondual, if you are going to enter [into views] you should enter into all [views], and if you are going to abandon [views] you should abandon all [views]. The following lines are all the same as this.

"If you can dwell within the eight difficult conditions [of birth] and not attain freedom from difficulty." To "dwell" means not to abandon. "Freedom from difficulty" refers to the fruits [of nirvana] without remainder. The two schools are all in agreement with this interpretation. If you understand that the eight difficult conditions are empty and lack that which can be abandoned, and that freedom from difficulty is not something to be attained, then this is truly a field of eradication. But Subhūti believes that the eight difficult conditions can be abandoned and freedom from difficulty can be realized—this is attachment to perceptual attributes, still carrying the fruits of bondage. How can he be a field of eradication [of entanglements]? One

37a interpretation says that Subhūti believes that ordinary people dwell within the eight difficult conditions [of birth] but that he himself has realized freedom from difficulty—a serious false view. Hence this is all the more reason that he dwells within the eight difficult conditions and cannot attain freedom from difficulty. These two lines show that he does not possess the function of a field of eradication.

"If you are one with the mental afflictions and abandon the truth of purity." "One with" means "to not be in opposition." "Abandon" is "not to be attached." The text is interpreted as above. One school of thought agrees with this interpretation. "If you attain the *samādhi* of no-strife and all sentient beings also attain it." This also is because emptiness is nondual. These two lines show that he is not a field of knowing.

From "those who give you alms" is the second aspect, criticizing Subhūti's belief that he possesses the function of a field of merit. "If you are not called a field of merit by those who give you alms." This is also because emptiness is nondual. One interpretation says that if you describe the ultimate underlying principle, it has a single attribute that is without distinction; it is precisely because Subhūti believes that some are fields of merit and some are not fields of merit that he has false views. Therefore, those who give him alms are not said to be giving alms to a field of merit. This line is criticism based on the function [of a field of merit] at the outset [of the practice of giving]. "If those who make offerings to you thereby fall into the three evil pathways" is again because emptiness has no differentiation. One interpretation says that it is precisely because Subhūti believes in discrimination that he himself has false views, and therefore those who make offerings to him will surely fall into the three evil destinies. This line is criticism based on the function [of a field of merit] as the outcome [of the practice of giving].

From "[If you join hands] with the legions of Māra" is the third part, concluding [the first part of the fourth actual criticism, that Subhūti] lacks the essential nature of a field of merit. "If you join hands with the legions of Māra and make the various defilements your companions." Subhūti reckons that Māra is endowed with both entanglements and karma, and therefore is not a field of eradication. However, he thinks that he himself has success-fully eradicated [entanglements and karma], and so he is possessed of the essential nature of a field of eradication. Within the underlying principle, however, emptiness is nondual and thus there is also no distinction between Subhūti and Māra. This line concludes the above [critique that Subhūti] does not possess the essential nature of a field of eradication. One school agrees with this. "If you can be equal to and no different from the legions of Māra, the many troubles and afflictions of the world, [. . . then you can accept the food]." Subhūti believes that he possesses pure knowing but again, because emptiness is nondual, they are equal and without distinction. One school also agrees with this. This line concludes the above [critique that Subhūti] does not possess the essential nature of a field of knowing.

From "[If you can have a hostile mind] toward all sentient beings" is the fourth part, concluding the above second [criticism that Subhūti] lacks the function of a field a merit, [which is itself the fourth aspect of the actual criticism of Subhūti]. "If you can have a hostile mind toward all sentient beings, [. . . then you can accept the food]." Subhūti reckons that those on non-Buddhist paths are of no benefit to almsgivers and therefore they have a hostile mind toward all sentient beings. Because emptiness is also non-dual, however, he is the same as those on non-Buddhist paths. One school is also in agreement with this.

"Slandering the buddhas, defaming the Dharma, not numbered among those in the assembly, and in the end not attaining ultimate nirvana." This again means that it is because emptiness is nondual. However, "in the end not attaining ultimate nirvana" says simply that in the end he does not enable the almsgiver to attain ultimate nirvana. One interpretation says that it is Subhūti who in the end does not attain ultimate nirvana. The interpretation of the text is as above. "If you are able to do this, then you can accept the [alms]food." This is as was explained above.

From "At that time, World-honored One, I [heard these words]" is the third aspect of the actual clarification of the criticism, showing how [Su-bhūti] felt when he heard Vimalakīrti's criticism. From "Vimalakīrti said to me" is the fourth aspect, Vimalakīrti's encouragement in response [to Subhūti's doubts]. This also has four parts. The first is the actual encour-agement, "Subhūti, take your [alsm]bowl without being afraid." The second,

37b

from "What is the meaning of this?", uses a metaphor to question Subhūti. The third part is Subhūti's response, "'No,' I said." The fourth is from "Vimalakīrti [said, 'All phenomena']," and is Vimalakīrti's further encouragement, bringing together [the previous metaphor and an explanation of all phenomena].

This has three aspects. The first is the direct encouragement to not be afraid. The second explains this encouragement, and the third, from "Why is this?", is further explanation. What is the reason for saying that you should not be afraid of something like a magical apparition? "Not different from these perceptual attributes" means "apparitional attributes." Knowledgable ones are not attached to words and letters, thus there is nothing to which to be attached; therefore it says that Subhūti should not be afraid. The third aspect is further explanation of why one should not be attached to words and letters. "The nature of words and letters is separate [from their perceptual attributes]—words and letters do not exist." This means that the nature of words and letters is empty and so there is no attachment; they do not exist and so there is no attachment. "This is liberation" means that it is liberation because both linguistic designations and essential natures are empty and unfettered. One interpretation says that emptiness is the condition of liberation, and so emptiness is what is called liberation.

From "[When] Vimalakīrti [gave this teaching]" is the third part of the explanation of [Subhūti's] declining [to visit Vimalakīrti], describing the benefits obtained by the multitudes [of heavenly beings] when Subhūti was criticized. "Therefore, I am not worthy of visiting him and inquiring after his illness" is the third part of [Subhūti's] declining as unworthy, the conclusion that he is not worthy.

The fifth [disciple] asked [to visit Vimalakīrti] was Pūrṇa [Maitrāyaniputra]. Maitrāyani was his mother's name. He was foremost among the ten disciples in expounding the Dharma. This also has [the two main parts of] the Buddha's request and [Pūrṇa Maitrāyaniputra] declining. The three parts of the declining are also as above. The second part, the explanation of why Pūrṇa Maitrāyaniputra declined [to visit Vimalakīrti], also has four aspects. The first gives the situation leading to the criticism; the second, from "At that time Vimalakīrti," is the actual criticism. The third, from "At that time Vimalakīrti entered into *samādhi*," describes Vimalakīrti entering into a state of concentration and enabling the *bhikṣu*s to know their former lives. The fourth, from "I thought that a *śrāvaka* [who cannot see people's capacity]," describes how Vimalakīrti's criticism caused Pūrṇa Maitrāyaniputra to arouse an unprecedented resolve. The reason that Pūrṇa Maitrāyaniputra was criticized was for not ascertaining the ability and nature of those he was teaching—he expounded the Hinayana to them even though they possessed the spiritual capacity of the Mahayana. Therefore, he was criticized by Vimalakīrti.

The second aspect, the actual criticism, has two items: the first is Vimalakīrti's instruction regarding what to do before teaching; the second, from "Do not put rotten food [into precious vessels]," is the actual criticism. "First you should enter into concentration and contemplate the minds of the people, and only after that should you expound the Dharma." This means that in order to expound the Dharma for people, you must [enter a state of concentration and contemplation] just like this. The second item, the actual criticism, has four sections. The first criticizes Pūrṇa Maitrāyaniputra for not knowing the abilities and natures [of beings] of the three worlds. The second, from "If you wish to travel the Great Way," criticizes the difference between his teaching and the spiritual capacity [of the audience]. The third, from "Pūrṇa, these *bhikṣu*s [aroused the mind of the Mahayana long ago]," concludes the second section, the difference between his teaching and the spiritual capacity [of the audience]. The fourth, from "I discern the discerning awareness of the Hinayana [to be insignificant and shallow]," concludes the first section, not knowing the abilities and natures [of beings] of the three worlds.

37c

"Do not put rotten food into precious vessels" means that you should not give the Hinayana to those with the spiritual capacity for the Mahayana. "You should know the thoughts in the minds of those *bhikṣu*s" means that he should ascertain the thoughts in the minds of those *bhikṣu*s and then teach them. This line criticizes Pūrṇa's not knowing the present spiritual capacity [of the *bhikṣu*s]. "Do not take lapis lazuli to be the same as crystal." This also means that he should not regard the Hinayana to be the same as the spiritual capacity for the Mahayana. One interpretation says that "lapis lazuli" is a metaphor for the spiritual capacity for the Mahayana and that "crystal" is a metaphor for the teachings of the Hinayana, and that this means that we cannot compare them.

"You are not able to know the abilities and foundations of sentient beings." This is to say that Pūrṇa did not know people's abilities. This line criticizes him for not knowing their prior abilities and natures. "Do not arouse them with the teachings of the Hinayana." This means that he should not expound the Hinayana to them and cause them to arouse a lesser aspiration. "They are without injury—do not hurt them." This is to say that those *bhikṣu*s are originally without the disease of the Hinayana and so Pūrṇa should not now expound the Hinayana and thereby cause them to give rise to the wound of the Hinayana. This line criticizes him for not knowing future benefits.

From "If you wish to travel the Great Way" is the second section, criticizing Pūrṇa for the difference between his teaching and the spiritual capacity [of the audience]. This has three lines, all of which illustrate the point by means of an external metaphor; these can be understood. From "[Pūrṇa,] these *bhikṣu*s [aroused the mind of the Mahayana long ago]" is the third section, concluding the second section above, critiquing the difference between Pūrṇa's teaching and the spiritual capacity of the audience. From "I see [the discerning awareness] of the Hinayana [to be insignificant and shallow]" is the fourth section, concluding the first section, criticizing Pūrṇa for not ascertaining the abilities and natures of those to whom he was teaching. One interpretation says that from "Pūrṇa, [these *bhikṣu*s aroused the mind of the Mahayana long ago]" up to "[Why do you] teach and lead them [with the teachings of the Hinayana]?" goes with the two preceding metaphors of the small path and the ox's footprint, and that from "I see [the discerning awareness] of the Hinayana [to be insignificant and shallow]" separately goes with the metaphor of the firefly. This doesn't go against the overall meaning and so you can interpret it as you wish.

From "At that time Vimalakīrti [entered into *samādhi*]" is the third aspect of the explanation of why Pūrṇa Maitrāyaniputra declined [to visit Vimalakīrti], describing how Vimalakīrti entered into a state of concentration and enabled the *bhikṣu*s to know their former lives. This has three parts. The first is the actual description of [Vimalakīrti's] entrance into a state of concentration and making it possible for the *bhikṣu*s to know past events. The second is from "At that, [all of the *bhikṣu*s bowed their heads,]" and shows all the *bhikṣu*s revering Vimalakīrti in response. The third is from "At that time

Vimalakīrti [expounded the Dharma for them]," and describes how Vimala-kīrti expounded the Dharma for them and thereby strengthened their resolve for the Mahayana.

From "I thought that a *śrāvaka* [who cannot see people's capacity]" is the fourth aspect of the explanation of Pūrṇa's declining, showing how Vimalakīrti's criticism caused Pūrṇa Maitrāyaniputra to arouse an unprece-dented resolve. From "Therefore [I am not worthy to visit Vimalakīrti]" is the third part of Pūrṇa's refusal, the conclusion that he is not worthy.

The sixth [disciple] told to visit [Vimalakīrti] and inquire after his ill-ness was Katyāyana, foremost among the ten disciples in elucidating doc-trinal points. This also has both the request [to visit Vimalakīrti] and [Katyāyana's] declining. As with the [disciples] already described, the declin-ing has three aspects; the second aspect, the explanation of why he declined, also has three parts. The first part gives the situation leading to his criticism; the second part, from "At that time Vimalakīrti," is the actual criticism incurred [by Katyāyana]; the third, from "When Vimalakīrti had expounded this Dharma," describes how the bystanders benefited as a result of this criticism.

38a

The first part, the description of the situation leading to his criticism, is further divided into three. The first item describes that "the Buddha sum-marized the essentials of the Dharma for the *bhikṣu*." The five subjects that the Tathāgata explained are the essential explanations for entering the path, and so they are called the "essentials of the Dharma." The second item is "Afterward I developed and amplified these subjects" and describes Katyāyana's elaboration [of the Buddha's teaching]. The third item gives the teachings that he explained. The three marks [of all phenomena] are non-abiding and perishable; this is the "meaning of impermanence." The eight features [of life] are like the cutting of a sword; this is the "meaning of suf-fering." There is no inner self; this is the "meaning of emptiness." The five *skandha*s are not self-abiding; this is the "meaning of no-self." Annihilation of the body and the extinction of knowing—this is the "meaning of quies-cent extinction."

Katyāyana, however, merely passed on what the Buddha had taught. In short, he was criticized for two things. The first is with regard to the under-lying principle: the numerous *bhikṣu*s should certainly attain the same sal-vation as those three sages, and so Katyāyana was criticized even though he made no mistakes. The second is with regard to [the perceptual attributes of] things: when the Buddha spoke the audience had the spiritual capacity for understanding the existence of perceptual attributes, and so the Buddha also taught the existence of perceptual attributes. But when Katyāyana transmitted that teaching, the spiritual capacity of the audience had changed [and they were able to comprehend] the absence of perceptual attribute. Katyāyana, however, was unaware of this and so he expounded the existence of perceptual attributes—and for this reason he was criticized by Vimalakīrti.

The second aspect, the actual criticism incurred [by Katyāyana], has two parts. The first is the summary criticism. The second, from "Katyāyana, *dharma*s ultimately [are neither born nor extinguished]," gives the criticism of each subject separately. "Do not expound the true attributes of *dharma*s with a mind involved with birth and extinction." There are four ways to understand this. The first says that when the five subjects were taught, Katyāyana's mind experienced birth and extinction with regard to the five subjects; therefore Vimalakīrti told him "Do not expound the true attributes of *dharma*s with a mind involved with birth and extinction." The second says that a mind [involved with] perceptual attributes conditions the impermanent object, and names arise from those objects; therefore it is called a "mind involved with birth and extinction." Moreover, [when teaching], Katyāyana should not have a mind involved with "suffering" [or any of the other five subjects] on up to "quiescent extinction." The third says that you should not have a mind that is involved with birth and extinction taken to be the true perceptual attributes of *dharma*s. Certainly, you must teach that the true perceptual attributes of *dharma*s are that the functions of the mind are none other than emptiness. The fourth says that you should not speak of the absence of perceptual attributes while your mind is nonetheless involved with the birth and extinction of *dharma*s that possess perceptual attributes. Truly you should teach this with a mind conditioned by the absence of perceptual attributes.

As for the "true attributes of *dharma*s" expounded during the twelve years of teaching [the Āgamas], the five subjects were taken as the highest teaching about the true attributes of [conditioned] things like birth and extinction up to the unconditioned, such as the extinction of the body; and [the teaching that] provisional designations are not at all the true attributes [of phenomena]. Vimalakīrti's criticism here is to say that both the provisional and the true are empty and that this is the true attribute of *dharma*s. Dharma Master Sengzhao says, "The true attribute is mysterious and profound, exhausting the ordinary realm. It is not something that is known by the discriminating minds of sentient beings, it is not something that can be spoken of by those who discuss things." When Katyāyāna heard the Buddha speak of the five subjects, he thought that *dharma*s had the attributes of birth and extinction; therefore Vimalakīrti criticized him, saying, "Do not expound [the true attributes of *dharma*s] with a mind involved with birth and extinction." 38b

From "Katyāyāna" is the second part, the specific criticisms. "*Dharma*s ultimately are neither born nor extinguished—this is the meaning of impermanence." This means that the essential nature of the three kinds of *dharma*s is empty on its own and without birth and extinction, and that this is the meaning of impermanence. But Katyāyana only sees the birth and extinction of things and takes that to be the meaning of impermanence. In other words, he doesn't know the reason that things are impermanent. "The five appropriating *skandha*s are in the end empty, without arising—this is the meaning of suffering." As above, this means that the root of suffering is empty. But Katyāyana takes a mind burdened by objects to be the meaning of suffering. He does not know the root of the meaning of suffering. "The many *dharma*s are ultimately nonexistent—this is the meaning of emptiness." This means that the many *dharma*s are ultimately empty and without existence, and this is the meaning of emptiness.

But Katyāyana only knows that within [*dharma*s] there is no self and therefore they are empty—he does not know the meaning of emptiness.

"There is no duality of self and no-self—this is the meaning of no-self." This means that the five *skandha*s are not self-abiding in the soul, in which those on non-Buddhist paths believe, and that therefore there is no self. That all is empty and nondual—this is the meaning of no-self. One interpretation says that "no-self" means a "no-self" other than the soul [believed in by non-Buddhists, e.g., the no-self of the Hinayana]. Another says that "duality" refers to the provisional self and the emptiness of self. Katyāyana knows only that the five *skandha*s are not self-abiding and are therefore "no-self." In other words, he does not know the reason for no-self. "*Dharma*s have never been on fire from the beginning and so are without extinguishing—

this is the meaning of quiescent extinction." The essential nature of birth is unattained, and so it says that there is no birth. How could there be a later extinction if there is originally no birth? Therefore it says "no extinguishing." The underlying principle is originally without birth or extinction—this is the meaning of quiescent extinction. Katyāyana only knows the extinction of the body and the end of the mind and takes this to be the meaning of quiescent extinction. In other words, he does not know the reason for quiescent extinction.

From "When Vimalakīrti expounded this teaching" is the third part of the explanation of Katyāyana's declining, describing the merit attained by the bystanders because of the criticism. "Therefore I am not fit to inquire of his illness" is the third aspect of his declining, the conclusion that he is not up to the task.

The seventh [disciple] told [to visit Vimalakīrti] was Aniruddha, foremost among the ten disciples in divine sight. This also has [the two parts of] the request and the declining. The three parts of the declining are also as above. The second part, the explanation of Aniruddha's declining, is further divided into four items. The first is the description of the situation leading to the criticism; the second, from "At that time Vimalakīrti," is the actual criticism. The third item explains the nature of incurring the criticism; the fourth, from "those myriads of Brahmās," describes the Brahmā kings' inquiring about the ultimate divine sight.

The first item, describing the situation leading to the criticism, also has three parts. The first clarifies where he was "taking a walk." Because Aniruddha was taking a walking break along the road, it says "taking a walk." The second part describes the Brahmā kings coming to ask the extent of Aniruddha's divine sight. The third part gives Aniruddha's reply. These can be understood.

The reason that Aniruddha was criticized is because the Buddha always praised his attainment of divine sight as the best. The Brahmā king calculated that he too had obtained divine sight; however, if Aniruddha's divine sight was superior to the Brahmā king's, then he would study with him. But if it was not superior, then why did the Buddha praise him? Aniruddha, unaware of the Brahmā king's intention, simply told him what he saw. Vimalakīrti criticized Anirudhha because he should have told the Brahmā king about the Buddha's true divine sight, devoid of perceptual attributes; instead, he simply answered him with a description of what he saw, which possessed perceptual attributes. Therefore, Vimalakīrti came to criticize him.

The actual description of his criticism has two aspects: the first gives two propositions in order to initially determine their nature [as conditioned or unconditioned]; the second, from "If it is that of a constructed attribute," explains both propositions, objecting to each in the end. "Ah, Aniruddha, is the divine sight that of a constructed attribute?" This asks whether he sees things as having the perceptual attributes of constructed worldly truth. "Or is it that of an unconstructed attribute?" This asks whether he sees things as the unconstructed ultimate truth, devoid of perceptual attributes. From "If it is that of a constructed attribute" is the second aspect, the explanations that end with objections. "If it is that of a constructed attribute, then it is the same as the five supernatural powers of the non-Buddhist paths." This explains the first proposition: if you believe in the five sense objects and see things like that, then it is the same as those on non-Buddhist paths. What would be so wonderful about such [a path] that he would teach it to the Brahmā kings? "If it is that of an unconstructed attribute, then it is unconditioned and nothing should be seen." This means that if you do not believe in the five sense objects then the divine sight is unconditioned and nothing should be seen. What [then] could he teach to the Brahmā kings?

From "World-honored One, at that time I was silent" is the third item, explaining the nature of [Aniruddha] incurring the criticism. Aniruddha feared that if he said he saw things to be of a constructed attribute he would be the same as the those on non-Buddhist paths; but if he said that he saw things to be of an unconstructed attribute, then it would be as Vimalakīrti had already replied, [and there would be nothing that he could see]. Therefore he remained silent—this shows that he did not know the gist of things.

From "Those Brahmā kings" is the fourth item, the Brahmā kings' inquiry about the ultimate divine sight. This has four parts. The first is the Brahmā kings' inquiry about the ultimate divine sight. The second is Vimalakīrti's answer regarding the Buddha's true divine sight. The third is the benefit attained by the Brahmā kings. The fourth is the Brahmā kings paying their respects and leaving. These can be understood. "Therefore I am not fit to inquire of his illness" is the third aspect of his declining, the conclusion that he is not up to the task.

39a The eighth [disciple] directed [to visit Vimalakīrti] was Upāli, foremost of the ten disciples of the Buddha in observing the precepts. This [part of the scripture] also has both the [Buddha's] request [that Upāli visit Vimalakīrti and his] declining [to go]. As with the previous [disciples, Upāli's] declining has three aspects; the second, the explanation of his refusal to go, further unfolds in five parts. The first gives the situation leading to the criticism; the second, from "At that time Vimalakīrti," gives the actual criticisms; the third, from "Thereupon, the two *bhikṣus*," is the praise of Vimalakīrti by the two *bhikṣus*; the fourth, from "I answered, saying . . . ," is Upāli's praise [of Vimalakīrti]; and the fifth, from "Those *bhikṣus*. . . ," describes the benefits obtained by the two *bhikṣus*.

The first part, the situation leading to [Vimalakīrti's] criticism [of Upāli], also has three aspects. The first describes the nature of the *bhikṣus*' remorse for having broken their precepts: "There were two *bhikṣus* whose conduct violated the precepts; they were truly ashamed but did not dare ask the Buddha about it." The second is the actual inquiry. The third is Upāli's answer, based on the precepts.

If the transgression of the two *bhikṣus* was of the first category [of Vinaya offenses,] the *bhikṣus* would not be able to obtain absolution, and so we can know that it belonged to the second category of offense. Violating the precepts is an extreme among evil things; there is no higher or lower [offense], you should be completely ashamed for violating any of them. There are two reasons the *bhikṣus* were embarrassed [to ask] the Tathāgata but were not embarrassed [to ask] Upāli. The first is that the Buddha was the founding teacher as well as the master from whom they had received the precepts—therefore their shame was exceedingly deep. Upāli was neither the founding teacher nor the master who gave them the precepts, and so their sense of shame [before him] was bearable. The second meaning is that the Tathāgata had already extinguished the three poisons and had long since eliminated any remaining karmic forces; he was completely free of violations and infractions. Because of this, too, their shame was deep. Upāli, however, still had karmic residue and had also committed infractions. Because he seemed more like them, their shame was more tolerable. For these two reasons they could ask Upāli, although they were embarrassed to ask the Tathāgata.

102

From "They came to ask me, saying . . ." is the second aspect, the actual question. Their question had, in brief, three points. The first is asking the question—they wanted to ask about the gravity of their transgression because they didn't know to which category it belonged. The second point is that they wanted to be taught about the proper way of performing repentance. In general there are four kinds of remorse: 1) remorse that one has abandoned one's original purpose, 2) remorse that one has gone against the Buddha's wishes and teachings, 3) remorse that one is in a disturbed state of mind, and 4) remorse for the future fruits of suffering that one will reap. The third point was their asking how they can repent their mistakes and thereby be forgiven for their offense.

"I then taught them according to the Dharma" is the third part, Upāli's answer based upon the precepts. This shows that the *bhikṣus*' infraction   39b belonged to the second category of violations of the precepts. One can be pardoned for [this type of] offense if one confesses and repents the transgression to a group of twenty people. This answered the three points that the *bhikṣus* had inquired about. The reason, then, that Upāli was criticized by Vimalakīrti is that he based his answer to the *bhikṣus* on the existence of perceptual attributes, when he should have replied to them based on the absence of perceptual attribute—hence [Vimalakīrti's] criticism.

The second part, the actual criticism, has three items. The first is the actual criticism; the second is from "What is the reason?" and explains the criticism; the third is from "The one who knows this" and concludes the criticism.

"Do not increase the offenses of these two *bhikṣus*" means that the two *bhikṣus* had violated the precepts and were attached to the reality of their offense, and that is why they came to question Upāli. But Upāli too was thinking about perceptual attributes when he taught them about the retribution for their offense. Thus the attachment in their minds would grow more firm and they would commit new offenses. Therefore, it says, "Do not increase [the offenses of these two *bhikṣus*]." "You should immediately extinguish [their offenses] and not confuse their minds" means that Upāli shouldn't teach them the existence of perceptual attributes and thereby confuse them, but rather he must teach them the absence of perceptual attributes and thereby eliminate the old offenses to which they were attached.

The second part, the explanation [of the criticism], also has two items. The first initially clarifies that the essential nature of the offense is empty. The second, from "Upāli, wrongheaded thinking is defilement," shows that the many *dharma*s are empty and thereby demonstrates the emptiness of the offenses. The first item, the emptiness of the essential nature of the offense, has three points. The first directly states the emptiness of the essential nature of the offense. The second, from "As the Buddha has taught," shows that the source of the offense—the mind—is empty. The third, from "Just so, Upāli," gives a question and answer in order to show that the mind—the source of the offense—is empty.

In "The nature of that offense is not within," "within" refers to the body and the six sense organs, as these are the causes of the offense. In "Nor without," "without" refers to objects and the six sense fields; these are the conditions for the offense. This shows that within ultimate truth, the essential nature of offenses is empty and cannot be found. Therefore it says that it is not within the cause or condition, neither within nor without. In "Nor is it in between," "in between" means the various factors and six sense consciousnesses that produce offenses; the interpretation of the text is as above.

From "As the Buddha has taught" is the second point, showing that the mind—the source of the offense—is empty. This shows that the mind is certainly the source of the arising of virtue and sin. That is to say, if the mind that gives birth [to things] is already known to be empty, then of course the essential nature of the offense born thereof is likewise surely empty. There are three parts to this. The first wants to show that the mind is empty, and so it begins by explaining that the mind is the source of sentient beings, purity, and defilement: "As the Buddha has taught, sentient beings are defiled because of a defiled mind; sentient beings are pure because of a pure mind."

The second part is the actual illustration of the emptiness of the mind. "The mind is not within" means that it is not within the six sense organs; "not without" means that it is not within the six sense fields; "not in between" means that it is not in the six sense consciousnesses. From "As is the mind just like this" is the third part, the general conclusion that as with the emptiness of the mind, so too the ten thousand *dharma*s are empty. "As the mind is just like this, so too are offenses and defilement" means that if the root—the mind—is empty, then the branch—the offense—will naturally be empty.

39c

104

"The myriad *dharma*s are likewise just like this, not apart from suchness" means that not only are the mind and offenses empty, but all *dharma*s are entirely empty, not apart from suchness.

From "Just so, Upāli" is the third point, corroborating the above two aspects with a question and answer; this has three parts. The first is the question "Just so, Upāli, when one gains liberation through [the purification] of the attributes of mind, does any defilement remain or not?" There are two parts to the interpretation of "liberation [through the purification] of the attributes of mind"; the first is simply asking if when one contemplates the mind and attains liberation, the mind that is contemplated retains any defilement or not. The second part is the answer, "I replied, 'No.'" The essential nature of the mind is empty—how could there be defilement in emptiness? Therefore [Upāli] replied, "No." The second [interpretation] is from Dharma Master Sengzhao: "'When one gains liberation' means when one first becomes an arhat one gains the first liberation. At that time ignorance of the mind is dispelled, which means that there will be no more attributes of mind." Hence the answer, "No." The third part, "The mental attributes of all sentient beings are likewise without defilement," enables [Upāli] to understand that, similarly, the minds of all sentient beings are empty.

From "Ah, Upāli, wrong-headed thinking is defilement" is the second item of the explanation of the criticism, showing that the many *dharma*s are empty and thereby demonstrating the emptiness of offenses. This unfolds in two parts. The first is the initial clarification of purity and impurity. Although the above clarified that the mind is the source of purity and impurity, the "attributes" [of the mind] have not yet been discussed. Beings wonder, "What is it that is called purity? What is it that is called impurity?" Hence this clarifies that the three delusions are impurity and that the absence of the three delusions is purity. The second part is from "Upāli, all *dharma*s [are born and pass away into extinction]" and is the actual explanation of the emptiness of the many *dharma*s, thereby demonstrating the emptiness of offenses.

The first part, the distinction of purity and impurity, is comprised of three lines. "Deluded thoughts are impurity, the absence of deluded thoughts is purity" clarifies wrong thoughts. "Wrong-headed thinking is impurity, the lack of wrong-headed thinking is purity" clarifies wrong mind. "Clinging to self is impurity, not clinging to self is purity" clarifies wrong views.

In general, the [three] wrongs are what is meant by impurity and the absence of these three wrongs is what is meant by purity. If, however, we are talking about the underlying principle, we cannot distinguish between "wrong" and "not wrong." Therefore, we say that the offenses are empty.

From "Upāli, [all *dharmas* are born and pass away into extinction]" is the second part, the actual explanation of the emptiness of the many *dharmas*, thereby demonstrating the emptiness of offenses. This explains that because the many *dharmas* are all like this (i.e., empty), the offenses are also empty. This critique has two meanings. "The one who knows this is called 'upholder of the precepts'" is to say that one who can understand that the offenses and the mind are entirely empty can be called foremost in observing the precepts and one whose practice is complete. "The one who knows this is said to 'understand well'" means that if you can eliminate the offense of others in this manner then you are said to well understand the meaning of the Dharma and your practice of transforming others is complete.

From "Thereupon, the two *bhikṣus*" is the third part, showing the two praises of Vimalakīrti by the *bhikṣus*. From "I answered, saying. . ." is the fourth part, Upāli's praise of Vimalakīrti. From "At that time those two *bhikṣus*" is the fifth part, describing the benefits that the two *bhikṣus* obtained as a result of Vimalakīrti's critique. This is divided into two; the first straight-away describes the benefits that were obtained: "Their doubts and remorse were eliminated and they aroused the resolve [to achieve] the unsurpassed mind." The second illuminates their arousing the vow: "May all sentient beings obtain such eloquence!" "Therefore I am not worthy to visit him and inquire about his illness" is the third aspect of Upāli's declining [the Buddha's request], the conclusion that he is not suitable.

The ninth [disciple] directed [to visit Vimalakīrti] was Rāhula. He was foremost of the ten disciples in observing morality. As above, this has both the directive [to visit Vimalakīrti] and [Rāhula's] declining [to go]. Within the description [of Rāhula's] declining, there are the three aspects, also as before. The second level, the explanation of his declining, further unfolds in three parts: the first gives the situation leading to [Vimalakīrti's] criticism; the second, from "Vimalakīrti [approached me and said]," presents the actual criticism; the third, from "Thereupon Vimalakīrti [said to the sons of

40a

the elders]," is Vimalakīrti's exhortation to the elders' [sons] to leave home and become *bhikṣu*s.

The first part, the situation leading to the criticism, has two divisions. The first clarifies the [sons of] the elders asking Rāhula about the benefits of leaving home to become a *bhikṣu*. The second is Rāhula's answer, "I explained for them the benefits of the merits obtained by leaving home to become a *bhikṣu.*" This refers to obtaining the merit of the four fruits of the renunciant path, nirvana, the benefit of the factors of the path, and the like.

One interpretation is that the factors of the path are the merit, and the fruits [of nirvana] without remainder constitute the benefit. This means cultivating the merit of the factors of the path at the beginning, and in the end obtaining the benefit of the fruits of [nirvana] without remainder. Another interpretation is that merit means the essential nature of the two kinds of nirvana, [that is, nirvana with remainder and nirvana without remainder,] and benefit refers to the cause. What led Vimalakīrti to criticize [Rāhula], however, was that contrary to the elder's [son's] spiritual capacity for hearing of the Mahayana renunciation devoid of perceptual attributes, Rāhula taught them the merit and benefits of the Hinayana renunciation of the householder's life replete with perceptual attributes. Hence Vimalakīrti was led to criticize him.

The second part, the actual criticism, itself has three divisions. The first is the general statement of the two types of Mahayana renunciation of the householder's life devoid of perceptual attributes; straightaway Rāhula is criticized for [teaching] the Hinayana renunciation of the householder's life replete with perceptual attributes. The second, from "Why," is the explanation of his criticism. The third, from "If you can do this," is the summary conclusion of the criticism.

"You should not preach of the benefits of the merit of leaving home to become a *bhikṣu*" means that you should not preach the benefits of the merit of the Hinayana renunciation of the householder's life replete with perceptual attributes in mistaken understanding of the spiritual capacity of the audience.

The second division, the explanation of the criticism, itself has two parts: the first gives the renunciation of the householder's life devoid of perceptual attributes, and criticizes Rāhula for [teaching] the renunciation of the householder's life replete with perceptual attributes. The second, from "Rāhula, renunciation of the householder's life," gives the Mahayana renunciation of the householder's life, and criticizes the Hinayana renunciation of the householder's life. A question: Why shouldn't the benefits of the merit of the renunciation of the householder's life be taught? "No benefit and no merit—this is renunciation of the householder's life" explains that the renunciation of the householder's life devoid of perceptual attributes is just like this—therefore this is not the teaching given [by Rāhula that dealt with] the renunciation of the householder's life replete with perceptual attributes. This gives an affirmation and illumines a negation.

40b

"Conditioned *dharma*s can be taught as having benefit and having merit" refers precisely to the renunciation of the householder life replete with perceptual attributes. This gives a negation and illumines an affirmation. "Renunciation of the householder's life is an unconditioned *dharma,* and there is neither benefit nor merit within the unconditioned *dharma*s" refers to arousing the resolve to renounce the householder's life within the absence of perceptual attributes.

From "Rāhula, renouncing the householder's life" is the second, giving the Mahayana renunciation of the householder's life, and criticizing the Hinayana renunciation of the householder's life. This has two points: the first explains the meaning of the Mahayana renunciation according to one's own practice; the second, from "subduing hosts of Māras," explains the meaning of the Mahayana renunciation according to the transformation of others.

"Rāhula, renunciation of the householder's life is not there, not here, and not in between." "There" means nirvana. "Here" means samsara. If "there" and "here" exist, it would mean that of course "in between" also exists; therefore it says "in between." This explains the Mahayana renunciation of the householder's life. Regarding one's own practice, the Mahayana renunciation devoid of perceptual attributes is called "true renunciation." Now, the spiritual capacity [of the elders' sons] who stood before Rāhula was such that they should have been taught the Mahayana renunciation devoid of perceptual attributes, but he taught them the Hinayana renunciation replete with perceptual attributes—this was wrong.

"Abandoning the sixty-two wrong views and dwelling in nirvana" also illustrates the meaning of the Mahayana renunciation. "It is accepted by the knowledgeable and practiced by the sages" means that the above two lines are accepted and practiced by the myriad sages.

From "Defeating hosts of Māras" is the second point, explaining the meaning of the Mahayana renunciation according to the transformation of others. This has two elements: the first is the explanation of subduing Māras, and the second, from "subjugating all those on non-Buddhist paths," illustrates the restraining of those on non-Buddhist paths.

The first element, subduing Māras, is further divided into two aspects. The first immediately clarifies [the meaning] of subduing Māras. The line about defeating Māra illustrates that the purpose of establishing the Mahayana renunciation of the householder's life is certainly in order to subdue [the Māras] and have them enter the buddha path. Dharma Master Sengzhao says, "When the true path has been made smooth, the false ways are blocked off of their own accord. The scripture says, 'When one person renounces the householder's life, all of Māra's palaces tremble.'" This is what it is saying.

The six verses from "Crossed over the five paths of existence" explain a question and thereby illuminate the Māras' benefit. That is, when beings hear of overcoming Māras, they wonder if this is so because of an intentional wish to harass them. Therefore it is interpreted to mean that it is not from a wish to harass them but rather a wish to make them virtuous. The two lines "Crossing over the five paths of existence and purifying the five eyes" give the results, and the two lines "Gaining the five powers and establishing the five roots of goodness" describe the cause; these four lines truly illustrate the benefit obtained by the Māras. "Not bothering others, separated from mistakes and evils" is the concrete explanation of the question, showing that there is no intention to overcome [others] but rather the wish to eliminate evil. We can also say that all six lines clarify the benefit [obtained by the Māras] and explain the question [about whether there was an intention to harass the Māras by vanquishing them].

One interpretation is that the six lines from "Crossed over the five paths of existence" mean that the reason the hosts of Māras are skillfully subdued 40c is just because of the full completion of knowing and the eradication [of entanglements]. [According to this interpretation,] the six lines are divided into two: the first four lines clarify knowing and the latter two lines clarify the eradication [of entanglements]. "Crossed over the five paths of existence" means "below, transform and nurture living beings"; "purifying the five eyes" means "above, seeking the path of the Buddha." "Establishing the five roots of goodness" is the cause—this means that from the initial step of [establishing] faith there is never retrogression. "Obtained the five powers" is the result—this means that the five roots of goodness grow with a graceful abundance of strength and hence are called "powers." The last two lines clarify eradication [of entanglements]. "Not bothering others" means not arousing anger in others. "Separated from mistakes and evils" means eliminating one's own entanglements.

From "Subjugating those on non-Buddhist paths" is the second element; that is, subjugating those on non-Buddhist paths. This has two aspects. The first is the immediate subjugation of those on non-Buddhist paths. This means that the purpose of establishing the Mahayana renunciation of the householder's life is to prevail over the non-Buddhist paths, to overturn the false and return to the true. Dharma Master Sengzhao says, "The sun and moon do not anticipate making the darkness go away, yet the darkness is naturally eliminated; those who renounce the life of a householder do not [do so] in anticipation of subjugating those on non-Buddhist paths, yet the non-Buddhist paths are naturally eliminated."

From "Transcending provisional designations" also clarifies a doubt and thereby illumines what is obtained by those on non-Buddhist paths. This shows that they subjugate them because of a simple desire to have them abandon evil and acquire virtue, and not from a particular desire to harass [anyone]. "Transcending provisional designations" shows that the desire is to make them understand the emptiness of both the provisional and the real and not believe in [the true existence of] perceptual attributes.

"Leaves the mud and muck" means wishing to free them of the mud and muck of the five *skandha*s. "Without bonds or attachments" likewise means wishing to free them of their belief in and attachment to the five *skandha*s. "Without the properties of the self" also means that they want to make them not believe in anything pertaining to the properties of the self. "Without possessions" too refers to the desire to free them of the six sense objects. These five lines actually describe what will be obtained by those on non-Buddhist paths.

"Without confusion or disorder" means to have no desire to bother others; "joyous of heart" means to have no internal jealousy or envy. "Guarding the minds of others" simply means the desire to reverse false ideas and enter into the truth. "Following meditative concentration and avoiding myriad mistakes and evils" again shows the desire to have them obtain virtue and abandon evil. These five lines clarify the issue and show that they subjugate [non-Buddhists] because they simply want them to obtain virtue and abandon evil, not because they wish to harass them.

It is also possible that these ten lines together illustrate and explain the question [about whether those on non-Buddhist paths are being harassed] and the benefits they receive. One interpretation is that the seven lines from "transcend provisional names" shows that those on non-Buddhist paths are able to be well subjugated because of the full accomplishment of both knowing and the eradication [of entanglements]—hence they are able to subjugate [them]. The seven lines can be divided into two parts: the first six lines illustrate the eradication [of entanglements], and the seventh line, "joyous of heart," illustrates knowing. "Guarding the minds of others, following meditative concentration, and avoiding myriad mistakes and evils" together conclude the above [full accomplishment of] both the virtues of knowing and the eradication [of entanglements].

"If you can do it like this, it is truly renouncing the householder's life." This refers to the third division [of the actual criticism of Rāhula], the summary conclusion that in the Mahayana way of renouncing the householder's life, both one's own practices and the practice of transforming others, are fully accomplished; therefore it is called "truly renouncing the householder's life."

From "Thereupon Vimalakīrti [addressed the sons of the elders]" is the third part of the explanation of [Rāhula's] declining [to visit Vimalakīrti],   41a that is, Vimalakīrti's encouragement to the [sons] of the elders to renounce the householder's life. This has four further aspects: the first is immediately encouraging them to physically renounce the life of a householder; the second is their declining because they [first] need their parent's [permission]; the third is Vimalakīrti's exhorting them to renounce the householder's life in their hearts and minds; and the fourth is [the sons] of the elders giving rise to the determination to leave the householder's life in accord with this teaching. This can be understood.

"Therefore I am not worthy to visit him and inquire of his illness" is the third level [of Rāhula's] declining [the Buddha's request], the conclusion that he is not suitable.

The tenth [disciple] directed [to visit Vimalakīrti] was Ānanda, foremost among the ten disciples of the Buddha in his total retention [of the Buddha's teachings]. This too has both the directive [to visit Vimalakīrti] and [Ānanda's] declining [to go]. Within [Ānanda's] declining there are, as above, three levels; the second level, the explanation of why he declined, is further divided into four parts. Part one gives the situation leading to [Vimalakīrti's] criticism; the second part, from "Vimalakīrti [approached me]," gives the actual criticism; the third, from "At that time, World-honored One," describes his inner feelings [of confusion] after being criticized; the fourth, from "Then I heard [a voice] in the sky," describes the voice that was heard in the sky and reconciles Ānanda's confusion.

The first part, the situation leading to [Vimalakīrti's] criticism, also has three divisions: the first describes [Ānanda's] begging for milk, the second is Vimalakīrti's question, and the third is Ānanda's reply—these can be understood.

As other scriptures say, the Buddha knew that the brahmans would fall into endless hell and he thus wished to save them. Therefore he appeared as though he was ill and had Ānanda go begging for milk; he also wished to show *bhikṣu*s of later ages the way to beg for medicine. As for the reason he was criticized by Vimalakīrti, the *Ruguanjing* says that seven sages together saved one person: 1) the Buddha, [whose request for milk resulted in the others being saved]; 2) Ānanda, who begged for milk; 3) Vimalakīrti, who criticized [Ānanda]; 4) the mother cow, who explained the verse; 5) the calf, who explained the verse; 6) the voice in the sky; 7) the deity who manifested as a human and drew the milk.

If we discuss this, there are four points to Vimalakīrti's criticism: the first is that the Dharma body does not need milk; the second is that although the trace manifestation receives [things] it is not the real [Buddha]; the third point is that [Ānanda's begging for milk] will cause non-Buddhists to slander [the Buddha]; the fourth point is that it will cause the disciples to be embarrassed.

The second part, the actual critique, has three further points. The first straightaway clarifies that the Dharma body does not get ill; the second, from "Ānanda, a wheel-turning sage-king (*cakravartin*). . . ," explains the reason for not getting ill; the third, from "Ānanda, you should know," exhorts [Ānanda] to understand the meaning of the Dharma body. One interpretation understands the three points as: 1) the actual critique from the point of the underlying principle, 2) using the lack of illness of [the kings of the] world as an example, and 3) concluding Vimalakīrti's critique by returning to [a discussion of] the underlying principle. Another interpretation is that because Ānanda is called upon five times in the text [to do this or that], there are five levels [to the interpretation] itself. In general, all of these interpretations are the same and you can use any of them as you wish.

"Stop, stop, Ānanda." With one sentence [Ānanda] has already committed [the above] four errors. To be mistaken about the underlying principle is very serious and that is why Vimalakīrti says several times, "Stop, stop."

"The Tathāgata's body is the essence of diamond" means that the Dharma body cannot be destroyed. "All evil has already been eradicated" means that   41b the virtue of eradication [of entanglements] has been fully accomplished. "Myriad good qualities accumulated" means that the virtue of knowing has been fully accomplished. "How could there be illness?" means that internally there is no trouble. "How could there be vexation?" means that externally it is without annoyance.

One interpretation has it that "All evil has already been eradicated" means the absence of the cause of suffering and that "Myriad good qualities accumulated" means the presence of the cause of joy; "How could there be illness?" means the absence of the fruit of suffering and "How could there be vexation?" means the presence of the fruit of bliss.

"Go, Ānanda, in silence, and do not slander the Tathāgata" means that Ānanda should go in silence and get the milk [for the Buddha]—he should not say that the Tathāgata is ill. One interpretation is that "Go" means "to leave," and that Ānanda should leave silently. "Do not let other people hear these crude words" means that he shouldn't let those on non-Buddhist paths hear him.

From "Ānanda, a wheel-turning sage-king. . ." is the second point of the actual criticism [of Ānanda], explaining the reason the Dharma body does not become ill. Another interpretation has it this is using the lack of ill-ness of the [kings of the] world as an example [to illustrate why the Dharma body does not become ill]. This can be understood.

From "Ānanda, you should know" is the third point of the actual criti-cism [of Ānanda], exhorting him to understand the meaning of the Dharma body. We could also say that this concludes Vimalakīrti's critique by com-ing back to [a discussion of] the underlying principle. [In "The body of the Tathāgata is not a body of thoughts or desire,"] "thought" means "karma" and "desire" means "affliction." These two lines straightaway show that the Dharma body does not have karma or mental afflictions.

"The Buddha is the World-honored One, beyond the three worlds" means that the Buddha is removed from the cause and effect of the three worlds. One interpretation takes this to mean beyond the cause and effect of sec-ondary [afflictions] of the three worlds. "The Buddha's body is without out-flows; all of the outflows have already been exhausted" means that the Buddha has completely exhausted all causes. We could also say that the attributes of the root [afflictions] have been extinguished. "The Buddha's body is unconditioned and does not fall into any of the myriad analytic calculations" means that it is removed from the fruits and rewards of conditioned exis-tence. These two lines are the actual explanation of the Dharma body.

"How could a body like this become ill?" This concludes [the teaching] that the Dharma body is without illness. The main point of the text in all of this is that the myriad evils have already been eradicated and that it is dia-mondlike and cannot be destroyed. If the myriad evils have already been eradicated and it is diamondlike and cannot be destroyed, does this not mean that it is the explanation of eternally abiding? In the previous commentary in the chapter "Skillful Means," we have noted that even if it is within the teaching of the preface or the dissemination parts of this scripture—those parts of the teaching that did not actually take place in Vimalakīrti's room—there still is no problem [with understanding this as] describing the eternally abiding [nature of the Tathāgata]. So it is!

From "At that time, World-honored One. . ." is the third part of the explanation of why [Ānanda] declined [the Buddha's request], describing his inner feelings after he had been criticized.

From "Thereupon I heard [a voice] in the sky" is the fourth part of the explanation, describing the voice heard in the sky that reconciled Ānanda's confusion. "It is as the layman said" refers to Vimalakīrti saying that the profound essence is without illness. "However, it is in order to teach and liberate sentient beings that the Buddha has appeared in this evil world of the five impurities and is now practicing this Dharma." This means that within the [Buddha's] manifestation for Ānanda, it is not the case that there is no manifestation of illness or begging for milk. "Go now, Ānanda, and fetch the milk without feeling ashamed" means that there is no error in his response [to the Buddha's request] and so he should not feel ashamed. One interpretation says that from "Go now" shows that in the manifestation [of the Buddha's illness] for Ānanda's response it is not the case that there was no illness and that everything before this is about Vimalakīrti's describing the profound essence as free of illness. From "World-honored One" is the third level of [Ānanda's] declining [to visit Vimalakīrti], his conclusion that he is not worthy.

41c

From "In this way, five hundred [great disciples declined]" is the second part of the chapter "The Disciples," the conclusion that none [of the five hundred disciples] are worthy [to visit Vimalakīrti and inquire about his illness].

Chapter Four

The Bodhisattvas

This is the second aspect [of the third part of the specific introduction], in which Vimalakīrti's virtues are manifested; that is, the directives [given by the Buddha] to the bodhisattvas to [visit Vimalakīrti and] inquire about his illness, thus the title of the chapter. This part unfolds in two levels: the first is the specific directives to four people; the second is the overall conclusion that none of the eight thousand people are worthy [to visit Vimalakīrti and inquire about his illness].

The first one to be directed [to visit Vimalakīrti] was Maitreya Bodhisattva; this section further includes both [the Buddha's] directive and [Maitreya's] declining [to go]. As before, his declining is unpacked in three aspects, the second of which is the explanation of his declining; this is further divided into three parts. The first explains the situation leading to [Vimalakīrti's] criticism; the second, from "At that time, Vimalakīrti. . . ," gives the actual criticism; the third, from "When Vimalakīrti gave this teaching," describes the many benefits received by the assembly at that time as a result of [Vimalakīrti's] criticism [of Maitreya].

The situation that led to [Maitreya] being criticized is that he was already a bodhisattva occupying the place of succession, [that is, the bodhisattva who is to follow Śākyamuni as the next buddha in this world. In the text it says that] in the past he had already explained the practices of the three nonretrogressive stages of the eighth level and above for the deities of the Tuṣita Heaven. One interpretation of this is that although it is actually the eighth level that is called "nonretrogressive," it is in the seventh level and below that the causes of the eighth level are produced; this is what is being called "practices." Here Maitreya is described as teaching the practices of the seventh level, and therefore it says "practices for the nonretrogressive stages."

Now, what was it that led Vimalakīrti to criticize him? Maitreya had four attachments: 1) [attachment to] his belief that his practice was superior, 2) [attachment to] his belief in the prediction [of his future buddhahood],

3) [attachment to] his belief in the fruits of *bodhi*, 4) and [attachment to] his beliefs about extinction and nirvana. The first two of these are attachment to the cause, and the latter two are attachment to the result. Now the spiritual capacity of the deities [he taught in the Tuṣita Heaven] was such that he should have taught them the practices of emptiness devoid of perceptual attributes, but instead he taught them [on the basis of his attachment] to these four beliefs. Thus his teaching was at odds with the spiritual capacity [of the audience] and this is what led Vimalakīrti to criticize him.

The second item, the actual criticism [of Maitreya], initially unfolds in two items. The first is from the beginning up to "[*Bodhi*] cannot be attained with the body or mind" and rejects the four things [to which Maitreya] was attached. The second, from "quiescent extinction is *bodhi*," broadly explains the nature of *bodhi*. The first item, rejecting the four things [to which Maitreya was attached], has three further elements: the first uses "birth" to show that there can be no prediction [of attaining perfect *bodhi*] in just "one more birth." The second, from "If, Maitreya, you receive a prediction," uses a sequence [of rhetorical questions] to reject the four things [to which Maitreya] was attached. The third, from "Maitreya, you should make these gods [discard discriminating views of *bodhi*]," is the concluding exhortation to abandon attachments; it can also be said to explain getting rid of the closed mind.

The first element, using "birth" to show that there can be no receiving a prediction [of attaining perfect *bodhi*] in just "one more birth," is further unpacked in three parts. The first shows that with regard to existence birth is not fixed, and so there can be no receiving a prediction [of perfect *bodhi* in "one more birth"]. It also could be that the teaching of impermanence shows that there is no receiving a prediction. The second, from "If [this prediction] refers to birthlessness," shows that with regard to emptiness birth too is empty, and therefore there can be no receiving a future prediction [of perfect *bodhi* in "one more birth"]. The third part, from "Was it because of the birth of suchness [that you received a prediction about your future *bodhi*]?", takes the teaching on the unity of emptiness and existence and shows that because birth is empty there can be no receiving a prediction.

42a

The first part, showing that there is no receiving of a prediction with regard to existence, opens up into three areas. The first straightaway problematizes [the possibility of "one more birth"] in any of the three worlds [of past, present, and future]. The second, from "[Did you receive your prediction] about a past [birth]?", is comprised of three lines, separately refuting the determination of which of the three worlds [of past, present, or future "one more birth" could refer to]. The third, from "If it was about a birth in the past," again takes up the lack of a fixed existence of the three worlds and gives a negative appraisal [of the possibility that "birth" could refer to any of them].

"Birth" is summarily interpreted in two ways. The first says that after departing this [world Maitreya] will be born a single time in the celestial palaces and attain buddhahood. The other says that from the celestial palaces he will fall for a single birth into a royal family and attain buddhahood. The second problem, separately refuting the determination [of the prediction referring to a birth in the past, present, or future], can be understood.

The third area of discussion demonstrates that the three worlds are without a fixed existence and gives a negative appraisal [of the possibility that "birth" can refer to birth in any of them]. "If it refers to a past birth, that birth is already extinguished," and so there can be no prediction [of Maitreya attaining perfect *bodhi* in that birth]. "If it refers to a future birth, that future birth has not yet arrived," and so there can be no prediction [of attaining perfect *bodhi* in that birth]. "If it refers to the present birth, this birth is nonabiding, changing, and passing into extinction moment by moment," and so, again, there can be no prediction [of attaining perfect *bodhi* in this birth]. The genuine words of the Buddha are then quoted as proof: "At this very moment you are born, grow old, and die." This shows that there is no abiding or resting even for a brief moment. Now, the reason that the authentic words of the Buddha are quoted as proof for only the example of the present is that past and future [lifetimes] are only ideas and not actually [existing at the moment], and so this one quote should be trusted [to also refer to the past and future]. However, precisely because of the actuality of the present, it is difficult to reject it with a single sentence, and therefore the Buddha's words were quoted as proof.

From "If [your prediction of attaining perfect *bodhi*] refers to birthlessness" is the second part, using emptiness to show that there can be no receiving a prediction [of attaining perfect *bodhi* in just "one more birth"]. This part begins with "If your prediction of attaining [perfect *bodhi*] refers to birthlessness."

"Birthlessness is none other than the stage of certainty" means that the comprehension of birthlessness is none other than the stage of certainty of [attaining] suchness. "Within the stage of certainty there is neither the receiving of predictions nor the attainment of *bodhi*" shows that there is definitely no receiving of a prediction [of attaining *bodhi*]. This is to say that within the stage of certainty—emptiness—you do not first receive a prediction and then later attain *bodhi*. "How, then, Maitreya, can you have received a prediction [of attaining perfect *bodhi*] in one lifetime?" concludes the explanation of birth as empty and therefore without receiving predictions [of the attainment of *bodhi*].

From "Was it because of the birth of suchness [that you received a prediction about your future *bodhi*]?" is the third part, using the teaching on the unity of emptiness and existence to show that because birth is empty there is no receiving a prediction. The above has only used the separate teachings of emptiness and existence in order to clarify that there is no prediction [of future attainment] because birth is empty. Beings might think that when emptiness and existence are brought together they will then attain [the prediction of *bodhi*]; this shows that even when emptiness and existence are brought together there is no possibility of attainment. Within this there are three further points: the first establishes the criticism of a determined [existence]; the second, from "If it was because of the birth of suchness," uses the underlying principle to explain the criticism; the third point, from "all sentient beings are entirely suchlike," concludes the criticism by giving four [examples of] suchness.

"Was it because of the birth of suchness that you received a prediction [about your future *bodhi*]?" "Suchness" is another name for emptiness. "Birth" is another term for existence. That is to say, does Maitreya reckon that if he brings suchness and birth together he can thereby attain a prediction [of future buddhahood]? "Was it because of the extinction of suchness that you attained a prediction [about your future *bodhi*]?" "Extinction" is also another name for existence. On the other hand, does Maitreya reckon that if he brings suchness and extinction together he can thereby attain a prediction [of future buddhahood]?

One interpretation has it that Maitreya reckons that the underlying principle of suchness gives birth to a knowing that destroys the mental

42b

afflictions, and thus he wishes to bring together a determined [existence and the underlying principle of suchness]. Therefore, this is asking if Maitreya reckons that it is because the underlying principle of suchness gives rise to knowledge that a prediction is attained. Or is it that a prediction is attained because the underlying principle of suchness gives rise to a knowing that extinguishes afflictions?

From "If it was because of the birth of suchness" is the second point, using the underlying principle to explain the criticism. "If it was because of the birth of suchness that you received a prediction, [you should know that] suchness has no birth" means that suchness is fundamentally birthless. Who could become one with suchness and receive a prediction of [future *bodhi*]? One interpretation is that this means that if you [think that you] can receive a prediction [of future buddhahood] because the underlying principle of suchness gives rise to knowing, [you should know that] in suchness there is no knowing that can be born. "If it was because of extinction that you received a prediction, [you should know that] in suchness there is no extinction" means that suchness is fundamentally without extinction—who could it be that unites with suchness and receives a prediction? One interpretation is that this means that if you [think that you] can receive a prediction [of future buddhahood] because the underlying principle of suchness gives birth to a knowing that extinguishes mental afflictions, [you should know that] in suchness there are no mental afflictions that can be extinguished.

From "All sentient beings are entirely suchlike" is the third point, concluding the critique by giving four [examples of] suchness. There are four lines divided into two pairs. "All sentient beings [are entirely suchlike] and all *dharma*s are also suchlike." These two lines put the self and the properties of the self together and show that they are empty, without differentiation; we could also say that this puts sentient beings together with non-sentient [things]. "The myriad wise and holy ones are all also suchlike; even you, Maitreya, are also suchlike." These two lines put self and other together and show that they are [empty], without differentiation; we could also say that [these two lines] put guest and host together. Now, showing that all four of these are all empty and without differentiation is to ask how, within non-differentiated emptiness, he could possibly teach the gods about a prediction of obtaining *bodhi* within one lifetime.

My interpretation is a little different. First of all, the initial point—that because birth is empty there is no receiving of a prediction—unfolds in only two parts. The first shows that with regard to [the world of] existence there is no receiving of a prediction, and the second shows that with regard to emptiness there is no receiving of a prediction. As for there being no receiving a prediction in [the world of] existence, "existence" is interpreted as above. The [second point], however—showing that with regard to emptiness there is no receiving of a prediction—has two parts: the first is straightaway showing that there is no receiving of a prediction within emptiness; the second part, from "Was it because of the birth of suchness," is a rejection of the reckoning that with regard to emptiness you die "here" and are born "there." The term "extinction" means "to die." This is to say that within emptiness there is fundamentally no dying "here" and being born "there."

From "If, Maitreya [you received a prediction]" is the second aspect of the rejection of the four things to which [Maitreya] is attached, actually using a sequence [of rhetorical questions] to reject the four things [to which Maitreya] is attached. The rejection of these four things itself has four aspects. The first is the rejection of the prediction. "If, Maitreya, you received a prediction, then all sentient beings should also receive a prediction [of future awakening]" sets up the comparison. From "Why?" explains the comparison, showing that because the nature of both Maitreya and sentient beings is empty and nondual, the receiving and non-receiving of a prediction [of awakening] is likewise the same.

The second aspect is the rejection of *bodhi:* "If, Maitreya, you were to obtain *bodhi*, then all sentient beings too should obtain it." This sets up the comparison and "[Because] all sentient beings have the attribute of *bodhi*" explains the comparison. There are four ways to understand "Sentient beings have the attribute of *bodhi*." The first says that *bodhi* is the unsurpassed knowing of the Buddha; that is to say that within ultimate truth the emptiness of Maitreya and the emptiness of sentient beings is of one attribute and not two, and there is no distinction between attainment and non-attainment. Therefore it says, "If, Maitreya, you were to obtain *bodhi,* then all sentient beings would also attain it." The second way to understand this is to say that the term *bodhi* means "ultimate truth." Because Maitreya and sentient beings all [equally participate in] ultimate truth, it says that "all sentient beings also

42c

attain it." The third understanding is to say that the empty nature of sentient beings is none other than the emptiness of the knowing that is devoid of perceptual attributes; hence it says that "all sentient beings also attain it." The fourth way to understand this is to say that all sentient beings entirely are possessed of the underlying principle of knowing *bodhi*; hence it says that "all sentient beings also attain it."

[The third aspect is the rejection of extinction:] "If, Maitreya, you attain extinction then all sentient beings also will be extinct." There are also four ways to understand this line. The first is as above: because emptiness is nondual, [if Maitreya] attains [extinction], then [all sentient beings should] likewise attain the same [extinction; if Maitreya] does not attain [extinction], then [all sentient beings should] likewise [not attain extinction]. The empty nature of sentient beings is originally empty of its own accord—there is no further extinction and achievement of nirvana. Thus they would say, "without further extinction." The second understanding is that the empty nature of sentient beings is none other than the emptiness of nirvana—there is no further extinction and achievement [of nirvana]. Thus they would say, "without further extinction, none other than the attribute of nirvana." The third understanding takes the empty nature of sentient beings to be nirvana; hence they would say, "none other than the attribute of nirvana, without further extinction." The fourth understanding says that sentient beings fundamentally possess the underlying principle of extinction; hence they would say, "none other than the attribute of nirvana; there is no further extinction and achievement [of nirvana]."

From "Therefore, [Maitreya]" is the fourth aspect, the rejection of [Maitreya's belief that his teaching is evidence of] his superior practice. "Do not instruct these gods with this teaching." "This teaching" refers to Maitreya's belief in his teaching of the superior practices for the three nonretrogressive stages.

"Truly there is no one who arouses the mind of *bodhi* nor is there anyone who retrogresses." "[No one who] arouses the mind [of *bodhi*]" refers to Maitreya, while "nor is there anyone who retrogresses" refers to other beings in the category of those who have not yet aroused the mind [of *bodhi*]. One interpretation is that "arouse the mind [of *bodhi*]" refers to the initial generation of the mind in the abodes below; "no one who retrogresses" refers to the three stages of nonretrogression from the eighth stage and above. Another interpretation has it that "Do not instruct these gods with this teaching" is the summary conclusion that Maitreya should not instruct the gods by means of the above three things in which he believed, [that is, his prediction, *bodhi*, and extinction,] and that from "Truly there is nobody who arouses the mind [of *bodhi*]" is the actual rejection of Maitreya's belief [that his teaching is evidence of his] superior practice.

From "Maitreya, you should make these gods [discard discriminating views of *bodhi*]" is the third point within the rejection of the four things to which [Maitreya] was attached, the concluding exhortation to abandon attachments. Some say that what comes before this is the rejection of the four things to which [Maitreya] was attached, and from here is the rejection of the closed mind. This has two aspects: the first is the straightforward exhortation to abandon attachment; the second, from "Why?", is the explanation of the exhortation to abandon attachments. This explains that because *bodhi* is not form, it "cannot be attained through the body"; because it is not mind, it "cannot be attained through the mind." One interpretation is that because *bodhi* is empty it cannot [be attained] through the body or mind.

43a

From "Quiescent extinction is *bodhi*" is the second point in the actual criticism of Maitreya, the broad clarification of the attributes of *bodhi*.

The above removes and cleanses the myriad attributes—all are empty and unattainable, there is no basis for beings' thoughts. Therefore this shows that with regard to names, the attribute of that which is devoid of attribute is the profound attribute of *bodhi*. One interpretation says that the above clarifies the emptiness of the person who attains the fruit, and that from "You should make these these gods [discard discriminating views of *bodhi*]" explains the emptiness of the fruits of *bodhi* that are attained. In all, this is divided into twenty-five lines, each of which is different. Here I will follow the text with appropriate commentary.

"Quiescent extinction is *bodhi*." *Bodhi* is the Indian pronunciation and is a word for the omniscience [of the bodhisattvas that knows] the type of path [that each sentient being requires for salvation]. This knowing illuminates the realm of quiescent extinction; because it takes its name from this realm, it is said that "quiescent extinction is *bodhi*."

124

"Because it is the extinction of perceptual attributes." This explains the reason that "quiescent extinction is *bodhi*." This shows that it is because the various perceptual attributes do not exist. One interpretation says that the essential nature of knowing is none other than emptiness, and that is why it says that "Because it is the extinction of perceptual attributes, quiescent extinction is *bodhi*." Omniscience is born of the realm [of quiescent extinction], and because the essential nature of knowing is already quiescent no perceptual attributes are attained; hence it says, "Because it is the extinction of perceptual attributes."

"Non-contemplation is *bodhi*" refers to the knowledge that there exists no object of perception that can be contemplated. "Because it is separated from the many conditions" means that because the essential nature of conditions is already empty it cannot be contemplated. One interpretation is that this means that because the essential nature of contemplation is empty, it says "non-contemplation." "Because it is separated from the many conditions" means that because the essential nature of contemplation is empty it is not conditioned by many conditions.

"Non-acting is *bodhi*." [This means that] knowing does not act on the objects of perception. "Because it is without mental recollections" means that it is because [*bodhi*] is without objects of perception which could give rise to mental recollections [that "non-acting is *bodhi*."] One interpretation is that because the essential nature of acting is empty, there is no acting. "Because it is without mental recollections," there is no acting.

"Eradication is *bodhi*." [This means that] exhausting and leaving behind the many views is *bodhi*. Why? Because [*bodhi*] is the abandonment of the many views. "Eradication," however, does not refer to omniscience but is an adornment of that knowing. Because of that adornment, *bodhi* is illuminated. Another understanding is that this is simply saying that knowing is capable of eliminating the many views, and so it says, "Eradication is *bodhi*."

"Abandoning is *bodhi,* because it abandons the many false views." This means that the essential nature of knowing is the profound severance of false ideas and confused thinking. One interpretation is that "eradication" and "abandoning" are both different names for emptiness. "Eradication is *bodhi*" also refers to emptiness, and "Abandoning is *bodhi*" means that the five views are empty, and therefore this too [refers to emptiness].

"Obstructions are *bodhi,* because they obstruct aspiration." Knowing obstructs samsaric aspirations.

"Non-entry is *bodhi,* because it is without desire and attachment." Knowing is without desire and attachment; it does not cavort with the perceptual attributes of the six sense objects and [thereby] enter into samsara. Therefore it says, "non-entry is *bodhi.*" One interpretation has it that the realization of the emptiness of the mental afflictions leads to not seeing the twelve sense fields (the six sense objects and six sense organs) coming together with each other.

43b   "Accordance is *bodhi,* because it accords with suchness." Knowing is empty in accordance with suchness.

"Abiding is *bodhi,* because it abides in the Dharma-nature." Knowing abides in the nature of true emptiness. The essential nature of knowing is empty and it never departs from the Dharma-nature of emptiness.

"Arriving is *bodhi,* for it arrives at the limits of reality" means that knowing arrives and illumines the limits of reality. One interpretation has it that the essential nature of knowing is emptiness and that the ultimate limits are the same as the limits of emptiness.

"Nonduality is *bodhi,* because it is separated from both thoughts and *dharma*s." This means that knowing contemplates the underlying principle of nonduality. "Thoughts" refer to knowing and "*dharma*s" refer to objects; "separated" refers to emptiness. Both knowing and objects are empty and nondual.

"Equality is *bodhi,* because of the equality of empty space" means that knowing contemplates the underlying principle of impartiality, without highs or lows, as in empty space. One interpretation takes it that this means that both knowing and objects are empty and without distinctions, as in empty space.

"The unconditioned is *bodhi,* because it is without birth, abiding, or extinction." This means that knowing contemplates the underlying principle of emptiness and does not see the conditioning of the three states [of birth, abiding, and extinction]. One interpretation is that both knowing and objects are empty and thus unconditioned—the unconditioned is without birth, abiding, or extinction. This is *bodhi.*

"Knowlege is *bodhi,* for it completely knows the mental activities of sentient beings." This means that the full and perfect knowing of the fruits of buddhahood is fully enlightened about all of the distinct mental activities of sentient beings—this is *bodhi.*

"Non-engagement is *bodhi,* for entrances to the senses do not engage." Knowing does not see the [six] senses and their objects—the twelve sense fields—engaging with each other.

"Not coming together is *bodhi,* for it is separated from the karmic influence of the mental afflictions." Knowing contemplates the mental afflictions as empty and so too there are no residual karmic influences [of afflictions]. Hence there is no samsara, which is the aggregation of mental afflictions. One interpretation is that not coming together with the objects of the six senses is *bodhi,* because when there is no coming together [with sense objects] the karmic influences of the mental afflictions are well eliminated.

"Non-location is *bodhi,* because it is without shape or form." This means that in the contemplation of emptiness there is no seeing shapes or forms that exist in some location—this is *bodhi.*

"Provisional designations are *bodhi,* because names and words are empty." This means that knowing contemplates all names and words as empty.

"To be like an apparition is *bodhi,* because there is neither grasping nor rejecting." This means that all things are empty. One interpretation has it that because the essential nature of knowing is empty, like an apparition, there is neither grasping nor rejecting.

"The absence of agitation is *bodhi,* because it is forever calm in and of itself." The Buddha's state of concentration is forever calm, and this is *bodhi.* The essential nature of knowing is none other than emptiness that severs movement and agitation. This is because the underlying principle of the ultimate truth is forever calm in and of itself.

"Excellent quiescence is *bodhi,* because its nature is pure." This means that the Buddha is in accord with the underlying principle of quiescent extinction and is forever pure. One interpretation says that the essential nature of knowing is excellent quiescence, primordially pure.

"Non-grasping is *bodhi,* because it is separated from the conditioned objects of grasping." This means not seeing objects of perception as things to be grasped. "Because it is separated from the conditioned objects of grasping" means that [non-grasping is *bodhi*], because the essential nature of the conditioned objects of grasping is none other than emptiness. One interpretation is

that this means that the essential nature of knowing is none other than emptiness and without grasping, because it is separated from the conditioned
objects of grasping.

"Nondifferentiation is *bodhi*" means that it does not see objects of perception as able to be differentiated. "Because all *dharma*s are the same" means
because everything is empty and equal. One interpretation is that this means
that because the Buddha's merits are all equal it says "nondifferentiated."
Because of the equality of the ten powers and four fearlessnesses it says
"because all *dharma*s are the same."

"Incomparability is *bodhi,* because it bears no analogy." There are no
analogies that extend to knowing. One interpretation has it that buddhas cannot be compared to anything below the diamond [stage], and so it says,
"Incomparability."

"The subtle and sublime is *bodhi,* because *dharma*s are difficult to know."
The essential nature of knowing is subtle and sublime and severs worldly
entanglements; it cannot be fathomed by lesser minds—therefore it is said
to be difficult to know.

From "World-honored One" is the third item, describing the many benefits received at that time as a result [of Vimalakīrti criticizing Maitreya]. "Therefore I am not worthy to visit Vimalakīrti and inquire about his illness" is the
third part of [Maitreya's] declining, the conclusion that he is not suitable.

The second [bodhisattva] instructed [to visit Vimalakīrti] was Shining
Adornment Bodhisattva; this section also contains both the Buddha's request
and [Shining Adornment's] declining. As before, declining [to visit Vimala-
kīrti] has three levels, the second of which, the explanation of why he declined,
also has three parts: the first gives the situation leading to Vimalakīrti's criticizing him; the second, from "A sincere mind is the site of awakening," is
the actual criticism; the third, from "When he taught this Dharma," describes
the benefits that were received as a result of this criticism.

There are four aspects of the situation that led to [Vimalakīrti's] criticism [of Shining Adornment]: the first describes Vimalakīrti meeting Shining Adornment; the second aspect is Shining Adornment's paying his respects
and inquiring as to where Vimalakīrti was coming from; the third is Vimalakīrti's reply that he was coming from the site of awakening; the fourth is
Shining Adornment's then asking where the site of awakening is located.

The reason Shining Adornment was criticized is that if we speak of the underlying principle, then the ten thousand activities of the great beings all skillfully benefit sentient beings because they all lead to the fruit of buddhahood—there are none that are not the site of awakening. But Shining Adornment knew only of Magadha, the site of awakening where Śākyamuni obtained the path. That is, he wondered if Vimalakīrti had come in haste from a distant place or if there were a site of awakening nearby; thus he asked, "Where is that place?" This is the reason that Vimalakīrti criticized his narrow understanding [of the meaning of "site of awakening"].

The second part [of the explanation of Shining Adornment's declining the Buddha's request] is the actual criticism, which has five further levels. The first, from the beginning up to "because of discarding conditioned [*dharma*s]," describes the site of awakening with regard to various activities. The second, from "The four truths are the site of awakening," describes the site of awakening in terms of conditions. The third, from "subduing Māras," describes the site of awakening in terms of transforming others. The fourth, from "the ten powers and [four] fearlessnesses are the site of awakening," describes the site of awakening in terms of turning to the study of the stage of buddhahood. The fifth level, from "Like this, good son," is the summary conclusion of the above four levels.

"A sincere mind is the site of awakening, because it is without falsity." "Awakening" means penetration (i.e., insight); "site" means judgment. "Awakening" refers to the full and perfect knowing that is the fruit of buddhahood. "Site" is explained as the stage of training, and means that the sincere mind during the training stages is well able to judge virtue and evil and the far-off experience of buddhahood. Hence it says, "The sincere mind is the site of awakening." "Because it is without falsity" is interpreted to mean that the faith is honest and straightforward, without any falsity.

From here down to "The thirty-seven factors of enlightenment are the site of awakening, because of discarding conditioned *dharma*s" all describe the delightful practices of mental cultivation, the impartial place of spreading the buddha path.

"The resolve to act is the site of awakening, because it is able to skillfully distinguish things." Having already established a sincere mind, one is able to skillfully resolve to cultivate myriad virtues. The reason that one is

44a

able to skillfully resolve to act is because one is able to skillfully distinguish things.

"The profound mind is the site of awakening, because it increases merit." When myriad virtues have been accumulated, the mind becomes profound; when the mind becomes profound, the many merits increase.

"*Bodhi*-mind is the site of awakening, because of the lack of confusion and mistakes." Because of the sincere mind one is able to skillfully resolve to act; because of the resolve to act virtuously the mind becomes the profound mind, and it is the profound mind that transforms into the *bodhi*-mind. The reason is that [the two practices of] "above, broaden the path of the Buddha" and "below, transform and nurture living beings" are without any confusion or error.

[The next six items,] the six perfections, bring together self-cultivation and transformation of others, and therefore they all are the delightful sites of true awakening. [The next four items,] the four immeasurable minds, are the requisite practices by which the great beings extensively transform sentient beings; hence they are noble sites of awakening.

"The spiritual powers" refer to the five spiritual powers of the causal realm that skillfully enable the six spiritual powers of the result [realm]; hence they "are the site of awakening." "Liberation" means the eight liberations. "Skillful means" indicates that because the skilled investigation of the medicine and the disease is appropriate, multitudes are transformed and they enter the path. "The four means of attraction" completely lead [sentient beings] and transform [them]. These [latter] two items are both skillful activities used by the great beings to transform beings—they are the requisite practices for perfecting awakening, and therefore it says that they "are the site of awakening." "A disciplined mind" refers to cultivating the mind according to the underlying principle of the two truths, understanding in line with the underlying principle, and in accordance with correct insight. If one skillfully accomplishes "the [thirty-seven] factors of enlightenment," then one will be able to abandon the conditioned *dharma*s of samsara; hence they "are the site of awakening."

From "The four truths are the site of awakening" is the second [of the five levels of criticism], that is, describing the site of awakening in terms of conditions. "The four truths are the site of awakening, because there is no deceiving the world." Conditioned by the Four Noble Truths, knowing and understanding are born, and in the end the Tathāgata's fruit of nondeception is obtained. Another interpretation is that the four truths are true and real and not worldly deception.

"Conditioned arising is the site of awakening, because everything from ignorance up to old age and death is unexhausted." "Conditioned arising" means the twelve limbs of conditioned arising, and causes and conditions affect each other without exhaustion. We could also say that causes and conditions are none other than emptiness, and emptiness cannot be exhausted. If we are able to awaken to the basis of cause and condition, knowing will shine of its own accord. If the knowing mind has been illuminated, then the mind of awakening will be perfected of its own accord. Thus it says that "Conditioned arising is the site of awakening."

"The mental afflictions are the site of awakening, because of knowing reality as it is." Understanding that mental afflictions are none other than emptiness gives birth to clear understanding and the obtaining of buddhahood.

"Sentient beings are the site of awakening, because of knowing no-self. All *dharma*s are the site of awakening, because of knowing the many *dharma*s to be empty." Both of these lines explain mental afflictions in the same way.

From "Subduing Māras" is the third level, explaining the place [of enlightenment] in terms of transforming others.

"Vanquishing Māras is the site of awakening, because of being unmoved." This explains being unmoved by Māras. The Māras are not vanquished because [of a desire] to overpower and harass them but rather a wish to make them change their evil [ways], follow the virtuous, give rise to faith, and enter the path. This is how we understand the activity of transforming others.   44b

"The three worlds are the site of awakening, because there is nothing that arises." Although [buddhas] exist in the three worlds, there is no karma that binds them because there is simply the wish to transform beings; thus it says that "there is nothing that arises." "The lion's roar is the site of awakening, because there is nothing that is feared." In teaching the Dharma and saving the masses there is not a single thing that is feared, like the roar of a lion.

From "The [ten] powers and [four] fearlessnesses are the site of awakening" is the fourth level, describing the site [of awakening] in terms of turning to the study of the merits of the stage of buddhahood.

"The [ten] powers, the [four] fearlessnesses, and the [eighteen] unique traits [of a buddha] are the site of awakening, because there is no error." There is no error because evil has long ago been ended. "The three illuminations are the site of awakening, because there is no lingering obscuration." The many obscurations have long ago been exhausted and there are no obstructions. "Knowledge of all *dharmas* in a single thought is the site of awakening, because of the accomplishment of omniscience." "Knowledge of all *dharmas* in a single thought" refers to the diamondlike mind. "The accomplishment of omniscience" refers to turning to the study of the omniscience which is the fruit of buddhahood.

From "Like this, good son" is the fifth level, the summary conclusion of the above four levels.

"If bodhisattvas are in accord with the many perfections" means that bodhisattvas above the eighth level illuminate existence and nonexistence equally and are long without any difference in entering or leaving [the ordinary world and the buddha worlds]. Because they are able to mutually accord with the eighty thousand perfections, it says "the many perfections"; this line describes their self-cultivation.

From "Teach and transform sentient beings" describes their transformation of others. "All of their actions, even lifting their foot or putting it down, come from the site of awakening." All things done by bodhisattvas above the eighth level come from the practice of the ten thousand virtuous merits and lead to buddhahood. "Abide in the Buddha-Dharma" means to reach buddhahood and dwell there. Viewed from the result of buddhahood, it is taken as "comes from"; viewed from the cause, it is taken as "leaving." Another interpretation is that "abide" means that there is no forward movement or cessation [of movement] that does not exist within the Buddha-Dharma.

From "When he taught this Dharma" is the third part, the benefits that resulted from [Vimalakīrti's] criticism [of the bodhisattva Shining Adornment]. "Therefore I am not worthy to visit him and inquire about his illness" is the third level [of Shining Adornment's] declining, the conclusion that he is not suitable.

The third [bodhisattva] directed [to visit Vimalakīrti] was Maintains the World Bodhisattva. This also has [the Buddha's] directive and [the bodhisattva's] declining; the three levels of the declining are also as before. The second level, the explanation of the declining, further has four parts: the first gives the situation that led to [Vimalakīrti's] criticism; the second, from "[I] had not even finished speaking," gives the actual criticism; the third, from "He then said to Māra," describes Vimalakīrti's demanding the women from Māra; the fourth, from "At that time Vimalakīrti," is Vimalakīrti's teaching the Dharma for the goddesses.

The first level, the situation that led to the criticism, also has four parts: the first describes how Māra arrived; the second is Maintains the World [Bodhisattva] not recognizing Māra; the third, from "I thought," describes Māra offering the goddesses to Maintains the World [Bodhisattva]; the fourth, from "Thereupon he said to me," depicts Maintains the World [Bodhisattva's] declining to accept the goddesses.

44c

The reason Vimalakīrti criticized [Maintains the World Bodhisattva] is that Māra wanted to disturb Maintains the World [Bodhisattva's] meditation. However, he feared that Maintains the World [Bodhisattva] would not associate with him. Because Indra was the Buddha's benefactor and highly respected by his many disciples, [Māra] changed his form into that of Indra and went [to Maintains the World]. However, Maintains the World [Bodhisattva] didn't know this and so he was criticized by Vimalakīrti.

From "[I] had not even finished speaking" is the second part, the actual description of his being criticized. "This is not Indra" criticizes him straightaway for not knowing that Māra had disguised his form. "This is Māra who has come to disturb you." This criticizes him for not knowing Māra's purpose in coming.

From "He then said to Māra" is the third part, describing how Vimalakīrti demanded the women [from Māra]; this has four aspects. The first is his just asking [for the women]. The second, from "Māra was surprised and afraid," describes how Māra was afraid and wanted to get away. The third, from "A [voice] was heard in the sky," tells of a voice in the sky that urged [Māra] to give [the women to Vimalakīrti]. The fourth describes Māra presenting the women [to Vimalakīrti]: "Māra, frightened and looking this way and that, gave [the women to Vimalakīrti]."

"You can give [these women] to me; a person such as myself can accept them." This is to say that because Maintains the World [Bodhisattva] is a home-departed bodhisattva he should not accept them. Because Vimalakīrti is a white-robed layman it is alright for him to accept them. The next three parts can be understood.

From "At that time, Vimalakīrti" is the fourth part, [Vimalakīrti] teaching the Dharma to the goddesses. This also has two aspects: the first is the actual teaching of the Dharma; the second, from "At this, the devil Māra," describes how Māra, after seeing [Vimalakīrti] teach the Dharma, spoke to the goddesses and said that he wanted to return with them to the heavenly palaces. The first aspect, the actual teaching of the Dharma, has two further elements: the first is the actual teaching of the Dharma; the second, from "All of you have already aroused the intention for enlightenment," is a further teaching for them on how they can take delight in the Dharma in place of delighting in the five desires.

The actual teaching of the Dharma has three divisions: the first is [Vimalakīrti] letting them know that they belong to him; the second, from "Now, you [should arouse the mind for *anuttarā samyaksaṃbodhi*]," encourages them to generate the mental resolve [to attain perfect awakening]; the third, from "Thereupon and with a response appropriate [to their needs, Vimalakīrti taught the goddesses]," [explains] that he taught them in various ways in accordance with what was appropriate [for their needs].

From "Again he spoke to the goddesses" is the second element, the further teaching [to the goddesses] on the delight of the Dharma. The nature of women is to take delight in what is pleasing. If he did not explain the delight of the Dharma in place of taking delight in the five desires, there was a chance that it would be difficult for them to forget the delights of the five desires; hence [Vimalakīrti] explained how to take delight in the Dharma in place of delighting in the five desires.

Within this too there are four items. The first is Vimalakīrti disclosing the delight of the Dharma and exhorting them to follow it. The second is the goddesses asking about the attributes of delighting in the Dharma: "The goddesses thereupon asked, 'What is the delight in the Dharma?'" The third item is from, "He answered, 'Delight is always having faith in the Buddha,'" and is the extensive listing of the delights of the Dharma. The fourth is the conclusion: "These are the bodhisattva's delight in the Dharma."

45a

The third item, the extensive listing of the delights of the Dharma, further unfolds in four aspects. The first is explaining the delight of the Dharma with reference to the Three Jewels. The second, from "Delight is to abandon the five desires," clarifies the delight of the Dharma with regard to the teachings about renouncing evil. The third aspect, from "Delight is to be in accord with the intention for enlightenment," explains the delight of the Dharma with regard to the teachings about cultivating virtue. The fourth, from "Delight is to vanquish hosts of Māras," explains the delight of the Dharma with reference to sundry teachings on virtue and evil.

Although all things under heaven are woven together, it is still necessary to abandon evil and take up virtue. The basis for abandoning evil and taking up virtue is certainly the Three Jewels; hence the first thing explained is the Three Jewels. Wearying of evil, the second aspect, is purely about self-cultivation. The third aspect, cultivating virtue, illustrates both self-cultivation and the transformation of others; these can be understood. The fourth aspect, the sundry teachings [on virtue and evil], also includes the explanation of both self-cultivation and the transformation of others.

"The hosts of Māras" means the four Māras. "[Delight is hearing] the profound Dharma [without fear]" means the Mahayana Dharma; because the two vehicles fear [the profound Dharma], it says that "[Delight is hearing the profound Dharma] without fear." Another interpretation is that "profound Dharma" means the underlying principle of non-arising, which makes ordinary people feel fear and disbelief when they hear about it; therefore it says, "not fearing."

The "three gates of liberation" refer to the three gates of emptiness; "the wrong time" means the partial fruits of the two vehicles. "Fellow students" means those who have aroused *bodhicitta* and seek the same fruits of buddhahood. One interpretation is that "fellow students" refers in general to [those who share] one's own resolve. "[Those who are] not fellow students" means the [followers of the] two vehicles—because [their practices] are not the same as the practices of the great beings, they are called "not fellow students." Again, the other interpretation is that in general all those whose resolve is different from one's own are referred to as "not fellow students."

"Bad friends" are those who accept evil and do not follow the holy teachings. "Good friends" are those who are prudent and follow the holy teachings. "A mind that enjoys purity" means to rejoice in the virtue of others and not be jealous.

"This is the bodhisattva's delight in the Dharma" is the fourth item, the conclusion.

From "At this, the devil Māra" is the second aspect [of Vimalakīrti] teaching the Dharma [to the goddesses, describing how] Māra, after seeing [Vimalakīrti] teach the Dharma, told the goddesses that he wanted to return [with them] to the heavenly palaces. This has seven levels. The first is Māra telling the goddesses that he wants to return to the heavenly palaces. The second, from "The women said," is the goddesses telling him that they didn't want to return [to the heavenly palaces with Māra]. The third level, from "Māra said, 'Layman,'" is Māra's attempt to get Vimalakīrti to relinquish [the women]. The fourth level, from "Vimalakīrti said," is Vimalakīrti's letting them go. The fifth level, from "Thereupon the women asked," is the goddesses asking how they should behave when dwelling in the heavenly palaces. The sixth, from "Vimalakīrti replied," is the teaching for them on how they should behave when dwelling in the heavenly palaces. The seventh, from "Thereupon, the goddesses," describes the goddesses paying their respects and returning to the heavenly palaces with Māra.

"I want to return with you to the heavenly palace." When [Māra] heard the voice in the sky earlier and, fearful, gave [the goddesses to Vimalakīrti], he didn't really want to [give the goddesses away], so now he wishes to [take the goddesses back] and return [to the heavenly palaces]. The second and the third [of the seven levels] can be understood.

45b The fourth level is Vimalakīrti relinquishing them: "[Vimalakīrti said,] 'I have already let them go; you may take them and leave.'" Vimalakīrti had originally accepted [the goddesses] in order to preach the Dharma to them; now that he had finished preaching the Dharma, there was no reason for him to be reluctant [to let them go]. "Make all sentient beings entirely fulfill their Dharma aspirations." Just as Māra has gotten the women back and fulfilled his aspiration, great beings always cause aspirations to be aroused, hence it says "Make all sentient beings entirely fulfill their Dharma aspirations."

The fifth level is the goddesses asking how they should behave while dwelling in the heavenly palaces: "How should we stay in Māra's palace?" In the past they too were like Māra, but now they are bodhisattvas. In other words, there is a distinction between truth and falsity—how can they live together with Māra in his palace?

The sixth level is teaching them how to behave while dwelling with Māra; this has two points. The first is actually giving them the teaching on the inexhaustible lamp and encouraging them to study it; the second, from "Although you dwell in Māra's palace," encourages them to disseminate [the Dharma]. These can be understood.

From "At that time the goddesses" is the seventh level, describing the goddesses paying their respects [to Vimalakīrti] and returning to the heavenly palaces with Māra.

From "World-honored One" is the third level of [the explanation of why Maintains the World Bodhisattva] declined [the Buddha's request to visit Vimalakīrti], the conclusion that he is not suitable [for the task].

The fourth [bodhisattva] directed [to visit Vimalakīrti and inquire about his illness] was Good Virtue Bodhisattva. Within this there are again both the directive [to visit Vimalakīrti] and [Good Virtue's] declining. Within the declining there are also the three levels as above, within the second of which, [the explanation of the declining,] there are three further parts: the first gives the situation leading to [Vimalakīrti's] criticism [of Good Virtue]; the second, from "At that time, Vimalakīrti," gives the actual criticism; and the third, from "World-honored One, when [Vimalakīrti] taught this Dharma," describes the benefits attained as a result of the criticism.

Good Virtue [Bodhisattva] was criticized because he had come up with a plan to accumulate wealth for three years and then make a vast offering of it over a period of seven days. There are four points to Vimalakīrti's criticism: 1) although the offering of material wealth may be vast, it will be exhausted in the end; 2) material wealth does not benefit the spirit; 3) the first to arrive will receive the finer things and those who come later will get coarser things; 4) even when one gives away [material wealth] there will be those who receive first and those who receive later—[the donor] will not be able to give everything away equally at one time. For this reason, Vimalakīrti recommended the gift of the Dharma and criticized [Good Virtue's] material gifts. As was already noted, bodhisattvas bestow the teachings in accordance with spiritual capacity; hence there is nothing that is not done.

Moreover, giving is the first of the six perfections and is also included within the four means of attraction. What was the intent of [Vimalakīrti's] criticism? We can see that it was not because [Good Virtue Bodhisattva] should renounce giving material wealth—it was not that he should do this. It was simply that he thought that giving away his material wealth was the height [of giving]—this is what led Vimalakīrti to criticize him. If [Vimalakīrti] had wanted to criticize [the giving of material wealth] he would have criticized him earlier. The reason that he came to criticize him after seven days had already passed is because even if giving material wealth is not like the gift of the Dharma, in principle it is not the case that you should not practice [giving material wealth]. If the full seven days had not passed, then this point would have been lost; hence it was necessary to let the full seven days pass before coming to criticize him.

The second part, the actual criticism, unfolds in five sections. The first is straightaway recommending the gift of the Dharma and criticizing material giving. The second, from "I said, 'Layman,'" is Good Virtue [Bodhisattva's] asking about a gift of the Dharma; the third, from "An assembly for giving the Dharma," is a direct answer to the question with a brief summary of a gift of the Dharma. The fourth section is Good Virtue [Bodhisattva] again asking about the essential attributes of a gift of the Dharma: "What does this mean?" The fifth section, from "This means that with *bodhi*," is the extensive listing of the essential attributes of a gift of the Dharma.

45c

"You should not do a great offering assembly like this." This means that he should not accumulate material wealth for three years and then give it away in seven days. This line is the actual denial of the offering of material wealth. "You should have an assembly to give the Dharma." This means that in the beginning, the gift of the Dharma endows the spirit and aids our understanding; in the end, the highest fruits are attained, subtle and sublime. This line encourages the giving of the Dharma. "Of what use is this assembly to offer material wealth?" This is the conclusion that he should not make offerings of material wealth.

"I said, 'Layman, what is an assembly to give the Dharma?'" This is the second section, Good Virtue [Bodhisattva's] asking about a gift of the Dharma. From "An assembly to give the Dharma is . . ." onward comprises the third section, that is, a direct answer to the question with a brief summary of giving the Dharma.

"An assembly to give the Dharma makes offerings to all sentient beings simultaneously, with no before or after." This means that a gift of the Dharma is not the same as an offering of material wealth, which has four different inferiorities. When given a full explanation in a single word, sentient beings hear the same [Dharma] and each of them benefits, being endowed in the distant [future] with the wisdom-life of the Dharma body. "This is called an assembly to give the Dharma" is the conclusion about an assembly to give the Dharma. "What does this mean?" is the fourth section, Good Virtue's asking again about the essential attributes of a gift of the Dharma—although earlier he had heard that a gift of the Dharma was superior, with equal benefit received simultaneously, he had not yet heard about the essential attributes [of a gift of the Dharma]. Therefore he now asks again about the essential attributes. Some understand that "What does this mean" is not spoken by Excellence Attained [Bodhisattva] but rather that Vimalakīrti himself raises the question, "What does this mean," because he wishes to extensively explain the attributes of a gift of the Dharma.

From "With *bodhi*" is the fifth section, the extensive explanation of the essential attributes of a gift of the Dharma. This has two divisions: the first is the actual description of the essential attributes of a gift of the Dharma; the second, from "In this way, good son," is the concluding exhortation to [host an assembly] to offer the Dharma. The thirty-two lines of the first division, the actual description of the essential attributes of a gift of the Dharma, are divided into two groups: the first seventeen lines explain self-cultivation; the second group, the latter fifteen lines, from "with regard to body, life, and material wealth," describe the practice of transforming others.

"This means that through *bodhi*, arouse a mind of kindness." There are two ways to understand this. One interpretation says that you should give rise to a mind of kindness because of the wish to transform sentient beings and cause them to attain the fruits of *bodhi*. Another interpretation is that this means that if, with the aspiration for *bodhi*, you see people in front of you and want to give to the assembly, then you should teach and transform them, making them give rise to a mind of kindness. The lines that come below are of a similar [meaning]; you can follow [either interpretation] as you wish.

"Through saving sentient beings, arouse a mind of great compassion." This means that great compassion is a requisite for removing suffering. "Through upholding the true Dharma, arouse a mind of joy." This is to say that jealousy and envy obstruct the many virtues; therefore one should give rise to a mind of joy. "Through the embrace of discerning awareness, arouse

46a   a mind of equanimity." Discerning awareness is the true understanding of the absence of perceptual attribute; without a mind of equanimity there is no basis for embracing true knowing. Therefore one [should] give rise to a mind of equanimity.

"Through the control of parsimony and greed, arouse the perfection of *dāna* (charity)" teaches to arouse the practice of giving. "Through transforming those who violate morality, arouse the perfection of *śīla* (morality)" teaches that one ought to give rise to the practice of upholding the precepts. "Through the Dharma of no-self, arouse the perfection of *kṣānti* (serene acceptance)" means that without serene acceptance one will believe in self and other and it is not possible to be even-minded; therefore, [one should] give rise to serene acceptance. "Through abandoning the attributes of body and mind, arouse the perfection of *vīrya* (effort)." This is to say that being able to not believe in body and mind is the requisite cause of attaining [the perfection of] effort. Another interpretation is that if you believe in body and mind then you will not accomplish [the perfection of] effort.

"Through the attribute of *bodhi,* arouse the perfection of *dhyāna* (meditative concentration)." This is because meditative concentration is always attained from the fruits of *bodhi.* "Through omniscience, arouse the perfection of *prajñā* (discerning awareness)." Omniscience is the result; *prajñā* is the cause. This means that knowing as the result surely is accomplished by means of understanding as the cause. "Through teaching and transforming sentient beings, arouse the [understanding of] emptiness." This is because, although one might wish to transform beings, if you are not [established in] emptiness then that transformation will be one-sided.

"Without abandoning conditioned *dharmas*, arouse that which is devoid of perceptual attributes." This is to say that existence and nonexistence function together and complete all of the ten thousand things. "Manifesting the experience of birth, arouse the uncreated." The uncreated is emptiness; this is the same as the above line. "Upholding and protecting the true Dharma, arouse the power of skillful means." The true Dharma is the Tathāgata's two teachings of exhortation [to cultivate virtue] and admonition [to avoid evil]. It is not different from the underlying principle of things, and so it is called "true"; because it makes the rules for beings, it is termed "Dharma." Without skillful means there can be no upholding and mastering the true Dharma. "Through saving sentient beings, arouse the four means of attraction." The "four means of attraction" are the requisite practice for transformation of beings. "Through respect for all things, arouse the elimination of pride." This can be understood.

From "with regard to body, life, and material wealth" is the second group, describing the transformation of others.

"With regard to body, life, and material wealth, arouse the three substantial *dharma*s." This means forsaking the body, life, and material wealth [characterized by] mental afflictions, and [instead] cultivating the Dharma body, wisdom-life, and Dharma wealth. "With regard to the six recollections, arouse the method of thoughtful recollection." [This means that] with regard to morality, giving, heaven, the Buddha, the Dharma, and the Sangha, one thoughtfully remembers and does not forget. "With regard to the six kinds of respectful harmony, arouse an honest and sincere mind." Body, speech, and mind are three [of the six kinds of respectful harmony]; the fourth is sharing nourishment with others when it is received; the fifth is to hold the precepts with purity; and the sixth is cultivation of awareness and exhausting the contaminations. If you practice these six, you will be harmonious with beings and respected; if you do not have a sincere mind, then you cannot accomplish these six practices.

"Correctly practicing the virtuous Dharma, arouse pure livelihood." This means that if you wish to correctly practice the virtuous Dharma you will not make your livelihood with an evil mind; hence it says, "arouse pure livelihood." Attaining wealth in accord with Dharma is "pure livelihood." "A mind pure and joyous [leads to] being near the wise and holy." This means to purify people's minds and make them calm and happy; associating with foolish [people] gives rise to trouble and suffering. "Not despising evil people, arouse a disciplined mind." If you are able to discipline your own mind   46b the three poisons will not arise; hence you will not despise evil people.

"Through the way of leaving home, arouse the profound mind." Leaving home is a difficult thing; it cannot be accomplished with a shallow mind, and therefore it says, "arouse the profound mind." "Through practicing according to the teaching, arouse wide learning." Although one may wish to practice according to the teachings, without extensive learning there is no basis to do so. "Through the way of non-contention, establish the dwelling place of the forest retreat." This is because forest retreats are wonderfully free of contention. "Turning toward a buddha's knowledge, establish tranquil sitting." This is because there is no basis for turning toward a buddha's knowledge without a concentrated mind. "Through releasing sentient beings from their fetters, establish the stages of practice." If one is not able to engage in self-cultivation, how can one save the masses?

"By becoming complete in the [thirty-two] attributes and [eighty] signs [of a buddha's body] and purifying the buddha land, establish meritorious karma." This is because you cannot complete [the auspicious marks and signs of a buddha's body and the purification of a buddha land] if [your karma] is not meritorious. "Knowing the minds and thoughts of all sentient beings and preaching the Dharma to them appropriately, establish the karma of knowing." Without cultivating the karma of knowing within the causal [stages], there is no basis for attaining the fruits of buddhahood. This line is an explanation based on existence. "Knowing all *dharma*s without grasping or abandoning and entering the gate of the one attribute, establish the karma of knowledge." This is the explanation based on emptiness. Those who wish to attain the fruit of buddhahood put an end to conceptualization, and truly understand—their attainment will certainly be due to their having cultivated the karma of [discerning] awareness within the causal [stage].

"Eradicating all mental afflictions, all obstructions, and all nonvirtuous *dharma*s, establish all virtuous karma." Only virtue is able to drive away various evils. "Through attaining omniscience and all virtuous *dharma*s, establish all the *dharma*s that aid along the buddha path." The *dharma*s [that help one along] the buddha path are the uncontaminated Mahayana *dharma*s.

From "Like this, good son" is the second division of the extensive explanation of a gift of the Dharma, the concluding exhortation to give the gift of the Dharma. This itself has two parts: the first is the conclusion, "This is called an assembly for giving the Dharma." The second, from "If a bodhisattva," is the exhortation; this shows how, personally, one will acquire the title "Great Donor"; for others, one will be a field of merit for all. For this reason, one should give the gift of the Dharma.

From "World-honored One, [when] Vimalakīrti [taught this Dharma]" is the third part of the explanation of [Good Virtue Bodhisattva's] declining; that is, the benefits attained as a result of the criticism. This has two further divisions: the first explains the benefits that the assembly attained at that time: "Within the assembly of brahmans two hundred people all aroused *bodhicitta*." The second division, from "At that time my mind attained a purity," shows the benefit that Good Virtue [Bodhisattva] himself acquired. This has three further aspects. The first is straightaway stating the benefit that he himself attained: "At that time my mind attained a purity. . . ." The second is praise by means of the three actions: "exclaimed to be unprecedented" is the action of speech, and "bowing to [Vimalakīrti's] feet" is the action of the body. If there were no inner intention, there would be no basis upon which the two actions of body and speech could be generated; thus, we can know that the action of thought was also present.

The third aspect, from "Thereupon I removed my necklace," is [Good Virtue Bodhisattva's] repaying [Vimalakīrti's] kindness with [a gift of] material wealth. This also has six items. The first describes [Good Virtue's] repaying [Vimalakīrti's] kindness by removing his necklace [and offering it to Vimalakīrti]. The second describes Vimalakīrti not accepting it, for two reasons: the first is that [Good Virtue Bodhisattva] should acquire the [proper] mindset of a donor; the second is that [he should learn to] accept the will of the recipient. The third item is Good Virtue Bodhisattva's asking [Vimalakīrti] to accept [the necklace and telling him to use it as he wished]—this showed that [Good Virtue had developed] the mindset of a donor and that he accepted the will of the recipient. This is [the part of the text] from "I said, 'Layman.'"

The fourth item describes Vimalakīrti accepting the necklace and skillfully using it to make an offering of material wealth. It has already been said above that an offering of material wealth is not [the same as] a gift of the Dharma. Now, however, Good Virtue [Bodhisattva] has made an offering of material wealth to Vimalakīrti. The reason that Vimalakīrti has accepted it is the desire to have him again reveal the meaning of a skillful offering of material wealth and to cause that assembly to abandon their biased minds. The reason is that the Tathāgata is already worthy of the highest respect;

46c

beggars are worthy of the greatest sympathy. Although noble and base are different, giving rise to virtue is not different. Thus Vimalakīrti divided the necklace into two parts, offering one to the Tathāgata and giving one to the beggars. If such is the case, the Tathāgata was not worthy of many offerings [simply] because of his nobility, nor the beggars worthy of just a few gifts [simply] because of their lowly [status]. Again, although it was a gift of material wealth, if it is performed in this way, impartial to superior and inferior, then it can be called a skillful offering of material wealth. Not only was giving illustrated but the Dharma body of the Pure Land and the many and various adornments were also revealed—the reason was the wish to show that if in this way you are able to make an impartial offering of material wealth, in the end you will certainly obtain a reward such as this.

"The necklace changed into a jeweled dais with four pillars" shows that when the practice is fulfilled and buddhahood achieved, the four impartial [virtues] universally envelop the four kinds of birth. "The four sides were unobstructed" means that the four [unhindered capabilities] of speech transform beings without obstruction.

From "At that time, Vimalakīrti" is the fifth item, another offering of material wealth and the broad promulgation of the gift of the Dharma; this has five lines. "If the donor's mind is even and he gives to the lowliest beggar as though they possessed the attributes of the Tathāgata's field of merit, with no discrimination . . . [this is called 'the complete gift of the Dharma']." Citing the inferior as equal to the superior explains "impartial." This is telling us that our sympathy for beggars is equal in importance to our respectful attitude toward the Buddha. "Equal in great compassion and without seeking reward." Citing the superior as equal to the inferior explains "impartial." This is telling us that respecting the Buddha is equal in importance to our compassionate attitude toward the beggars. "This is called 'the complete gift of the Dharma'" is the conclusion.

From "The impoverished in the city," is the sixth item, describing how the impoverished people, seeing Vimalakīrti's miraculous transformations and hearing his teachings, aroused their minds [to attain perfect awakening] and attained benefits. "Therefore I am not worthy to visit him and inquire about his illness" is the third level of [Good Virtue's] declining, the conclusion that he is not suitable.

From "In this way the many bodhisattvas" is the second level in this chapter [of the second aspect of the third part of the specific introduction that introduces Vimalakīrti's virtues; that is to say], the overall conclusion that none [of the bodhisattvas in the assembly] were worthy [of visiting Vimalakīrti and inquiring about his illness].

Chapter Five   47a

Mañjuśrī's Inquiring
about the Illness

So far it has been described how five hundred *śrāvaka*s and eight thousand bodhisattvas were directed [to visit Vimalakīrti and inquire about his illness], but each of them told how in the past they had been humiliated [by Vimalakīrti] and so all had declined, saying that they were not worthy. Since not a single one was willing to go, there was nobody to inquire about the illness. At that point, however, Mañjuśrī accepted the instruction to visit Vimalakīrti in his room, to fully set forth the Buddha's thoughts and inquire about the illness. Hence the title of the chapter.

From this chapter up to where it says, "When this was finished, [Akṣobhya's realm Abhirati] returned to its original place, and all of the assembly saw it" in the chapter "Seeing Akṣobhya Buddha," is the second part of the three main sections of this scripture, that is, the main teaching. This unfolds in two parts: the first is from this chapter up through the chapter "[The Buddha] Accumulated Fragrances," altogether six chapters that actually take place in Vimalakīrti's room, in which he himself expounds the inconceivable, the principle of the two knowledges of the conventional and the real, and the transformation of people of the three capacities. The second part, from the chapter "Practices of the Bodhisattvas" up to "all of the assembly saw it" in the chapter "Seeing Akṣobhya Buddha," describes how [the entire assembly] went from Vimalakīrti's room back to Āmrapālī and, together with the Buddha, clarified all manner of profound Dharma and corroborated the inconceivable teachings that had been given in Vimalakīrti's room.

One interpretation has it that the main teaching is comprised solely of the first six chapters [after the introduction, chapters five through ten]. From the chapter "Practices of the Bodhisattva" onward is the dissemination of the teachings. I will explain this when we get there. The first part of the main teaching was given when Vimalakīrti was actually in his room and concerns the transformation of people of the three capacities; this naturally has three

                                     147

levels. The first is the transformation of people of superior capacity and consists of the two chapters "[Mañjuśrī's] Inquiring about the Illness" and "The Inconceivable." The second is the transformation of people of middling capacity, and consists of the two chapters "Contemplating Sentient Beings" and "The Way of the Buddha." The third level is the transformation of people of inferior capacity, and consists of the two chapters "Entering the Dharma Gate of Nonduality" and "[The Buddha] Accumulated Fragrances."

There are also two aspects to the first level, the two chapters that concern the transformation of [those of] superior capacity. Within the first, the chapter "[Mañjuśrī's] Inquiring about the Illness," there is only the one person, Vimalakīrti, and only one matter of concern, [the explanation of why Vimalakīrti] manifested the illness. Therefore, it is called a condensed explanation of the inconceivable. Within the second, the chapter "The Inconceivable," many buddhas and bodhisattvas appear and all manner of inconceivable things are extensively explained; hence it is called the extensive explanation of the inconceivable. When people of superior capacity hear these two teachings of the extensive and condensed [explanations of the inconceivable], they give rise to faith, enhance their understanding, and the ordinary is changed into the sagely.

Another interpretation takes it that the exposition of the inconceivable while actually in Vimalakīrti's room only has two levels. The single chapter "[Mañjuśrī's] Inquiring about the Illness" is the condensed explanation
47b of the inconceivable, and the five chapters from the chapter "The Inconceivable" comprise the extensive explanation of the inconceivable. The five chapters, in other words, derive from the earlier matter and so the text is divided—and the chapters should be interpreted likewise. Here, however, we are going to follow the prior interpretation.

The chapter "[Mañjuśrī's] Inquiring about the Illness" initially unfolds in two levels: the first is from the beginning up to "[that which is seen] can be seen no more" and is called the background details concerning [Mañjuśrī's] inquiring about the illness; the second, from "Let us put aside this matter," is the actual description of [Mañjuśrī's] inquiry about [Vimalakīrti's] illness. The first level, the background details concerning [Mañjuśrī's] inquiring about the illness, opens up in six items. The first is the Buddha's directive; the second is Mañjuśrī's accepting the mandate; the third, from "within the assembly [many wished to accompany Mañjuśrī]," describes how the great assembly wished to go with Mañjuśrī; the fourth, from "Thereupon, Mañjuśrī," describes Mañjuśrī entering Vimalakīrti's room together with a great assembly; the fifth, from "At that time the elder," explains how Vimalakīrti knew of Mañjuśrī's coming along with a great assembly and emptied his room; the sixth, from "Vimalakīrti said," shows Vimalakīrti and Mañjuśrī exchanging the brief courtesies of host and guest and [engaging in] a repartee that cleared away doubts.

The first item can be understood. The second item, [Mañjuśrī's] assent to the mandate, also has two parts. The first extols the virtues of the difficulty of responding to Vimalakīrti; the second, from "Nonetheless," describes the actual acceptance of [the Buddha's] mandate that he should go [visit Vimalakīrti]. The first part, extolling the difficulty of responding to [Vimalakīrti], also has two levels: the first is the overall praise: "That eminent man is difficult to respond to." The second level, from "he has deeply penetrated the true attribute," is a separate praise of the gate of the Dharma, consisting of nine lines divided into three layers: the first is the initial four lines that praise him according to [his mastery of] the four [unhindered] capabilities of expression; the second layer is the next four lines that praise him for [his mastery of] miscellaneous teachings; the third is the one line that concludes with praise of [his perfection of] the two knowledges.

"Deeply penetrated the true attribute" [is praise of his unhindered] expression of the meaning. The truth of the underlying principle sunders falsity and transcends the existence of perceptual attributes, therefore it says "true attribute." "Skilled at teaching the essentials of the Dharma" refers to [Mañjuśrī's] language and expression; "His expression is unrestricted" refers to his unhindered ease of teaching; and "his discerning awareness is unobstructed" refers to his [unhindered] expression of the Dharma.

The four lines from "[He knows all the rules of] bodhisattva [conduct]" are the second level, praise of [his mastery of] miscellaneous teachings. "He knows all the rules of bodhisattva conduct" means that he has skillfully penetrated all of the many practices of the causal stages. "There is no secret storehouse of the buddhas to which he has not obtained entrance" means that he has skillfully penetrated the twelve meanings of the result stage that have been taught. Dharma Master Sengzhao says, "Close by he knows the etiquette of bodhisattavas, far off he enters the secret storehouses of the many buddhas. 'Secret storehouse' means the secret storehouses of the Buddha's body, speech, and mind." These two lines compare cause and effect and show that there is nothing in the principle of cause and effect that is not penetrated.

"Subdued hosts of Māras" means that [Vimalakīrti] has subdued the four Māras; this line praises his strong approach, and it also can refer to his practice of transformation of others.

"Sports and plays with the spiritual powers" means that in transforming beings he avails himself of the five spiritual powers as he wishes; the meaning is the same as "sports and plays." This line praises his flexible approach, and it can also refer to his self-cultivation. These two lines compare his strength and agility and show that there is no feat of strength or agility of which he is incapable. "He is already perfect in discerning awareness and skillful means" is the third level, the concluding praise of his [perfection of] the two knowledges. "Discerning awareness" means knowing truth; "skillful means" refers to knowledge of the conventional. This shows that because he is complete in these two knowledges he has also entirely purified the many virtues for which he was praised above.

From "Nonetheless, [I will accept the Buddha's holy mandate and visit him and inquire about his illness]" is the second item in the acceptance of the [Buddha's] mandate, actually accepting that he should go [visit Vimalakīrti]. The third and fourth items can be understood. The fifth item, Vimalakīrti's knowing that Mañjuśrī was coming with a great assembly and [therefore] emptying his room, has two divisions. The first shows Vimalakīrti emptying out his room in order to begin their discussion; the second, from "[Mañjuśrī] then entered the house," describes Mañjuśrī seeing the empty room.

To discuss the heart of the matter concerning Vimalakīrti's manifesting an illness, it was because he wished to cause the newly trained bodhisattvas, who might encounter the suffering of illness, to arouse great compassion and a peaceful mind so as to transform beings without experiencing fatigue. He emptied his room because he truly wanted to rid sentient beings of their confusions of right and wrong. If we discuss the specifics, however, five things were born of his emptying the room and six discussions were born of his manifesting an illness.

As for the five things born of Vimalakīrti's emptying his room, the first is Mañjuśrī seeing that the room is empty and asking Vimalakīrti, "Layman, why is this room empty?" Vimalakīrti replied, "Not only my room, but the many buddha realms are likewise all empty." The second is Mañjuśrī's question, "Why are there no servants?" Vimalakīrti replied, "All the hosts of Māras and every one of those [beings] on non-Buddhist paths are all my servants." The third is Śāriputra seeing that the room was empty and wondering, "Where will all these many bodhisattvas and great disciples sit?" Vimalakīrti knew his thoughts and first spoke of the ultimate underlying principle, scolding him for looking for chairs, saying, "Ah, Śāriputra, [did you come] for the sake of the Dharma or for the sake of a chair?" Then, by borrowing seats from [Sumeru] Lamp King, he broadly illustrated the underlying principle of all manner of the bodhisattva's inconceivable [activities].

The fourth thing is that the bodhisattva Universally Manifested Form Body saw that the room was empty and asked Vimalakīrti, "Layman, your father, your mother, your wife, your child, your friends—who are they? Your elephants, horses, carriages, servants and attendants—where are they?" Vimalakīrti replied that, "The perfection of discerning awareness is the bodhisattva's mother, and skillful means is the father." That is to say, he broadly proclaimed all manner of the great being's practices. The fifth thing is Śāriputra's seeing that the room was empty and wondering, "It is already noon— what are these many bodhisattvas going to eat?" Vimalakīrti knew his thoughts and initially, by means of the eight liberations, scolded him, saying, "The Buddha has taught the eight liberations; you, good sir, should accept and practice them. Why do you mix up your desire for food with listening to the Dharma?" Then he requested food from [the Buddha] in the fragrant land and, with a single meal, fed everybody [in the great assembly]. Thereby he revealed the meaning of all manner of doing a buddha's work. In short, these 48a are the five things born of Vimalakīrti's emptying his room.

Six discussions were born of his manifesting an illness. The first was Mañjuśrī asking, "Layman, what is the cause of this illness?" Vimalakīrti replied, "A bodhisattva's illness is caused by their great compassion." The second discussion is occasioned by Mañjuśrī asking, "Layman, have you long been ill like this?" Vimalakīrti replied, "Because of ignorance there is attachment; hence the birth of my illness." The third is Mañjuśrī asking,

"Layman, how can this illness be extinguished?" Vimalakīrti replied, "My illness is caused by the illness of all sentient beings; if the illness of all sentient beings is extinguished, then my illness will be extinguished."

The fourth discussion is Mañjuśrī asking, "Layman, what are the attributes of this illness?" Vimalakīrti replied, "My illness has no form and cannot be seen." The fifth discussion is Mañjuśrī asking, "How should a bodhisattva comfort and instruct a bodhisattva who is ill?" Vimalakīrti replied that they should be comforted and instructed with truths such as "Explain that the body is impermanent, but do not teach that you should despise or abandon this body." The sixth discussion is when Mañjuśrī asks, "How should a bodhisattva who is ill discipline their mind?" Vimalakīrti replied, "Bodhisattvas who are ill should think: 'My present illness entirely stems from the deluded thoughts, confused thinking, and many mental afflictions of my previous lives; there are no real *dharma*s—who could experience illness?'" First, one should be made to know the cause of the illness, and afterward be taught to see things [like this]. In short, this is how the six discussions are born of [Vimalakīrti's manifesting an] illness.

The reason that Mañjuśrī and [the bodhisattva] Universally Manifested [Form Body] revealed their questions aloud but Śāriputra only thought [to himself about his questions] is because these two great beings and Vimalakīrti were all of the Mahayana—thus, even if they harbored a question in their minds they could ask it aloud without embarrassment. Śāriputra, however, was a Hinayana follower and found it difficult to engage in the give-and-take among the many great beings; hence he could not ask [his questions] out loud but only thought [to himself about them].

From "At that time, Vimalakīrti said" is the sixth item [of the background details of Mañjuśrī's inquiry], the brief exchange of courtesies between host and guest. This also has two parts. The first is the host's initial commendation of the guest; the second, from "Just so, layman," is the guest's humble reply. The first part, the host's commending the guest, itself has two meanings. The first is, "Welcome, Mañjuśrī," straightaway commending his coming. In correspondence to the spiritual capacity of beings, profound benefits will surely be had.

"Going" and "coming" are words that refer to backward and forward. From Vimalakīrti's room looking [back] toward Āmrapālī, [Mañjuśrī] is "coming"; from Āmrapālī looking [forward] toward Vimalakīrti's room, [Mañjuśrī] is "going." "You have come without the attribute of coming." If we speak from the point of view of truth, in crossing over from Āmrapālī there is leaving but not arriving at Vimalakīrti's room; therefore it says, "without the attribute of coming." However, if we speak from the point of view of the conventional, the crossing over from Āmrapālī is continuous without ceasing, and so there is the coming to Vimalakīrti's room; therefore it says "You have come."

The second meaning is, "You see [me] without the attribute of seeing." Again, to speak from the point of view of truth, the Mañjuśrī that was in Āmrapālī has left and arrived at Vimalakīrti's room, nonetheless there is no seeing [Vimalakīrti]; therefore it says, "without the attribute of seeing." How- 48b ever, from the point of view of the conventional, the Mañjuśrī of Āmrapālī continues on, without ceasing, eventually arriving at Vimalakīrti's room and seeing him; therefore it says, "You see [me]." These two lines laud the lack of perceptual attributes in [Mañjuśrī's] coming [to visit Vimalakīrti].

From "Mañjuśrī said" is the second part, the guest's humble reply. This has two further aspects: the first is the simple statement, "Just so, layman"; the second is the explanation of this statement, "Just so, [layman]," and indicates that there is nothing said by the layman that is not correct with regard to the underlying principle.

"If one has already come, there is no more coming." If within the provisional [truth] one has completed [the act of] coming, then in the [ultimate] truth there is no more coming. "If one has already gone, there is no more going." This is the same [as above]. This should be followed by, "If one has already seen, there is no more seeing," but the text is simply abridged.

From "Why" is the second aspect, the explanation [of the above statements]; it expresses a question as to why coming and going are without a fixed existence. "One who comes, comes from nowhere." To talk about the one who comes within the provisional [realm] from the point of view of reality, the crossing over from Āmrapālī ends in Āmrapālī—the crossing over to Vimalakīrti's room arises only at Vimalakīrti's room; therefore it says "comes from nowhere." "One who leaves, goes nowhere." To talk about the one who leaves within the provisional [realm] from the point of view of reality, the Mañjuśrī of Āmrapālī has himself been extinguished in Āmrapālī—

there is no leaving and arriving at Vimalakīrti's room; therefore it says, "goes nowhere."

"That which is seen [cannot be seen again]" refers to the fact that, although in the realm of provisional designations both Āmrapālī and Vimala-kīrti's room are seen, if we speak from the point of view of [ultimate] truth, the seeing of Āmrapālī is extinguished [at Āmrapālī] and does not carry over to Vimalakīrti's room. That and this—each arises and each passes away. Mañjuśrī does not have the role of one who sees, nor does Vimalakīrti have the function of the one who is seen; hence it says, "cannot be seen again."

From "Let us put aside this matter" is the second level [of this chapter], the actual description of [Mañjuśrī's] inquiry about [Vimalakīrti's] illness. This further unfolds in three parts: the first is initially passing on the gist of the Buddha's inquiry; the second, from "Layman, what is the cause of this illness?", sets forth Mañjuśrī's own concerns; the third, from "When he spoke these words," gives the benefits received by the assembly at that time.

"Let us put aside this matter." Because he wanted to convey the Buddha's inquiry about his condition, he sought to end the initial discussion. From "Layman, [can you endure this illness]" is the actual expression of the nature of the Buddha's inquiry. There were three questions: 1) "Layman, can you bear this illness or not?", 2) "Does the treatment hurt?", and 3) "Is it not getting worse?"

"The World-honored One has made innumerable courteous inquiries about you." This conveys the Tathāgata's deep concern. What is being said is not only in these three questions, but in his great compassion he is broadly and limitlessly questioning all.

From "Layman, [what is the cause] of this illness?" is the second part [of the actual description of Mañjuśrī's inquiry about Vimalakīrti's illness] and relates Mañjuśrī's own concerns. This also is unpacked in two parts: the first discusses only the situation in Vimalakīrti's room; the second, from "At that time Mañjuśrī asked Vimalakīrti, saying 'How should a bodhisattva comfort and instruct a bodhisattva who is ill?'", is the general discussion for the sake of the other, newly trained bodhisattvas.

As for the first part, the discussion of just the things in Vimalakīrti's room, this too unfolds in three [parts]: the first is the discussion about the cause of the illness; the second, from "Mañjuśrī said, 'Layman, why is this

48c

room empty?", discusses the reason that the room is empty; the third, from "Layman, what are the attributes of your illness?", is a discussion about the cause of [the medical diagnoses of the] cold and hot attributes of Vimala-kīrti's illness.

The first, the discussion about the cause of the illness, also has two parts: the first is asking Vimalakīrti about three things; the second is Vimalakīrti replying to those three things. The first of the three questions is "Layman, what is the cause of this illness?" This line asks about the cause of Vimala-kīrti's illness. This is the first of the six discussions born of [Vimalakīrti's manifesting] an illness. The second question is "Layman, have you long been ill like this?" This line asks how many days have passed since he became ill, whether it has been a long or short time. This is the second of the six dis-cussions born of [Vimalakīrti's manifesting] an illness. The third question is "How can it be extinguished?" This line asks about whether healing the illness will take a long or short time. This is the third discussion of the six discussions occasioned by [Vimalakīrti's manifesting] an illness.

The second part, Vimalakīrti's reply to these three questions, has two further divisions. The first is the initial response to the latter two questions; the second, from "He again spoke, ['from what cause does] this illness [arise]?'", adds a reply to the first question.

The first division, the initial response to the latter two questions, also has three parts. The first is the actual answer to the latter two questions. The sec-ond, from "Why?", lists his explanations. The third, from "For example, it is like an elder," uses an example to further elucidate the meaning of his reply.

The second question above, "Have you long been ill like this?", is here answered with, "Because of ignorance there is attachment; hence my illness arises." Because sentient beings have the real illnesses of ignorance and attach-ment, bodhisattvas are moved—hence the bodhisattvas are also ill in response.

The third question above, "How can it be extinguished?", is here answered with, "My illness is caused by the illness of all sentient beings; if the illness of all sentient beings is extinguished, then my illness will be extinguished." This means that if the real illnesses of ignorance and attachment of sentient beings that cause the bodhisattvas to be moved are extinguished, then the illness that the bodhisattvas have in response [to sentient beings] will like-wise be extinguished.

From "Why?" is the second part, that is, the listing of [Vimalakīrti's] explanations; it expresses a question. "Because of ignorance there is attachment; hence my illness arises. . . . [If] sentient beings' illness is extinguished, my illness will be extinguished—what is the reason?" Bodhisattvas enter samsara because of the real illnesses of sentient beings' ignorance and attachment. Because there is samsara, bodhisattvas also are ill in response. Therefore it says, "Because of ignorance there is attachment; hence my illness arises." Further, if the real illnesses of sentient beings' ignorance and attachment are extinguished, then the bodhisattvas too will have no residue of illness. Therefore it says, "if the illness of [all] sentient beings is extinguished, then my illness will be extinguished."

From "For example, it is like an elder" is the third part, using an example to further elucidate the meaning of his reply; there are two aspects, the opening and the combining [of the example with the teaching about the bodhisattva]. "For example, it is like an elder who has an only child; the child falls ill and the father and mother also fall ill." This illustrates the above, "Because of ignorance there is attachment; hence the birth of my illness." "If the child's illness is cured then the father and mother's illness will also be cured" illustrates the above, "If the illness of all sentient beings is extinguished, then my illness will be extinguished." The second aspect, the combining [of the example and the teaching about the bodhisattva], can be understood.

From "He again spoke, ['From what cause does this illness arise?']" is the second division of the three questions, the additional answer to the first question about the cause [of the illness]. "He again spoke, 'From what cause does this illness arise?'" This illustrates the above words, "A bodhisattva's illness is caused by their great compassion." This is the actual answer to the question. This means that without the great compassion of the profound source there would be no cause for the illness [of the bodhisattva] to arise in response. Thus it says, "caused by their great compassion."

In short, we can also list five questions and answers that give the intent of this [exchange]. The first question is, if the reason Mañjuśrī inquired of [Vimalakīrti's] illness was originally because of the Buddha's directive, why did Vimalakīrti only answer Mañjuśrī's personal questions here and not respond to the Buddha's inquiry? In short. there are three reasons why [Vimalakīrti] did not answer the Buddha's inquiry. The first is that after the

49a

business in Vimalakīrti's room is concluded, Vimalakīrti and Mañjuśrī will go together to see the Tathāgata and there, in front of [the Tathāgata], he will respectfully answer [the Tathāgata's inquiry]. Hence he did not answer [here]. The second is that after Mañjuśrī passed on the Buddha's directive he next set forth his own questions. There was no break in which to answer the Buddha's inquiry; hence [Vimalakīrti] did not respond [to the Buddha's inquiries]. The third reason is that if we speak from the point of view of truth, although these were Mañjuśrī's personal questions they were also none other than the Buddha's questions. The reason is that he had already said above, "The World-honored One has made innumerable courteous inquiries about you." Mañjuśrī understood the intent of this, and so when he made his own inquiries there was nothing in what he asked that was not the Buddha's intent. Thus neither did Vimalakīrti give a separate reply.

The second question is why, if the above three questions began with an inquiry about the cause of Vimalakīrti's illness, his reply began with an answer to the latter two questions. Interpreting this, we say that it had not yet been explained to the great assembly that the bodhisattva's illness was in response [to sentient beings' illness] and not real. If he had initially answered the first question about the cause, saying that the illness of the bodhisattva arises from his great compassion, then they would think that bodhisattvas have real illnesses that arise because of their great compassion. Thus he first answered the latter two questions, explaining that essentially bodhisattvas do not have real illnesses and only have illness in response [to sentient beings' illness—that is, they only manifest illness] in order to transform beings. Thereby sentient beings would truly understand that, this being the case, the bodhisattvas' illness was only a response and not real. Next he explained that the bodhisattvas' illnesses arise because of their great compassion and made them understand that the real illness of sentient beings arises because of ignorance and attachment, and that the bodhisattvas' illness in response [to sentient beings' illness] arises because of their great compassion. This is the reason he first answered the latter two questions and subsequently answered the first question.

The third question is that, this being so, Mañjuśrī should have first asked his second and third questions: "Have you long been [ill] like this?" and "How can [this illness] be extinguished?" Instead Mañjuśrī immediately

49b

came to the point and first asked about the cause. But it has already been stated that Vimalakīrti and Mañjuśrī were great sages who had already realized the same true awakening—how could there be any difference in the quality [of that realization]? Interpreting this, we say that the reason Mañjuśrī did not immediately come to the point and first asked about the cause is because he wished to show that great compassion is the source of the bodhisattvas' ten thousand transformations. That Vimalakīrti first answered the latter two questions is because he wanted to show that the illness of a great being is only a response [to sentient beings] and is not real. If Mañjuśrī had not first asked about the cause, there would be no reason for showing that great compassion is the source of the bodhisattvas' ten thousand transformations. If Vimalakīrti had not first responded to the latter two questions, then again there would be no reason to show that the bodhisattvas' illness was only in response [to the illness of sentient beings] and is not real. Thus it is likely that the two sages together knew the appropriate time and together brought forth [the sequence of questions and answers].

The fourth question is that if, as has been said, great beings are essentially without any real illness and are only ill for the sake of [saving] beings, and if [illness] arises because of ignorance and attachment, then [Vimalakīrti] should have answered thus to the first question, "From what cause does [this illness] arise?" Why doesn't he say that [illness] arises because of ignorance and attachment? Interpreting this, we say that sentient beings have the real illnesses of ignorance and attachment, and hence they move the bodhisattvas. Because bodhisattvas have a mind of great compassion they also are ill in response [to the illness of sentient beings]. Being ill in response [to the illness of sentient beings], there is already a remote causal connection with the ignorance and attachment of sentient beings. However, the great compassion of the bodhisattvas is already the proximate [cause], and so here the proximate [cause] is used for the answer to the first question about the cause of [the illness] arising.

The fifth question is if the reason the bodhisattvas are ill in response [to the illness of sentient beings] is because they possess a mind of great compassion—in other words, the illness that bodhisattvas experience in response [to the illness of sentient beings] arises because of their great compassion— why doesn't [Vimalakīrti] answer thus to the second question, "Have you long been [ill] like this?" In interpreting this, we say that he couldn't [answer in this way]. The reason is that, as already stated, great beings are essentially without any real illness and only are ill as a response in order to transform beings. Therefore he answered that his illness arises because there are sentient beings with the real illnesses of ignorance and attachment. Thus, too, the [bodhisattva's] healing must await the extinguishing of sentient beings' real illnesses of ignorance and attachment. If, in response to the second question, "Have you long been [ill] like this?", he had said that [the illness of bodhisattvas] arises from great compassion, then, because great compassion is a personal quality of the bodhisattvas, [it would appear] that their illness too arise from [the bodhisattvas] themselves and not because they were moved by the [suffering] of beings. If this were the case, then the import of [the bodhisattvas' illness only being in response to] the illness of beings would be lost. Moreover, because there is no time when [bodhisattvas] lack great compassion, they would always have to be resting in bed [because of being ill]. However, even though great compassion can never be exhausted, bodhisattvas are not always bedridden. Therefore, [in reply to the second question about how long he has been ill, Vimalakīrti] could not reply that [his illness] arises because of great compassion.

One interpretation says that the reason that the latter two of the three questions are answered first is that the source of the illness [is the bodhisattva's compassion] for the sake of beings, and so [Vimalakīrti] wanted to first reveal the meaning that [his illness] is for the sake of beings; therefore he answered [the latter two questions] first. It can also be said that if there is a manifestation, there is surely a source, but even if there is a source there is not yet necessarily a manifestation. Therefore [Vimalakīrti] first answered about the manifestation. Replying to the second question, "Have you long been [ill] like this?" by saying, "Because of ignorance there is attachment; hence the birth of my illness," shows that because sentient beings have the   49c
afflictions of ignorance and attachment they obtain the illness of samsara; hence they move the bodhisattvas [to respond]. Because bodhisattvas possess great compassion, they respond with the same illness. This means that because the ignorance and attachment of sentient beings is without beginning, the illness [caused by] the bodhisattvas' great compassion is also without beginning.

The answer to the third question, "How can it be extinguished?", says, "If the illness of [all] sentient beings is extinguished, then my illness will be extinguished." If [the number of ill] sentient beings is inexhaustible, when will Vimalakīrti's illness be extinguished? This means that the illness has no end. For this we should use the traditional understandings—if we check these interpretations, it is simply said that because the real illness of sentient beings' ignorance and attachment has neither beginning nor end, the [sympathetic] illness of the bodhisattvas in response also has neither beginning nor end.

However, there is also a new way of interpreting this. In general, there are two kinds of real illnesses that sentient beings have. In accordance with this, there are also two kinds of illnesses that bodhisattvas have in response. The first is the constant illness of samsaric mental afflictions. Because of this, bodhisattvas have the constant illness of entering samsara because of their great compassion. The second type is the specific illnesses of ignorance and attachment that can be extinguished by a bodhisattva manifesting as [an ill person] resting in bed. For this reason, too, bodhisattvas have specific illnesses that they manifest and they rest in bed. If we were to speak about the constant illness of their freely entering samsara, it would be just like this. But here the question is only about the manifested illnesses that should extinguish the specific illnesses of ignorance and attachment; the question is not about the constant illness of their freely entering samsara because of their great compassion. The reason is that if the constant illness of their entering samsara because of their great compassion necessarily led to their manifesting [an illness] and resting in bed, then all of the sages would surely be bedridden—not just Vimalakīrti alone. Moreover, if it was [a question of] the constant illness caused by their great compassion, then too Vimalakīrti would always be lying down. But there are times when he is not bedridden. Furthermore, if it is certainly the case that the constant illness [caused by the bodhisattva's great compassion] is without beginning or end, how could the concluding example say, "[when] the child's illness is cured, then the father and mother are also cured"? Because there surely is a time when a worldly child's illness is cured, [shouldn't the illness of the bodhisattva also have an end?]

However, the traditional understanding does not really exhaust the matter, as far as I have heard. Let me also give my own opinion. Sometimes he is constantly in bed, day and night, and sometimes he is not. I will also say that sometimes all the sages are bedridden and only Vimalakīrti is not. The reason is that being bedridden or not are not personal characteristics of the sage. That they are as they are is certainly because sentient beings have differing spiritual capacities in how they experience things. Some see that Vimalakīrti's illness is cured and he gets up and leaves [his house], and some see him resting in bed—this is what is meant by both constantly bedridden and also not in bed. Moreover, if there is a karmic connection then all the sages will manifest [illness and rest] in bed; if there is no karmic connection, then not even Vimalakīrti will be bedridden. Sentient beings too sometimes see all the sages ill in bed and sometimes they see only Vimalakīrti in bed and [the sages] not bedridden. How could this be predetermined? From this we can surmise that there is nothing wrong with the fact that, because sentient beings' real illnesses of ignorance and attachment are without beginning or end, the illnesses that the bodhisattvas have in response are also without beginning or end.

From "Mañjuśrī said, ['Layman, why is this room empty?']" is the second discussion of things in Vimalakīrti's room, the discussion caused by his emptying the room. This itself has two parts: the first gives Mañjuśrī's question to Vimalakīrti; the second gives Vimalakīrti's answer to Mañjuśrī's question. 50a

The first part, Mañjuśrī's query, itself has two questions. The first question is "Why is this room empty?" This import of this question is that [Vimalakīrti] must engage in the karmic activities of a white-robed [layman]; moreover, he is physically ill and so there surely should be offerings of provisions. But now there is not anything in the room—hence the question. This is the first of the six discussions born of the emptiness of [Vimalakīrti's] room. The second question is "Why are there no servants?" The import of this question is also that when [Vimalakīrti] is ill he would surely have someone watching over and caring for him, but now there are no servants at all—hence the question. This is the second of the six discussions born of his emptying his room.

The second part, Vimalakīrti's answer, also has two parts. The first answers the question about the emptiness of the room; the second answers the question about why there are no servants.

The first part, the answer to the question about the emptiness of the room, also has two items. The first gives the actual answer according to the emptiness of the underlying principle; the second, from "He asked again, 'With what was it emptied?'", gives an exchange of six questions and answers and eliminates the question.

The first item is the actual answer: "Vimalakīrti said, 'The many buddha realms are likewise all empty.'" This means that the many buddha realms are primordially empty. Why did [Mañjuśrī] ask again about the emptiness of the room? The question was about the emptiness of phenomena [in Vimalakīrti's room], and the answer was about the emptiness of the underlying principle [of the many buddha realms].

The second item, giving an exchange of six questions and answers and eliminating the question, is also divided into two. First, the initial three [questions and answers] clarify the emptiness of objects, and the latter three clarify the emptiness of knowing.

The first question is, "With what was it emptied?" Because there is nothing in the room, it is empty. Now, the many buddha realms are actually seen with various things—what does it mean to explain that they are empty? "He replied, saying, 'It was emptied with emptiness.'" The means that it was explained to be empty because ultimate truth is empty.

"[Mañjuśrī] inquired further, 'How can emptiness use emptiness?'" If the many buddha realms are primordially empty, then [everything] should be simply and straightforwardly empty in and of themselves—why then should [Vimalakīrti] empty the room in order to further clarify emptiness? "He replied, saying, 'It is empty because ultimate truth is without discrimination.'" Because [Vimalakīrti] wished to illustrate that nondiscrimination is empty, he emptied the room. If he had wished to illustrate that ultimate truth is empty by the room's emptiness, then there would be two emptinesses, the emptiness of ultimate truth and the emptiness of the room. Thus, "[Mañjuśrī] asked further, 'Can emptiness be discriminated?'" The underlying principle of the ultimate truth severs discrimination, therefore "[Vimalakīrti] replied, 'Discrimination is also empty.'"

The traditional understanding, however, is a little different. "With what was it emptied?" asks whether it is the emptiness of the underlying principle or of the phenomenal things that is the cause of the emptiness of the room. "He replied, 'It was emptied with emptiness.'" This means the emptiness that comes from knowing emptiness due to the emptiness of the underlying

principle. The prior emptiness is the emptiness of objects. The latter emptiness is the emptiness of knowing. "[Mañjuśrī inquired] further, 'How can emptiness use emptiness?'" This means that if the underlying principle is itself empty, how can we provisionally establish the knowing of emptiness? "He replied, 'It is empty because of nondiscriminating emptiness.'" This   50b
means that the underlying principle does not provisionally establish knowing. But if knowing is not [provisionally established] there is no cause for understanding. Therefore this emptiness is attained through the knowing of nondiscriminating emptiness. Knowing pertains to existent phenomena, and emptiness pertains to nonexistent phenomena. In other words, there are two attributes that can be discriminated, therefore "[Mañjuśrī further] inquired, 'Can emptiness be discriminated?'" Within emptiness there is nothing that can be discriminated as having [these] two attributes, therefore [Vimalakīrti] said, "Discrimination is also empty."

From "[Mañjuśrī] inquired further" is the second part, the three questions and answers that clarify the emptiness of knowing.

"[Mañjuśrī] inquired further, 'Where should emptiness be sought?'" There is the danger that some who are confused might see these two great beings eloquently discussing the meaning of emptiness and think that the meaning of emptiness is [only] in the true and not in the false. In other words, knowledge of emptiness can only be sought from these two great beings. Hence [Mañjuśrī] asked further, "Where should this knowledge of emptiness be sought?"

[Vimalakīrti] answered, saying that the sixty-two views are entirely empty and it can be sought therein—in other words, [knowledge of emptiness] can be sought within emptiness. This means, then, that there is nothing that can be sought. Beings, however, will then think that they should only seek it within non-Buddhist paths. Hence "[Mañjuśrī] asked further, 'Where should the sixty-two views be sought?'" [Vimalakīrti] answered that the emptiness of the buddhas' liberation is no different from the emptiness of the sixty-two views, and can be sought therein. However, beings might then reckon that it can only be sought from the buddhas, and so "[Mañjuśrī] asked further, 'Where should the liberation of the buddhas be sought?'" [Vimalakīrti] replied that the emptiness of the mental functions of sentient beings is no different from the emptiness of the buddhas' liberation, and can be sought therein. Exhausting the lofty and entirely completing the low and middling, it is impartial and devoid of perceptual attributes and without differentiating attributes. If you wish to seek true knowing then you should only seek it within impartial emptiness.

One school interprets this as mutually negating, meaning that you cannot seek true knowing within the sixty-two views. It is as if there is no knowledge that can be attained within that which is devoid of perceptual attributes. I think that knowledge of emptiness can only be attained with regard to the entirely empty [nature] of these three things, [that is, the emptiness of the sixty-two views, the liberation of the buddhas, and the mental functions of sentient beings].

From "You also asked [why there are no servants]" is the answer to the second question about [the lack of] servants [in Vimalakīrti's quarters]. This has two parts: 1) the actual answer, and 2) the interpretation. "You also asked why there are no servants" refers to the above question. "All the hosts of Māras and all those on non-Buddhist paths are all my servants." "Servants" means subordinated followers; all the hosts of Māras and those on non-Buddhist paths follow his transformative [teachings], and so it says they are "all my servants."

The second part is the interpretation. Why are all the [Māras and non-Buddhists also] his servants? "The hosts of Māras delight in samsara, and the bodhisattvas are in samsara and do not forsake it"—rather, they instruct and cause [the hosts of Māras] to enter the Way. "Non-Buddhists delight in the many views, but the bodhisattvas are unmoved by the many views"—instead, they transform and cause [non-Buddhists] to change and follow them. Therefore [Vimalakīrti] said that "they are all my servants."

From "Mañjuśrī said" is the third part of the discussion of just the things in Vimalakīrti's room, the discussion prompted by the attributes of [Vimalakīrti's] illness. This is [also] the fourth of the six discussions born of [Vimalakīrti's manifesting] an illness. Within this there are two parts, the question and answer. [Mañjuśrī] asked, "Layman, what are the attributes of your illness?" The perceptual attributes of an illness are chills, fever, weakness, and fatigue, and so [Mañjuśrī] is asking which of these symptoms [Vimalakīrti] has. One interpretation is that he is asking about which attributes of the four elements [are manifested in his illness].

50c

The second part, Vimalakīrti's answer, itself has three items. The first is simply saying that his illness has no perceptual attribute that can be seen. The second, from "[Mañjuśrī] asked further, 'Is this illness associated with the body?'", eliminates the doubts with an exchange of two questions and answers. The third, from "However, the illnesses of sentient beings," concludes [the explanation of why Vimalakīrti's] illness has no perceptual attributes.

"My illness has no form; it cannot be seen." The essential nature of [Vimalakīrti's] illness is empty; because there is no illness, it is without form or shape that can be seen. One interpretation takes it that this means that the ground of the Dharma body is primordially without any perceptual attributes of illness that can be seen.

The second item is the exchange that eliminates the doubts. "[Mañjuśrī] asked further, 'Is this illness associated with the body or associated with the mind?'" Some might hear, "My illness has no form; it cannot be seen" and think that there is one [particular kind of] illness that is without form and cannot be seen. Thus [Mañjuśrī] asked, "Is this illness associated with the body or associated with the mind?"

"[Vimalakīrti] replied, '[My illness] is not associated with the body, because it is removed from the attributes of the body.'" This means that the body is empty. "It is also not associated with the mind because the mind is like an illusion." This means that the mind is also empty. This shows that mind and body being empty, there is nothing with which the illness can be associated. One interpretation has it that beings will wonder if it is because the perceptual attributes of the illness are subtly associated with the body and mind that they cannot be seen; hence [Mañjuśrī] asked "[Is this illness] associated with the body or associated with the mind?" Then "[Vimalakīrti] replied, '[My illness] is not associated with the body because it is removed from the attributes of the body,'" meaning that the Dharma body is already devoid of the perceptual attributes of the body. "It is also not associated with the mind because the mind is like an illusion" means that [Vimalakīrti's] knowing is likewise without perceptual attribute. Dharma Master Sengzhao simply says that beings might hear "My illness has no form, it cannot be seen," and then think that because an illness of the mind has no form it cannot be seen, and because an illness of the body is subtle it cannot be seen—therefore giving rise to [Mañjuśrī's] question. The meaning of the reply is the same as before.

The second question asks to which of the four elements [Vimalakīrti's] illness is related. Beings might wonder if the illness relates to the four elements yet cannot be seen; hence the question about which of the four elements the illness relates to. "[Vimalakīrti] answered, '[This illness] is not related to the earth element." The essential nature of the earth [element] is empty. "It is also not removed from the earth element." This means that [things] other than earth are also empty. The other three elements are all just like this. One interpretation has it that there is this separate question because the source of disease is the four elements. "[Vimalakīrti] answered, '[This illness] is not related to the earth element'" means that the Dharma body is not related to the earth element, and "It is also not removed from the earth element" means that the illness [Vimalakīrti has manifested] in response [to the illness of sentient beings] is also not removed from the earth element.

From "However, the illnesses of sentient beings" is the third item, concluding [the explanation of why Vimalakīrti's] illness has no [attributes]. It can also [be said] that the conclusion is that the Dharma body is without any real perceptual attributes of illness that can be seen.

51a　　From "Mañjuśrī asked Vimalakīrti, ['How should a bodhisattva comfort and instruct a bodhisattva who is ill?']" is the second of Mañjuśrī's personal questions, the general discussion for the sake of other, newly trained bodhisattvas. This is further unpacked in two parts. The first explains how to comfort and instruct [bodhisattvas who are ill]; the second explains how [bodhisattvas who are ill should] discipline [their minds]. Comforting and instructing is the practice of transforming others; disciplining [the mind] is the self-cultivation [of bodhisattvas]. This is because the text asks how bodhisattvas should comfort bodhisattvas who are ill. As for discipline, the text asks, "How should bodhisattvas who are ill discipline their minds?" To "comfort" means to put at ease and console; to "instruct" means to reveal and make aware.

We can discuss three divisions of "comforting and instructing." The first is that although there are the differences of superior and inferior from the initial stage and above, the contemplation of truth and the understanding that is manifested are the same. Therefore, although one skillfully comforts others, one does not comfort oneself. The second is that from the sixth mind and below there is only self-comforting and not comforting others. The third is that although one enters the established ranks from the seventh mind and above, there is not yet true understanding and so, being ill [himself, the bodhisattva] is not able to excellently transform beings. Therefore [the bodhisattva] is comforted by others and also comforts others. One interpretation is that although there is contemplation of the truth [in the stages from] the seventh mind and below it is not yet constantly manifested, and so comforting is necessary.

"Comforting and instructing" is the fifth of the six discussions born of [Vimalakīrti's manifesting] his illness. There are two questions and answers. "Mañjuśrī asked Vimalakīrti, 'What should a bodhisattva who is not ill say to comfort and instruct a bodhisattva who is ill?'" When one becomes ill in body or mind, the weakened body is very tired and bothered by many troubles. Right thought becomes muddled and confused, and the mind is always in pain. How can you have the leisure to strive for the Way? Therefore it is necessary to be skillfully comforted by another person, [which helps one] calm the mind and advance toward the underlying principle. Thus [Mañjuśrī] asked, "What should a bodhisattva who is not ill say to comfort and instruct a bodhisattva who is ill?" Even if [the bodhisattvas] are of the same rank they may comfort each other.

There is a question, however. Here, Mañjuśrī has come to deliver [the Buddha's] message [of consolation]; that is, Mañjuśrī, who [has come to] inquire about [Vimalakīrti's] illness, should be comforting and instructing [Vimalakīrti]. What does it mean, then, that conversely he is asking [Vimalakīrti, who is ill, [this question]? There are, in short, three interpretations of the meaning [of this]. The first is that because [Vimalakīrti] is ill many people will gather, and in the knowledgeable one's comfort and instruction there surely will be skilled comfort and instruction. The second is that the person who is ill knows how to ease the illness himself—it cannot be understood by bystanders. The third is as Vimalakīrti has already explained; that is, Vimalakīrti himself is fundamentally not ill but is only ill for the sake of beings, and so too he comforts and instructs [them] skillfully. For these three reasons and contrary [to what you would expect], Vimalakīrti is asked [how to comfort the sick even though he is the one who seems to be ill].

But we aren't yet finished with these three [reasons]. The reason is that the point of this comfort and instruction is surely to put an end to delusion and enable one to attain correct resolve. What comfort is needed when one is at ease with being ill? Moreover, even if one is knowledgeable, when he is ill shouldn't you ask how to comfort and instruct him? The principle of what was taught above is that not only is Vimalakīrti skilled—Mañjuśrī, too, is accomplished in the same [realization]. Among those having the same skill, surely the one inquiring about the illness will properly comfort and instruct [the sick person]. Because of these problems, my interpretation is a little different. Investigating the reason that contrary to [what one would expect] Mañjuśrī asks Vimalakīrti [how to comfort bodhisattvas who are ill], it is because to accept and practice comfort and instruction, as well as to discipline [one's mind], just as these things were taught, will certainly be difficult to put into practice. If Mañjuśrī, a master of the Dharma, was not ill, then the assembly gathered at that time would not necessarily believe in [his] purity. Therefore Vimalakīrti, who was ill, was made to give the teachings himself and thereby encourage the newly trained [bodhisattvas].

51b

The second part, Vimalakīrti's answer, is also divided into two: 1) the actual answer, and 2) the conclusion of the answer. The first, the actual answer, is further divided into two parts: the first is the specific teachings that explain how to comfort and instruct [bodhisattvas who are ill]; the second is the miscellaneous teachings that explain how to comfort and instruct [them].

"Teach that the body is impermanent." For the [bodhisattvas who are] ill one should teach that the body is impermanent and that you should rid yourself of desire for and attachment to the body. "Do not teach aversion and rejection of the body." Again, although teaching [bodhisattvas who are ill] to contemplate impermanence, while they now remain in samsara they should extensively transform sentient beings. This also means that ordinary people reckon the constant [nature of the world] and so take delight in it and do not feel aversion or rejection [toward it]. [Followers of] the two vehicles contemplate impermanence and therefore feel aversion to the world and do not transform beings. All of these are contrary to the intention of the Buddha and both lose the Middle Way. Bodhisattvas contemplate impermanence and therefore they have neither attachment nor aversion [to the body]. Hence they remain in samsara and extensively transform sentient beings, unlike the prejudices of [those of] the two vehicles and ordinary people. As they marvelously attain the Middle Way, they teach in this way; this is called the meaning of comforting and instructing bodhisattvas who are ill. The next three lines are the same.

"Teach the suffering of the body but do not teach the aspiration for nirvana." Although you contemplate the suffering of the body, you should not be like [followers of] the two vehicles and believe only in your own salvation, abandoning the transformation of others. "Teach that the body is without self yet [also teach] the instruction and guidance of sentient beings." Although one contemplates no-self, one uses a provisional self to instruct and transform sentient beings—unlike [followers of] the two vehicles who contemplate no-self and abandon the transformation of others. "Teach the empty quiescence of the body but do not teach ultimate extinction." Although one contemplates empty quiescence, it is not like the [followers of the] two vehicles who only seize upon ultimate extinction and abandon the transformation of others.

From "Teach repentance of former transgressions" is the second [part of Vimalakīrti's answer], miscellaneous teachings that explain comforting and instructing. One interpretation has it that this explains comforting and instructing as the four pure strivings.

"Teach repentance of former transgressions but do not teach that they are relegated to the past." Although you should teach that illness is entirely a result of one's past karmic transgressions and that one should sincerely repent those mistakes, you should not teach that transgressions have a fixed nature and are thus relegated to the past. If you believe that the nature of the transgressions is relegated to the past, transgressions will not be extinguished. One interpretation has it that although you repent of your former transgressions, there is no extinguishing the body [that is a result of those] past [transgressions].

"Use your own illness to commiserate with the illnesses of others." You should teach by comparing yourself to others, [thinking] that even while your own minor suffering [is hard to bear], how much more difficult must be the heavy suffering of the three paths. Therefore you should endeavor to bestow the teachings [upon others]. Non-Buddhist texts say, "To be able to take what is near as an example can be called the art of humanity."   51c

"Know the suffering of innumerable *kalpa*s of suffering of past lives, and [thus] be mindful of benefiting all sentient beings." One should teach that knowing that the evil karma created in past lives is the reason for the present experience of the suffering of illness, you can infer that if you do not do evil now then in the future you will surely be without suffering, and you will earnestly [teach and] transform beings. Dharma Master Sengzhao says, "You should know the immeasurable suffering of previous lives; present suffering [is instantaneous]—how can our anxiety and suffering ever completely be exhausted? [Just exert yourself] to relieve that suffering."

"You should remember the good you have cultivated, be mindful of [engaging in] pure livelihood, and not give rise to anxiety and worry." This means that you should remember the good that you have done and take it as your precious treasure. You should only cultivate correct practices, be mindful of [engaging in] pure livelihood, and not take up a wrong livelihood in order to cure an illness of the body. "Wrong livelihood" is to embellish, flatter, and strive in order to preserve one's life.

"Always arouse diligent perseverance—you should become a physician king and cure the myriad illnesses." That is to say, strive for goodness and to transform beings. "Bodhisattvas who, in this way, comfort and instruct bodhisattvas who are ill, will make them happy." This is the second part, the conclusion of [Vimalakīrti's] answer. It means that bodhisattvas who are not ill should comfort and instruct those who are ill, as explained above; encourage them to remember self-cultivation and the transformation of others; and cause them to give rise to the mind that aspires to the Way. One interpretation has it that the first half of these verses illustrates true knowing and the latter half illustrates phenomenal knowledge. It is fine to understand this as you wish.

From "Mañjuśrī said, 'How should bodhisattvas who are ill control their minds?'" is the second part [of the second of Mañjuśrī's personal questions that make up the general discussion for the sake of the other, newly trained bodhisattvas], explaining [how bodhisattvas who are ill should] discipline [their minds]. "Disciplining" [the mind] has three further distinctions. The first is that although the sixth mind and below has the aspect of disciplining [the mind], there is not yet understanding of the underlying principle. Because there can be retrogression from this rank, the discipline may be lost or become unclear. The second is that although there are qualitative differences from the initial level and above, the contemplation of truth is the same, and so there is no recourse to [mental] discipline. The third is that although from the seventh mind up through the thirty [grades] of mind one has entered the established ranks, there is not yet true understanding and thus [mental] discipline is necessary. One interpretation has it that all [bodhisattvas] from the seventh mind and above, [as well as all bodhisattvas] below the seventh level, need [to cultivate mental] discipline. The reason is that we can know [bodhisattvas] prior to the [ten] abodes, but [bodhisattvas] from the initial stage to the seventh level are not yet able to completely illuminate both [emptiness and existence] even though they contemplate truth. Accordingly, because there are qualitative differences there is also the need to discipline [the mind].

This section also has two parts, the question and the answer. The question is this: when you are ill, the affliction of the illness muddles and confuses right thought and you are not able to be mindful of the Way. How then should you discipline your mind and strive for the Way?

Vimalakīrti's answer further unfolds in three parts. The first, from the beginning up to "The one who has simultaneously eliminated old age, sickness, and death is called a bodhisattva," explains disciplining [the mind] in terms of the two practices of self-cultivation and the transformation of others. The second, from "Those bodhisattvas who are ill should have this thought" up to "[the bodhisattva] does not [seek] eternal extinction—this is called expedient means," explains disciplining [the mind] by exhorting [the bodhisattvas] to eliminate attachment. The third, from "Mañjuśrī, thus should bodhisattvas who are ill discipline their minds" up to the end of the chapter, extensively clarifies the bodhisattvas' many and varied practices of the Middle Way and fully concludes the topic of [how bodhisattvas who are ill should] discipline [their minds].

52a

The first part, explaining disciplining [the mind] in terms of the two practices, further unfolds in three divisions. The first explains disciplining the mind by reflecting upon self-cultivation. The second, from "Bodhisattvas who are ill should use that which is not experienced to experience the various experiences," [explains] disciplining the mind by reflecting upon the transformation of others. The third, from "Mañjuśrī, this is how bodhisattvas who are ill [discipline their minds]," concludes both of the previous two divisions.

The first division, exhorting [bodhisattvas] to reflect upon self-cultivation, has two further parts. The first explains disciplining the mind by contemplating the emptiness of provisional designations. The second, from "In order to extinguish the conception of *dharma*s, those bodhisattvas who are ill [should have this thought]," explains disciplining the mind through the contemplation of the emptiness of real *dharma*s.

The first part, contemplating [the emptiness of] provisional designations, itself has three parts. The first is the direct explanation of contemplating the provisional and disciplining the mind. The second, from "Further, the arising of this illness," [explains] contemplating and knowing the source of the illness and thereby disciplining the mind. The third, from "You should give rise to the conception of *dharma*s," explains disciplining the mind by bringing up real *dharma*s and going beyond provisional designations.

The first part, directly explaining the contemplation of provisional designations and disciplining the mind, has two further aspects. The first is directly contemplating [that the bodhisattva's illness] is provisional and without reality and thereby disciplining the mind. The second is the interpretation.

"My present illness entirely stems from the deluded thoughts, confused thinking, and many mental afflictions of my previous lives." "Deluded thoughts" refers to the reckoning that the ten thousand *dharma*s are real. Cross-grained reckoning of the four alternatives is taken as "confused thinking." With deluded thoughts, confused thinking, and many mental afflictions as a cause, the body is born. This line explains the cause of the illness.

"There are no real *dharma*s—who could experience illness?" This is the actual explanation that there are only provisional and no real [*dharma*s]. That is to say, because there are only provisional and no real [*dharma*s], so too there is no practitioner who becomes ill. One interpretation has it that the prior line means that because the cause is unreal, "there are no real *dharma*s." "Who could experience illness?" means that the result is false. "There are no real *dharma*s" is common to both the first and second [lines].

The second aspect is the interpretation. A question is raised as to why there is nobody who experiences [illness]. [Vimalakīrti] explains that "Because of the four elements coming together, we provisionally designate this as a body. The four elements are without a master, and so too the body is without a self." Hence we say that there is no one who experiences suffering.

From "Further, the arising of this illness" is the second part, giving the source of the illness.

"Further, the arising of this illness is entirely due to attachment to self." This actually gives the source of the illness. "Therefore you should not give rise to attachment to self." This means that you should not be attached. "Knowing the source of the illness, you should eliminate the conception of self and the conception of sentient beings." This means that you should not be attached; you should contemplate no-self and thereby eliminate the self. Having gotten rid of the vexation of self, the sixteen views [of self] will simultaneously be destroyed. Therefore it says, "and [eliminate] the conception of sentient beings," abridging [all sixteen heretical views of self] into one.

From "You should give rise to the conception of *dharma*s" is the third part, disciplining the mind by going beyond provisional designations through the truth of *dharma*s. "You should give rise to the conception of *dharma*s" means that you should know that the body is only the coming together of the five *skandha*s; there is no real sentient being.

"The arising [of the body] is only the arising of *dharma*s; the extinction [of the body] is only the extinction of *dharma*s." This means that it is only the five *skandha*s that arise and pass into extinction—there is no separately fixed spirit or self of a sentient being that arises and passes into extinction. "Further, these *dharma*s do not know each other; when they arise, they do not say, 'I have arisen'; when they pass into extinction, they do not say, 'I have passed into extinction.'" This means that the *dharma*s of the five *skandha*s do not know one another. This shows that you should push your thinking as taught above and thereby discipline your mind.

From "The bodhisattva who is ill" is the second part of [the teaching of how to] discipline your mind through reflecting upon self-cultivation, the explanation of disciplining the mind through contemplation of the emptiness of real *dharma*s. This has three further aspects. The first shows that you should abandon the mind that reckons that *dharma*s are real. The second, from "What should be abandoned?", gives the *dharma*s that should be abandoned. The third, from "Attaining impartiality," concludes with ultimate emptiness.

"In order to extinguish the conception of *dharma*s, bodhisattvas who are ill [should have this thought]." That is to say, [they should have this thought] in order to extinguish belief in the concept of the reality of *dharma*s. "[The

52b

173

bodhisattva] should have this thought: 'this conception of *dharma*s is also confused thinking." This means that the mind that reckons that the five *skandha*s really exist is also confused. "Confused thinking itself is a great vexation—I should abandon it." This means that because of this confused thinking the future will surely bring suffering and vexation. Therefore one should cultivate the Way and abandon [confused thinking]. This teaches that [arising] from [such a] cause, the result too must be problems and vexation.

From "What should be abandoned?" is the second aspect, giving the *dharma*s that should be abandoned.

"What is to be abandoned? Abandon [the notions of] 'self' and 'properties of the self.'" Ordinary people take the five *skandha*s as properties of the self; holy people take nirvana as a property of the self. This refers to the sense of properties of the self held by both the ordinary and the holy. "What is it to abandon [the notions of] 'self' and 'properties of the self'? It is [to abandon] the two *dharma*s." This lists the essential nature of what is to be abandoned. The "two *dharma*s" are 1) the *dharma*s that ordinary people take as belonging to the self, and 2) the *dharma*s that the holy take as belonging to the self. "What is it to abandon the two *dharma*s? Do not think of either internal or external *dharma*s and practice impartiality." This gives the essential nature of what is to be abandoned. "Internal" means one's own sense of a property of the self. It can also be the internal sense of a property of the self held by both ordinary and holy people. "External" means others' sense of a property of the self. It can also mean the provisionally designated self of ordinary [people] and holy ones.

"What is practicing equality? It is called the equality of self and the equality of nirvana." This gives a name to what is to be abandoned. It means to take the superior and make it equal to the inferior, all entirely and equally empty. "Why? It is because both self and nirvana are empty." This explains the above "equality." "Why are they empty? They are but names and thus are empty." This is a second explanation that both are empty. It shows that [self and nirvana] are only names and without reality, therefore [both are] empty; they are not forcibly emptied. "Thus these two *dharma*s do not have a fixed nature." This concludes that the two *dharma*s of the five *skandha*s and nirvana are all empty and without a fixed nature. It is also said that "internal"

52c

refers to the five *skandha*s, and "external" refers to things like mountains, rivers, and the like.

One interpretation has it that everything up to "How to abandon the two *dharma*s? Do not think of either internal or external *dharma*s and practice impartiality" refers only to the sense of property of the self held by ordinary people. The "two *dharma*s" refer to the two karmic retributions, that is, circumstantial retribution and direct retribution. From "What is [practicing] impartiality?" illustrates that the ten thousand *dharma*s are all empty and equal. Here, then, when it says "Thus these two *dharma*s do not have a fixed nature," it is referring to self and nirvana as the "two [*dharma*s]." It could also be said that the above "two [*dharma*s]" refer to "self" and "property of the self."

From "When you attain this impartiality" is the third aspect, concluding with ultimate emptiness. It could also be concluding by using emptiness to remove emptiness.

"When you attain this impartiality there will be no other illness." The illness of belief in real existence will be forever exhausted. "There is only the illness of emptiness." There is only the illness of one-sided emptiness. "The illness of emptiness is also empty." This is to say that the [one-sided illness that] calculates emptiness is also empty. Generally, the hearts of beings are easily influenced, hence *dharma*s are first used to eliminate [the sense of] self; next emptiness is used to eliminate the *dharma*s; and finally, ultimate emptiness is used to empty emptiness—and this is the ultimate realm, with no vexation.

From "Bodhisattvas who are ill should use that which is not experienced [to experience the various experiences]" is the second [of the three divisions that] explain disciplining [the mind] in terms of the two practices, [that is,] explaining [how to] discipline the mind by reflecting upon the transformation of others. There are many scholarly understandings of this, and they should be outlined in order to interpret them. Here, however, I am not going to follow these divisions and will simply interpret according to the text; in other words, I am saying that I am going to skip what is unclear.

"Bodhisattvas who are ill should use that which is not experienced to experience the various experiences." This means that great beings are primordially without the karma [that would result in their] having a body that experiences [things]. It is only because of their desire to transform beings that they take up a body [in one of] the six paths [of samsara]. "They do not complete the Buddha-Dharma nor extinguish experience, yet they seize realization." This means that the sentient beings that are transformed are not yet complete in the Buddha-Dharma, and so in the end [the bodhisattvas] do not extinguish [experiences] individually, yet they seize their own realization. These two lines illustrate their kindness, which is able to bestow bliss.

"Given the suffering of the body, [the bodhisattva] is mindful of sentient beings in the evil destinies and arouses a mind of great compassion." This means that the great beings forget the suffering of their bodies, [yet they remember that sentient beings have] the same suffering and therefore [they strive] to transform [sentient beings]. This line illustrates their compassion, which is able to remove suffering. "Having disciplined myself, I should now discipline all sentient beings." This means that in this way, [the bodhisattva] should take [the suffering and joy] of all sentient beings to be the same as their own suffering and joy.

"Only eliminate the illness, but do not eliminate the *dharma*s." Above it simply said, "discipline [all] sentient beings," but it did not explain the nature of "discipline." Therefore, from here it explains the attributes of this "discipline." Above [it said that although] *dharma*s are themselves non-existent, deluded thinking takes them to be existent. Therefore it says that although you should just eliminate the illness of deluded thinking, there is no need to eliminate *dharma*s. One interpretation has it that you should just eliminate the illness of sentient beings' deluded thinking, but not eliminate the *dharma*s that are able to transform [and teach sentient beings]. Another interpretation says that bodhisattvas teach people: although they have eradicated the cause of samsara they remain within samsara, and through the four virtues they benefit beings. "But do not eliminate the *dharma*s." This is different from the annihilation of the body, extinction of the mind, and [thereby the] elimination of the calamity of samsaric *dharma*s that are taught to people in the two vehicles.

"[Bodhisattvas] teach and guide them (i.e., sentient beings) in order to eradicate the source of illness." Above it simply said that the illness should be eliminated but it did not clarify the means to eliminate [the illness]. From here, therefore, the means to eliminate [the illness] are explained. This has

53a

two parts: 1) initially setting out two sections, and 2), from "What [is the source of their illness]?", explaining the two sections. "In order to eradicate the source of illness" is the section that sets out the [motivation—that is, eliminating the] source of illness. "[Bodhisattvas] teach and guide them" is the section that establishes the means of eliminating [illness]. This means that because [bodhisattvas] wish to eradicate the source of beings' illnesses, they employ the means of eliminating [the source of illness], which is teaching and guiding them.

"What is meant by the source of their illness? It means grasping at objects of consciousness. Because there is grasping at objects of consciousness, there is the source of illness." This describes the deluded mind that by grasping at the various objects reckons [them] to exist where they do not exist. This creates the karma that is the source of their illness. This line is the actual explanation of the source of their illness. "What objects of consciousness are grasped? It is the triple world." This gives the things that are the objects of consciousness.

From "What is it to eradicate the grasping at objects of consciousness?" is the section that explains the method of eliminating [grasping at objects of consciousness].

"What is it to eradicate the grasping at objects of consciousness? It is to be without anything that is attained [by consciousness]. If there is nothing that is attained, then there is no grasping at objects of consciousness." This says that if you are able to understand that objects are empty and that there is nothing that is attained, then grasping at objects of consciousness will naturally abate. "What is meant by non-attainment? It means [eliminating] the two views. What is meant by the two views? It means the view that there is an internal [object] and the view that there is an external [object], where [in reality] there is nothing to be attained." This gives the object of non-attainment. One's own five *skandha*s are [the object of] the internalist view, and the five *skandha*s of others are the [object of] the externalist view. It can also be said that all of the objects outside of the five *skandha*s are the [objects of] the externalist view. This means that if you are able to thoroughly realize the emptiness of the two views, then the source of the illness will naturally die away.

From "Mañjuśrī, [this is how bodhisattvas who are ill control their minds]" is the third [of the three divisions that] explain disciplining [the mind] in terms of the two practices, concluding both of the [previous two divisions that describe] the two practices of self[-cultivation] and [the transformation of] others. This itself has two parts: 1) concluding by way of giving a doctrinal explanation, and 2) concluding by way of giving an example.

"This is how bodhisattavas who are ill discipline their minds." This means that, as explained above, if you clearly realize that the provisional and the real are empty, if there is attachment to nothing and you are also able to remember the practices of both self and other—this is the means whereby bodhisattvas who are ill discipline their minds. "This is the eradication of the suffering of old age, sickness, and death; this is the *bodhi* of the bodhisattva." This means that cultivating the practice as [explained] above and [thereby] eliminating the suffering of old age, sickness, and death for oneself as well as others is called the *bodhi* of the bodhisattva. "If it is not like this, then all of that [bodhisattva's] prior cultivation and restraint will be without [discerning] awareness or benefit." This means that although there might be cultivation of the practices, if one does not eradicate the suffering of both self and other there is neither sufficient [discerning] awareness internally nor sufficient benefit externally.

The second part concludes by giving an example. "For example, someone who is victorious over enemies is considered a hero." This means that those who overcome their own enemies and also vanquish the enemies of others are called brave. "Just like this, the one who has simultaneously eliminated old age, sickness, and death is called a bodhisattva." This brings together [the doctrine and the example] and can be understood.

From "Bodhisattvas who are ill should have this thought" is the second [of the three parts of Vimalakīrti's explanation of how to] discipline [the mind], the explanation of disciplining the mind by exhorting [bodhisattvas] to eliminate attachment. This teaches that even if you discipline [your mind] by thinking about self-cultivation and the transformation of others, if you believe in self and other as the two objects of your practice then your practice will not be extensive. You will not be able to identify with the suffering and joy of beings. Therefore [bodhisattvas who are ill] are exhorted to eliminate attachment. This also has four levels. The first is the actual exhortation

53b

[that bodhisattvas] should eliminate attachment. The second is the explanation. The third, from "[Those bodhisattvas] will be born without bonds," gives both bondage and freedom as illustrations of the prior explanation. The fourth, from "What is meant by bondage? What is meant by freedom?", further describes bondage and freedom.

"Just as my illness is neither real nor existent. . . ." [Illness] is provisional, and hence "not real"; that is, it is empty and therefore "not existent." This line exhorts [bodhisattvas] to not be attached to self. In the same way, the line "The illness of sentient beings is neither real nor existent" exhorts [bodhisattvas] to not be attached to others. These two lines exhort [bodhisattvas to contemplate] the unreal and provisional [nature of self and other]. "If, when engaging in this contemplation, great compassion for sentient beings arises based on affectionate views, it should be rejected." This means that while compassion [born of] affectionate views might be good, because it is based on a belief in perceptual attributes it is unable to equalize the two objects of self and other or extensively transform sentient beings; therefore it says that [great compassion based on affectionate views] should be rejected.

From "Why?" is the second level, the explanation. A question is expressed as to why compassion born of affectionate views should be rejected.

"Bodhisattvas eradicate and eliminate adventitious mental afflictions and give rise to great compassion." This means that because bodhisattvas eradicate the adventitious mental afflictions of self and other, they give rise to great compassion that is devoid of perceptual attributes. Wishing to deny compassion born of affectionate views, this line first affirms great compassion devoid of perceptual attributes. Interpretations of "adventitious" are not uniform. Some say that the root of the tree is the master and the branches are "adventitious." Others say that anything existing outside of the underlying principle is "adventitious." The meaning [I] will adopt is that anything that is not virtuous does not constantly abide in the underlying principle, and in the end those will be the things that are eliminated—hence, they are "adventitious."

"Compassion born of affectionate views will lead to a mind that feels fatigue and aversion toward samsara." This line explains that compassion born of affectionate views is a mistake and therefore should be eliminated. "If [the bodhisattva] is able to abandon this [kind of compassion], then there will be no fatigue and aversion and wherever he is born he will not be blinded by affectionate views." This line is the actual disclosure of the meaning of the exhortation to eliminate [attachment].

From "[Those bodhisattvas] will be born without bonds" is the third level, giving both bondage and freedom to illustrate the prior explanation. What is being said here is that transforming beings comes first from simply wishing to eliminate one's own evil. "[Those bodhisattvas] will be born without bonds and they will be able to teach the Dharma to sentient beings and free them from their bonds." This means that because their self-cultivation is pure they will be born able to free others from their bonds. Therefore it says that they will not be blinded by any affectionate views. This line is the actual disclosure of the above interpretation.

Next the authentic words of the Buddha are given as proof: "It is as the Buddha has explained: 'If a person has bonds themselves, there is no way they will be able to free others from their bonds. If a person has no bonds themselves, then it is possible for them to free others from their bonds.'" This means that the arising of both good and evil begins with oneself and not others. "Therefore, bodhisattvas should not give rise to bonds." This is the conclusion that one should not be attached.

Question: It is possible that an ordinary person with a scattered mind [nonetheless] gives a fine explanation of the way of meditation. A student examines the teaching, cultivates and practices it, and attains profound peace. Moreover, an ordinary person with a confused mind might give a teaching on the ten levels with only a shallow understanding, yet a student investigating and practicing [that teaching] might attain an understanding that progresses through the levels. Going by this, it is not entirely the case, as was said, that a person who themselves has bonds is not able to free others from their bonds. Further, the Tathāgata was the epitome of freedom from bondage, yet [his disciple] Sunakṣatra gave rise to heretical views. Also, Śāriputra was free of bonds, yet the delusions and fallacies of his two disciples grew ever greater. So it is also not always the case that [only] if one is without bonds [himself] is he able to free others of their bonds.

Explanation: In short, there are two ways of benefiting by following others: 1) following their practice, and 2) following their teachings. What is being explained here relates only to practice. The problem raised here is about benefiting from the teachings of an ordinary person with a scattered mind—it is perhaps like this because what is discussed [follows the ordinary person's] teachings but not their behavior in practice. If you follow their practice, your bonds will increase because their practice is [afflicted by] bonds. Increasing virtue, however, is explained only in terms of the teaching [given by a person who is] free of bonds. You mention Sunakṣatra's eradication of his virtuous roots in the present, but if it were not for the Tathāgata's [allowing him to be in the sangha] he would also have eradicated all causes for future [benefit]—how then can you say that Sunakṣatra did not benefit from the Buddha?

As for the ever-increasing confusion and fallacies of Śāriputra's two disciples, this was because they learned his erroneous teachings. If they had followed his practice, which was that of an [arhat who had reached the stage of] no more learning, then they too would have been able to reach [the stage] of no more learning. This is not so clear, however. Although there is practice and teaching, this is the practice and teaching of an ordinary person. If it is the practice and erroneous teachings of Śāriputra, how could it be that only his practice was ordinary but his teachings were not ordinary teachings? It also could be that while the practices were Śāriputra's, the erroneous teachings were not Śāriputra's [teachings].

In my opinion, if we look at the details—what isn't like this? It is like this because here we are simply discussing the way things are in this world. From the point of view of the way of worldly things, the rejection of evil and the pursuit of virtue must begin with oneself—then you can encourage [other] people [to do the same]. If you are unable to do this yourself, how will you be able to urge others forward? If we really want to discuss increasing virtue and giving rise to evil, although both ordinary people and holy ones can bring forth evil [in others, the evil caused by holy ones] is not as great as that caused by ordinary people. So, too, although both ordinary people and holy ones [bring about an] increase in virtue [in others, the virtue caused by ordinary people] is not nearly as beautiful as that brought about   54a
by holy ones. This being the principle [of how things are in this world], it indeed explains the reach of bondage and freedom.

From "What is meant by bondage? What is meant by freedom?" is the fourth level [of the second part of Vimalakīrti's three explanations of controlling the mind], the further description of the attributes of bondage and freedom. Above it simply spoke of bondage and freedom but did not illustrate their attributes, and so [the attributes] are [now more fully] described. This unfolds in three parts. The first simply uses meditative concentration and skillful means to straightaway illuminate the essential nature of bondage and freedom. The second, from "Further, [discerning] awareness without skillful means is bondage," takes up skillful means and discerning awareness in order to profoundly describe bondage and freedom. The third, from "Further, to contemplate the body . . . ," again summarizes skillful means and discerning awareness.

"What is meant by bondage? What is meant by freedom? Desire for and attachment to the taste of meditation is the bodhisattva's bondage." This means that if you are attached to the taste of meditation then you will not have mastery [over your destiny] and you will be born in accordance with your karma—this is the bodhisattva's bondage. "Being born though skillful means is the bodhisattva's freedom." This means not being born due to one's karma but taking birth only in response [to the need for] transforming beings. The ability to have mastery [over one's destiny]—this is the bodhisattva's freedom.

The second part, taking up skillful means and discerning awareness in order to profoundly describe bondage and freedom, is further divided into three. The first initially lays out four topics. The second, from "What is it to say that [discerning] awareness without skillful means is bondage?", is the explanation of the four topics in order. The third, from "Mañjuśrī, [those bodhisattvas who are ill should contemplate the *dharma*s in this way,]" concludes with an exhortation to contemplate freedom from bondage.

Skillful means is the mind that traverses existence and accumulates merit; moreover, it has the virtue of being able to aid the understanding of emptiness. Discerning awareness is the understanding that is able to illuminate; moreover, it has the power of being able to lead [all] existence. It is necessary that these two work together.

"[Discerning] awareness without skillful means is bondage." This is to say that if you do not have skillful means as an aid, then your understanding of emptiness will dwell in the realization of emptiness and you will not be able to guide [all] existence and transform beings. Hence, this is an understanding of emptiness that is in bondage because of emptiness. "[Discerning] awareness with skillful means is freedom." This means that if you have skillful means as an aid, then your understanding of emptiness does not dwell in a one-sided realization of emptiness. Further, you will be able to lead [all] existence and transform beings. Hence, this understanding [of emptiness] is freedom.

"Skillful means without [discerning] awareness is bondage." If the skillful means that [attempt] to guide [sentient beings] lacks the awareness of emptiness, then that skillful means will dwell in existence until the final day and never be able to eradicate the entanglements. Therefore this skillful means is in bondage because of existence. "Skillful means with [discerning] awareness is freedom." This refers to the guidance [given to sentient beings] with the awareness of emptiness—this skillful means is not in bondage to the mental afflictions, and therefore it attains to freedom.

The second part interprets these four topics; they are interpreted in order and can be understood.

"Mañjuśrī, those bodhisattvas who are ill should contemplate the *dharmas* in this way." This is the third aspect, the exhortation to contemplate freedom from bondage. From "Further, to contemplate the body. . ." is the third part of the description of bondage and freedom, the summary of skillful means and discerning awareness. Before it simply spoke of skillful means   54b and discerning awareness but had not illustrated their attributes. Therefore this is used to illustrate and summarize the attributes; it can be understood. [Where the text says, "This illness and this body are neither new nor old,"] the "new" refers to "prior" and the "old" refers to "after."

From "Mañjuśrī, this is how bodhisattvas who are ill should discipline their minds" is the third part of Vimalakīrti's answer to Mañjuśrī's question explaining [how bodhisattvas should] discipline [their minds], the extensive description of the bodhisattva's numerous and varied practices that concludes the topic of disciplining [the mind]. This has two sections. The first discloses the starting point of the Middle Way generally; the second, from "To be within samsara. . . ," lists various practices of the Middle Way.

The first section, disclosing the starting point [of the Middle Way], has three further parts. The first straightaway discloses the starting point; the second, from "What is the reason?", is the interpretation; the third, from "Therefore," is the concluding exhortation [to cultivate] the Middle Way.

"[Mañjuśrī,] this is how bodhisattvas who are ill should discipline their minds" discloses the starting point [of the Middle Way]. "[Those bodhisattvas who are ill] should not dwell within [the disciplined mind]." [The practice of the bodhisattva should] not be like the one-sided dwelling within self-control [practiced by followers] of the two vehicles. "Nor should they dwell within an undisciplined mind." Neither should [their practice] be like ordinary people's one-sided dwelling within an undisciplined [mind].

The second part is the interpretation. "To dwell in an undisciplined mind is the way of a foolish person" explains [what was said] above, "Nor should they dwell within an undisciplined mind." "To dwell in the disciplined mind is the way of the *śrāvaka*s" explains [what was said] above, "[Those bodhisattvas who are ill] should not dwell within [the disciplined mind]."

From "Therefore" is the third part, the concluding exhortation to [cultivate] the Middle Way; this can be understood. One interpretation has it that "[Those bodhisattvas who are ill] should not dwell within" means "do not be attached to that which has been taught so far."

From "To be within samsara. . ." is the second section [of the third part of Vimalakīrti's answer to Mañjuśrī's question regarding how bodhisattvas should discipline their minds], and lists various practices of the Middle Way.

"To be in samsara but not undertake polluted practices, to dwell within nirvana but not [dwell within] eternal extinction[—this is the bodhisattva's practice.] [Cultivating] neither the practices of ordinary people nor the practices of the wise sages[—this is the bodhisattva's practice.] [Engaging in] neither defiled practice nor pure practice[—this is the bodhisattva's practice]." These six lines all explain dwelling [within a mind that is] not one-sided.

"Although beyond the actions of Māra, one manifests as subduing Māra[—this is the bodhisattva's practice]." This means that in the present one is born in samsara and subdues Māra. "To seek omniscience but not to seek it at the wrong time[—this is the bodhisattva's practice]." The halfway fruits of realization of the two vehicles are what is meant by "the wrong time." It can also be said that [to attempt] to realize the fruits of perfection for oneself while [the task of] transforming beings is not yet finished is called "seeking at the wrong time."

"Although contemplating the various *dharma*s as non-arising, not entering the stage of certainty[—this is the bodhisattva's practice.] Although contemplating the twelve links of conditioned arising, entering into hetero-dox views[—this is the bodhisattva's practice.]" These lines mean that although one contemplates the various *dharma*s as none other than empti-ness, one does not dwell within a one-sided realization of emptiness. It can also [mean] that one is accomplished at transforming beings within [the realm of] existence.

"Although embracing all sentient beings, there is no affectionate attach-ment[—this is the bodhisattva's practice]." This means that [the bodhisattva] is different from ordinary people. "Although aspiring for detachment, there is no reliance on the elimination of body and mind[—this is the bodhisattva's practice]." This means that [the bodhisattva] is different from [followers of] the two vehicles. "Aspiration for detachment" means abandoning the men-tal afflictions. "Although practicing within the triple world, the Dharma-nature is not destroyed[—this is the bodhisattva's practice]." This means that emptiness is not discarded.

"Although practicing emptiness, there is also the planting of virtuous roots[—this is the bodhisattva's practice]. Although practicing that which is devoid of perceptual attribute, sentient beings are saved[—this is the bodhi- 54c
sattva's practice]. Although practicing the wishless, there is the manifesta-tion of a body[—this is the bodhisattva's practice]. Although practicing non-arising, there is the arising of good deeds[—this is the bodhisattva's practice]." These four lines all have the same meaning and can be understood. They can also mean that [the bodhisattva's practice] is not the same as the one-sided [practice] of ordinary people and [followers of] the two vehicles.

"Although practicing the six perfections, there is also the universal knowledge of the [minds and] mental attributes of sentient beings[—this is the bodhisattva's practice]." The six perfections are the practice devoid of perceptual attributes—yet still [bodhisattvas have] "universal knowledge of the [minds and] the mental attributes of sentient beings." Although [followers of] the two vehicles attain the sixth perfection of *prajñā,* they are not able to contemplate existence and transform beings.

"Although practicing the six powers, the outflows are not exhausted[—this is the bodhisattva's practice]. Although practicing the four immeasura-ble [states of mind], there is no desire or attachment to birth in the Brahmā worlds[—this is the bodhisattva's practice]. Although practicing meditation, concentration, liberation, and *samādhi,* there is no birth [in the heavens] that accord with that meditation." These three lines show that [the bodhisattva] surpasses ordinary people.

"Although practicing the four foundations of mindfulness, there is no permanent abandoning of body, sensations, mind, and *dharma*s[—this is the bodhisattva's practice]. Although practicing the four right efforts, there is no forsaking the exertion of body and mind[—this is the bodhisattva's practice]." These two lines show that [the bodhisattva's practice of] the four states of mindfulness and [four right] efforts are not the same as that of [followers of] the two vehicles, which only seeks to extinguish body and mind.

"Although practicing the four supernatural powers, there is attainment of mastery of the spiritual powers[—this is the bodhisattva's practice]." This means that although [the bodhisattva's] practice of the four supernatural powers is the same as that of [followers of the] two vehicles, [the bodhisattva] attains the Mahayana mastery of the spiritual powers.

"Although practicing the five faculties, there is discrimination of the sharp and dull faculties of sentient beings[—this is the bodhisattva's practice]." This means that although [the bodhisattva] is able [to dwell within] the emptiness of the five [sense] faculties, he is also able to discriminate the sharp and dull faculties [of sentient beings]. [Followers of] the two vehicles are able to know their own [faculties] but they are not able to know the faculties of others.

"Although practicing the five powers, there is also aspiration to seek [the Buddha's] ten powers[—this is the bodhisattva's practice]." This means that [the bodhisattva's practice] is not the same as the practice of the five powers in the two vehicles, which seeks to enter the perception of truth. "Although practicing the seven factors of awakening, there is also discrimination of the discerning awareness of the buddhas[—this is the bodhisattva's practice]." This means that [the bodhisattva's practice] is not the same as the practice of the seven factors of awakening in the two vehicles, which only seeks the fruits of arhatship.

"Although practicing the eightfold noble path, there is also aspiration to cultivate the immeasurable path of the buddhas[—this is the bodhisattva's practice]." This means that [the bodhisattva's practice] is not the same as the practice of the eightfold noble [path] in the two vehicles, which puts an end to the eight kinds of evil. "Although practicing tranquility and insight, the supporting factors of the path, there is no ultimate falling into quiescent extinction[—this is the bodhisattva's practice]." "Tranquility" refers to a state of concentration; "insight" refers to [discerning] awareness. These two are excellent factors that support the path. This means that although there is cultivation [of tranquility and insight], there is no falling into nirvana.

"Although practicing with the various *dharma*s as non-arising and non-extinguishing, there is the ornamentation of the body with the [thirty-two] marks and [eighty] auspicious signs [of a buddha—this is the bodhisattva's practice]." This means that [the bodhisattva's practice] is not like that of the two vehicles, in which emptiness is contemplated but practice within [the realm of] existence is not possible.

"Although practicing with the authority and decorum of the *śrāvaka* and *pratyekabuddha,* the Buddha-Dharma is not forsaken[—this is the bodhisattva's practice]. Although according with the ultimately pure attribute of the various *dharma*s, this body is manifested as needed[—this is the bodhisattva's practice]. Although contemplating the various buddha realms as eternally quiescent like space, the many and various pure buddha lands are manifested[—this is the bodhisattva's practice]." These three lines are the same and can be understood.

"Although attaining the buddha way, turning the wheel of Dharma, and entering into nirvana, the way of the bodhisattva is not forsaken[—this is the bodhisattva's practice]." This is to say that although bodhisattvas actually attain the buddha way, they do not forsake the practices of the bodhisattva. This means that even when attaining buddhahood they do not forsake [the practices of] the bodhisattva. Indeed, this means none other than to realize the Middle [Way].

From "When [Vimalakīrti] taught this Dharma" is the third part of the actual description of [Mañjuśrī's] inquiry about [Vimalakīrti's] illness, describing the benefits received by the assembly at that time.

55a

Chapter Six

The Inconceivable

This chapter explains the many and varied inconceivable activities of bodhi-sattvas, thus the title of the chapter. This is the second aspect of the [explanation of] the transformation of those of superior capacity—that is, the extensive explanation of the inconceivable. The meaning of "extensive" is as explained above; [that is, whereas the previous chapter was concerned only with Vimalakīrti, this teaching concerns the inconceivable activities of numerous buddhas and bodhisattvas].

Broadly speaking, this chapter unfolds in six parts. The first part, from the beginning up to "Where will this assembly sit?", describes Śāriputra's wondering about [the absence of chairs upon which] to sit. The second, from "[The elder Vimalakīrti] knew his thoughts" up to "Five hundred gods obtained purity of the Dharma eye," admonishes Śāriputra for seeking when he should not have been seeking. The third part, from "[Vimalakīrti asked] Mañjuśrī, 'Virtuous One'" up to "able to sit on the lion thrones," describes [how Vimalakīrti gave Śāriputra] what he was seeking by borrowing chairs from [Buddha Sumeru] Lamp King. As a result of Śāriputra's praise, the fourth part, from "Śāriputra said, 'Layman, this is unprecedented!'" up to "[If I were to extensively explain this,] I would exhaust an entire *kalpa* and still not finish," extensively describes how buddhas and bodhisattvas possess the two inconceivable knowledges of the conventional and real and are able to display inconceivable manifestations. The fifth part, from "At this [time,] Mahākāśyapa" up to "Thirty-two thousand gods aroused the aspiration to achieve [perfect] awakening," describes how Kāśyapa lamented the severing of his own capacity and exhorted the newly trained [bodhisattvas] to arouse the aspiration [to achieve perfect awakening]. The sixth part, from "Vimalakīrti said to Mahākāśyapa" to the end of the chapter, is Vimalakīrti's affirmative response to the above exclamation of Mahākāśyapa. All six of these levels comprise the third of the five discussions born of Vimalakīrti's emptying his room.

The first part, [Śāriputra's] wondering about the chairs, can be understood. The second part, admonishing [Śāriputra] for seeking [something], itself has four sections. The first initially asks Śāriputra why he came: "Which is it, Virtuous One—have you come for the Dharma or have you come looking for a chair to sit on?" The second section is Śāriputra's answer, "I have come for the Dharma, not for a place to sit." The third section, from "Vimalakīrti said," is the actual admonition of Śāriputra for seeking [something]. The fourth, from "When he gave this Dharma," describes the benefits attained [from this teaching]. The first two can be understood [from the text].

The third section, the actual admonition, also has two parts. The first criticizes [Śāriputra] for wondering about chairs; the second, from "Ah, Śāriputra, a seeker of the Dharma is not attached to the Buddha in their seeking," criticizes his [manner of] seeking the Dharma.

"Ah, Śāriputra, a seeker of the Dharma should not be concerned with life or limb, much less a chair to sit on." This means that a person seeking the Dharma despises their body and exhausts their life in their quest. Śāriputra has stated that he came for the Dharma—how then can he be seeking a chair? Moreover, his five *skandhas*, twelve entrances (*āyatanas*), eighteen realms (*dhātus*), and three realms are all empty. What body would he wish to rest such that he was seeking a chair?

The second part, criticizing Śāriputra's [manner of] coming [and seeking] the Dharma, itself has four sections. The first is the actual illustration that within the underlying principle there is no seeking. The second, from "Why is this?", explains "no seeking." The third, from "The Dharma is called 'quiescent extinction,'" uses various illustrations to explain how [the Dharma] is devoid of perceptual attribute. The fourth, from "Therefore," concludes that there should be no seeking.

That the seeker of the Dharma should not be attached to the Three Jewels nor to the four truths means that within the underlying principle there are no Three Jewels on which to rely, nor are there four truths that may be contemplated.

From "Why is this?" is the second section, the explanation [of no seeking], and can be understood. The third section, using various illustrations to explain [how the Dharma is devoid of perceptual attribute], and the fourth section, the conclusion, can be understood.

"If one seeks the Dharma there should be no seeking of any of the *dharma*s." This means that it is precisely seeking that is without seeking that can be called the truly wonderful seeking of the Dharma.

From "When he spoke these words" is the fourth section [of the second of the six parts of this chapter], admonishing [Śāriputra] for seeking [something], and describes the benefits that were received by the assembly at that time.

From "At that time, the elder Vimalakīrti" is the third of the six major parts, describing [how Vimalakīrti gave Śāriputra] what he was seeking by borrowing chairs from [Buddha Sumeru] Lamp King. This has six sections.

The first section describes how Vimalakīrti asked Mañjuśrī where there could be found wonderfully tall seats. The reason he asked his guest is that there is no place that Mañjuśrī has not been to in his extensive and limitless teaching, and so he would surely know where wonderfully tall seats could be found. Moreover, it was originally because of the guests that seats were being sought. Wanting to accord with the wishes of his guest, and contrary [to what you might expect], he thus asked [a guest where chairs might be found].

The second section, from "Mañjuśrī said," gives Mañjuśrī's answer. The third section, from "Vimalakīrti manifested his supernatural powers," describes how Vimalakīrti borrowed the seats from [Buddha Sumeru] Lamp King. The fourth section, from "At that time that buddha," depicts Buddha [Sumeru] Lamp King sending the seats. The fifth section, from "The bodhisattvas and great disciples," tells that the great assembly saw unprecedented things.

The sixth section, from "At that time, Vimalakīrti said to Mañjuśrī," describes Vimalakīrti inviting the great assembly to take a seat; this itself has two parts. The first is initially inviting the great assembly; the second is separately inviting Śāriputra [to take a seat]. Śāriputra was the main person who sought a seat and so he was invited [to take a seat] separately. The first part, inviting the great assembly [to take a seat], has three further sections. The first is the invitation; the second describes how those who had supernatural powers were able to ascend the seats; the third describes how newly declared [bodhisattvas] who had recently aroused [the aspiration for awakening] were not able to ascend the seats—these can be understood. The separate invitation to Śāriputra also has four parts: the first is the invitation; the second shows Śāriputra declining because he was not able [to ascend the

55c

high seat]; the third relates how Vimalakīrti instructed [Śāriputra and the
newly trained bodhisattvas] to worship [Buddha Sumeru] Lamp King; the
fourth describes how the great assembly was able to ascend the seats after
worshiping [Buddha Sumeru] Lamp King.

From "Śāriputra said, '[Layman,] this is unprecedented'" is the fourth
of the six major parts [of this chapter], in which Vimalakīrti, because of Śāriputra's praise [of his supernatural feat], extensively describes the two inconceivable knowledges of the conventional and the real that buddhas and bodhisattvas possess and how they are able to display inconceivable manifestations.
This has two further sections: the first gives the brief praise given by Śāriputra; the second, from "Vimalakīrti said," shows Vimalakīrti's response to
Śāriputra's praise, that is, the extensive description of the inconceivable manifestations [that buddhas and bodhisattvas display].

[The description of the inconceivable manifestations] has three further
parts. 1) Because [Vimalakīrti] wished to clarify the manifestations, he began
by giving the essence: "Buddhas and bodhisattvas have a liberation called
'inconceivable.'" "Liberation" refers to the two knowledges of the conventional and the real. These two knowledges both transcend the thousand fetters, and therefore [to possess these two knowledges] is called "liberation."
This means that the buddhas and bodhisattvas having the two knowledges
of the conventional and the real is the essence of the inconceivable; hence
they are able to display all manner of inconceivable manifestations.

The second part, from "When a bodhisattva dwells in this liberation,"
is the extensive explanation of the inconceivable manifestations. The third
part, from "Śāriputra, I have now briefly explained [the power of the bodhisattva's inconceivable emancipation]," is the conclusion. Enveloping mountains and absorbing oceans, inhaling the winds [of the entire universe], and
clothing himself with the flames [of the world's end], changing his voice
and transforming his nature, compressing the long and expanding the short—
all of these are inconceivable manifestations. There are three schools of interpretation of "inconceivable." One says that Mount Sumeru and a mustard
seed are similar in that both are hollow and empty; hence one can be put
inside the other. The second [interpretation] is that Mount Sumeru doesn't
really enter into the mustard seed, it is just that the sage's supernatural power
makes it appear that way to the onlooker. The third [interpretation] is that

we don't know that [Mount Sumeru] was really put into [the mustard seed], nor do we know that it wasn't. We don't know how that is, but nonetheless it is—therefore it is called "inconceivable."

From "At that time, Mahākāśyapa" is the fifth of the six major parts [of this chapter], showing Kāśyapa lamenting the severing of his own capacity and exhorting the newly trained [bodhisattvas] to arouse the mind [of *bodhi*]. This itself is divided into three. The first has the narrator describing Kāśyapa's exclamation that his hearing of the inconceivable was unprecedented. The second, from "[Mahākāśyapa] said to Śāriputra," gives his actual lament. The third, from "When Mahākāśyapa spoke these words," depicts the thirty-two thousand gods arousing the aspiration [to achieve perfect awakening].

The second part, the actual lament, itself has four sections. The first shows [Mahākāśyapa exclaiming] that the *śrāvaka*s have severed [their good roots] and are without the disposition for buddhahood; thus, they are like the   56a
blind. The second, from "Knowledgable ones," rejoices that bodhisattvas [who hear of the inconceivable] are able to arouse the aspiration [for perfect awakening]. The third, from "How is it that we [have long cut off our capacity?]," describes the extreme gravity of what was lost in the two vehicles, such that they all should cry out [with such a howl] that the trimegachiliocosm shakes. The fourth section, from "All the bodhisattvas," describes the magnitude of the benefit attained by the bodhisattvas, such that they should joyously celebrate. The reason is that if one [merely] hears of this underlying principle, one will transcend samsara and pass beyond the troubles of Māra—not to mention one who practices accordingly.

The third part [of the fifth major section], describing the benefits attained, can be understood.

From "At that time Vimalakīrti said to Mahākāśyapa" is the sixth of the six major parts of this chapter, Vimalakīrti's affirmative response to Kāśyapa's exclamation. Before Kāśyapa had said that if there are [bodhisattvas] who are able to have faith in the inconceivable, then Māra can do nothing to them. Now, however, he sees that the disturbances of Māra are actually created by bodhisattvas for the sake of [testing the resolution of] the newly trained [bodhisattvas]—why then does he say that they can do nothing? Therefore we interpret this as meaning that they are all bodhisattvas dwelling in the inconceivable liberation. "Ordinary people are inferior"—how could they act in such a way? This has four parts. The first explains that it is because bodhisattvas wish to transform beings that they manifest as Māra kings. The second, from "Why is that?", explains why they appear as Māra kings. The third, from "Ordinary beings [are inferior]," shows why ordinary beings are incapable [of acting in this way]. The fourth, from "This is called [the gate of discerning awareness and skillful means possessed by bodisattvas dwelling in the inconceivable liberation]," is the conclusion. All of this can be understood.

Chapter Seven

Contemplating Sentient Beings

This chapter depicts the bodhisattvas "contemplating sentient beings," hence the title of the chapter. The two chapters from here are concerned with the transformation of people of middling capacity, as was explained above [at the beginning of Chapter Three of the *Commentary*].

When people of middling capacity hear the [teachings in the] chapter "[Mañjuśrī's] Inquiring about the Illness," four doubts arise. [The first is in regard to] the reply to [Mañjuśrī's] inquiry about [Vimalakīrti's] illness, where it was stated that bodhisattvas are not really ill but only [appear to be] ill for the sake of [teaching] beings. [Beings of] middling capacity delight in existence; they are attached to the idea that there truly are sentient beings within the underlying principle, and therefore the reason [bodhisattvas] manifest illnesses is surely for the sake of sentient beings.

The second doubt arises when [beings of middling capacity] hear the bodhisattva's love for sentient beings likened to the love ordinary parents have for their own children. Although the love that ordinary parents have for their children is important, nonetheless it is one-sided. If the bodhisattvas were like this, their views of affection toward others would not yet be eliminated—how then could they transform beings impartially?

The third [doubt arises in regard to] the above [discussion of how bodhisattvas should] comfort and instruct [a bodhisattva who is ill]. There it was stated that although bodhisattvas contemplate impermanence they remain in samsara, serenely accept suffering, and save beings. In the discussion [of how bodhisattvas should] discipline [their minds], it was explained that although bodhisattvas do not have the karma for taking on a body, for the sake of transforming beings they take on a body within the six paths. Although their bodies experience suffering, when they think about the sentient beings in the evil destinies they arouse a mind of great compassion. People of middling capacity give rise to doubt about whether the issue of physically remaining in samsara, serenely accepting suffering, and saving beings is only for [bodhisattvas] of the upper ranks, and not something that newly declared [bodhisattvas] are able to bear.

So too, the [fourth] doubt arises because they learned above of the bodhisattvas' many and various practices of the Middle Way, which fully completed [the discussion of how bodhisattvas] should discipline [their minds.] In principle, if what ought to be done is done, and what ought not to be done is not done, then what is not fixed? In this way, there is hesitation and wavering about entering the Way, and the mind is uneasy. It is for this reason that this chapter is given and an explanation is made.

56b

Now, in order to remove these four doubts the text itself has four kinds [of explanations]. The first, from the beginning up to "The bodhisattva's contemplation of sentient beings is like this," shows that bodhisattvas contemplate sentient beings as empty, without reality, like an illusion, like a dream—this dispels the first anxious doubt about whether sentient beings truly exist.

The second is from "Mañjuśrī said, 'If a bodhisattva contemplates [sentient beings] thus, how should they cultivate kindness?'" This shows that a bodhisattva's kindness is none other than a kindness that is devoid of perceptual attributes. This dispels the doubt about whether [the bodhisattva's love for sentient beings] is the same as the one-sided love ordinary parents [have for their children].

The third, from "Mañjuśrī asked further, 'What should the bodhisattva who fears samsara rely on?'", extensively describes the meaning of abiding within the merits of the Buddha. This dispels the third doubt regarding whether physically remaining within samsara, serenely accepting suffering, and saving beings is only for [bodhisattvas] of the upper ranks and not something that newly declared [bodhisattvas] are able to undertake.

The fourth, from "At that time there was a goddess in Vimalakīrti's room," dispels the doubt about lack of a fixed existence [of any *dharmas*].

The first aspect, describing the contemplation of sentient beings as empty, gives a total of thirty examples by way of explanation. These are divided into three parts: the first example of an illusion is the overall opening. The second part, the fourteen examples from "Like a knowledgeable one," clarifies emptiness with specific teachings; they are called "specific" because they distinguish between the provisional and the true. [The first nine examples refer to the provisional, and the five] from [the eleventh example,] "like a fifth element," explain true emptiness. The third part, the fifteen examples from "Like form in the formless realm," explains emptiness as a shared teaching—it is called "shared" because [the examples] have the provisional and the true in common. These three parts all have two aspects: 1) the actual depiction of emptiness [by way of a metaphor], and 2) the conclusion that "[The bodhisattva's contemplation of sentient beings] is like this." These can be understood.

The second explanation is that the bodhisattva's kindness is a kindness that is devoid of perceptual attributes; this dispels the doubt about whether [the bodhisattva's love is] the same as the one-sided love of ordinary parents [for their own children]. This is made up of the two parts of a question and answer.

"Mañjuśrī asked, 'If a bodhisattva contemplates [sentient beings] thus, how should he cultivate kindness?'" This explains what kind of practice of kindness will apply to living beings if sentient beings are all contemplated as empty objects, without reality.

The second aspect, Vimalakīrti's answer, has three parts. The first is [Vimalakīrti's] immediate reply that when bodhisattvas are enlightened to the three emptinesses and thereby teach sentient beings, causing them to cultivate that which is devoid of perceptual attributes and ultimately to obtain the highest fruits—this is called true great kindness. The second part, from "[The bodhisattva] practices a kindness of quiescent extinction," is an extensive explanation of the essential nature of kindness devoid of perceptual attributes. The third part is the conclusion regarding kindness devoid of perceptual attributes. Within these, however, the point of Mañjuśrī's question was explicitly answered with the three emptinesses as described above, but in his mind the purpose was to dispel the doubts about whether [the kindness of the bodhisattva] is the same as the one-sided love of ordinary parents [for their own children].

The second part, the extensive explanation of the essential nature of   56c kindness, is also divided into four sections. The first uses the emptiness of the underlying principle in order to give examples of kindness. The second section, from "[The bodhisattva practices] the kindness of an arhat," uses the practitioners of the three vehicles as examples. The third, from "[The bodhisattva] practices a self-same kindness," takes buddhahood as an example. The fourth, from "[The bodhisattva] practices a kindness without revulsion," uses the ten thousand practices of the causal stage as examples.

The first section, using the underlying principle of emptiness as an example, comprises nine verses in total. The first verse, "[The bodhisattva] practices a kindness of quiescent extinction, because there is nothing that is born or dies," shows that the underlying principle of emptiness is quiescent, without birth and death. This means that the kindness of tranquil extinction, without birth and death, is also like the underlying principle of emptiness. The following eight verses parallel this interpretation. "Inner" means "sense organ," "outer" means [sense] "objects"; within the underlying principle of emptiness there is no coming together of sense organs and their objects.

The second section, using the practitioners of the three vehicles as examples, is itself comprised of four verses. The first verse, "[The bodhisattva] practices the kindness of an arhat, because he has destroyed the traitorous entanglements," shows that kindness like that of an arhat is able to destroy the traitorous entanglements; the following three verses are the same as this.

The third section, using buddhahood as an example, also has four verses. The first verse is "[The bodhisattva] practices a self-same kindness, because it is attained without cause."

Because buddhahood is without a teacher it is [a state that] is self-same and attained without cause. This means that because [the bodhisattva's] kindness is devoid of perceptual attributes it is without cause and thus like uncaused buddhahood. The following three verses can be understood in line with this.

The fourth section, using the ten thousand practices of the causal stage as examples, is further made up of eleven verses. The first verse is "[The bodhisattva] practices a kindness without revulsion, because of contemplating emptiness and no-self." Bodhisattvas contemplate emptiness and no-self and transform beings without revulsion; their kindness is also like this. The [meaning of the] following verses can also be inferred in line with this.

"Thus is the kindness of a bodhisattva" is the third part [of Vimalakīrti's answer], the conclusion.

Again, one understanding has it that all of these refer to [the bodhisattva] causing others to attain freedom. This means that a bodhisattva's kindness is called a kindness of quiescent extinction because it causes people to attain the underlying principle of quiescent extinction. "Because there is nothing that is born." The reason a bodhisattva's kindness is called "quiescent extinction" is because it makes people attain the underlying principle of the unborn tranquil extinction—therefore it is called quiescent extinction. The following verses are all similar to this and there is no difference in how you divide them.

Another understanding has it that [the verse] says simply that the bodhisattva's kindness is quiescent and extinct. The reason that it is called quiescent extinction is because the kindness [of bodhisattvas] has nothing that is born.

The next [three] questions and answers are given in order to explain compassion, joy, and equanimity, respectively; they can be understood.

From "Mañjuśrī asked further, 'What should the bodhisattva who fears samsara rely on?'" is the third [explanation], and explains the meaning of abiding within the merits of the Buddha. This removes the third [doubt] about whether physically remaining in samsara, serenely accepting suffering, and saving beings is only for [bodhisattvas] of the upper ranks and not something that newly declared [bodhisattvas] can undertake. This shows that even if they are newly declared bodhisattvas, because they dwell within the power of the Buddha's merits how could they be unable to bear [physically remaining in samsara, enduring suffering, and saving beings]? In all there are twelve questions and answers that deal with this, and they can all be understood if you investigate the text. 57a

"The body is the basis." This is to say that good and evil necessarily arise dependant upon the body of the five *skandha*s. "Desire" refers to the *skandha* of will (*samskāra*), "discrimination" refers to [the *skandha* of] the feeling (*vedanā*) mind, "confused thinking" refers to the [*skandha* of] the perceiving mind (*saṃjñā*), and "non-abiding" refers to the conscious mind (*vijñāna*). There is no mind prior to consciousness; therefore it says that consciousness is non-abiding. Perception has consciousness as its basis but prior to consciousness there is no mind, so what then could be the basis? Hence it says that "non-abiding is without basis." "Mañjuśrī, all *dharma*s are established on the non-abiding [basis]." This means that [all things] are born in order, dependent on consciousness, up to and including the body. Another way of looking at it is that non-abiding refers to the underlying principle of emptiness, and that all *dharma*s have the underlying principle of emptiness as their basis.

From "At that time [there was a goddess] in Vimalakīrti's [room]" removes the fourth doubt about the lack of a fixed existence [of any *dharma*]. This initially unfolds in three parts. In the first [part] the narrator describes how the goddess manifested herself and scattered flowers over the assembly, and thereupon began a discussion. The second part, from "At that time the goddess asked," presents the actual discussion between the goddess and Śāriputra, revealing the attributes of non-fixed existence, the underlying principle of the Middle Way. The third, from "At that time Vimalakīrti," gives Vimalakīrti's praise of the goddess's virtues and completes [the discussion of] the attributes of non-fixed existence.

However, the goddess is none other than a *mahāsattva* of the Dharma body. She manifested as a goddess because she wanted to transform beings by having a discussion about a woman's body. She scattered the flowers because she wished to thereby begin the discussion. Because of the goddess's supernatural powers the flowers adhered [to the the disciples] but did not stick [to the bodhisattvas]. She wanted to curb the discriminating and biased attachments of the newly declared [bodhisattvas] and the [followers of the] two vehicles with the practices of the nondiscriminating Middle Way of the *mahāsattva*.

From "At that time the goddess asked" is the second part, the actual discussion. Although there are many questions and answers, they all arise in sequence with each other and here we can put them in seven groups. The first is the discussion occasioned by the flowers adhering [to the disciples] but not [to the bodhisattvas]. The second, from "Śāriputra asked, 'Goddess, have you stayed in this room long?'", uses the question of whether she has been in the room a long or short time to further the discussion. The third, from "Śāriputra said, 'Excellent, excellent!'", bases the argument on the question of [the goddess's] attainment. The fourth, from "Śāriputra asked the goddess, 'Which of the three vehicles do you pursue?'", bases the discussion on the question of which [vehicle the goddess] pursues. The fifth, from "Why don't you change your female body?", creates the discussion about the question of transforming one's body. The sixth, from "Śāriputra asked the goddess, 'When you die here, where will you be born?'", uses the question of [the goddess's future] rebirth to construct the argument. The seventh, from "Śāriputra asked the goddess, 'How long will it be before you attain [perfect] *bodhi?*'", uses the question of the fruits attained to further the discussion. Although there are many questions and answers within these seven levels of exchange, all of them have [the nature of] non-fixed existence as their main point. That is to say, it is clear that this completes and concludes the [dis-   57b cussion of that which is] "devoid of perceptual attributes" mentioned above.

The first group [of questions and answers], that is, the discussion born of the scattering of the flowers, itself has three parts. The first is the goddess asking Śāriputra why he tried to remove the flowers. The second is Śāri-putra's answer that they were contrary to the Dharma of a home-departed one and so he wished to remove them. The third part is the goddess scolding Śāriputra—this constitutes four parts.

The first is the simple chastising [of Śāriputra, telling him] not to say that the flowers are contrary to the Dharma. The second part explains that "These flowers are without discrimination—it is you, Virtuous One, who gives rise to discrimination." This means that the flowers are empty, without mind—hence they are essentially [in need] neither of removal nor non-removal. That Śāriputra says that they are contrary to the Dharma is, on the other hand, [an example of] discrimination. The third part, from "If one who has left home within the Buddha-Dharma [discriminates]," reveals what it means to be in accord with the Dharma and contrary to the Dharma. The fourth part, from "See the bodhisattvas," explains why the flowers adhere [to some but] not [to others].

What is being said is that [the flowers] adhere because there is dis-crimination in the mind; if there is no discrimination [the flowers] do not stick. Again, if there is fear in the mind they adhere, and if there is no fear they do not. Further, if the latent entanglements are not yet done away with [the flowers] will adhere, but if the latent entanglements are exhausted, they will not. This can all be understood. Now, although they are called bodhi-sattvas, those below the seventh level have not yet exhausted the latent entan-glements. Why then are only the [followers of the] two vehicles made light of? Although bodhisattvas [below the seventh level] have not yet exhausted the latent entanglements, nonetheless, from the day they begin their practice they establish the intent to cut off all latent karmic impressions. Wishing to transform beings, they neither fear samsara nor [do they fear] physically remaining in the world—therefore it says that they have exhausted [the latent karmic impressions]. To discuss this in terms of reality, [the latent karmic residue has] not yet [been] exhausted. But those of the two vehicles fear samsara and are not able to transform beings. They wish only to cut off the actual afflictions and not latent karmic impressions. Therefore [only those of the two vehicles] are made light of.

From "Śāriputra said, 'Goddess, have you been in this room [long]?'" is the second discussion, born of the question of how long [the goddess] has been in the room. This has nine further levels. The first is Śāriputra asking the goddess if she has been in the room a long or short time. On being chastised by the goddess with an eloquence like that of Vimalakīrti, [Śāriputra] thought that she must have been in the room a long time and had frequently been perfumed by the echoing breezes of Vimalakīrti's [discourses]—therefore, she was able [to speak as eloquently] as he. So he asked this question. The second level is the goddess's reply [to Śāriputra]: "I have been in this room as many years as the liberation of the elder" has been realized—there are no attributes such as "long time" or "short time" that [apply to her being] in the room. The third level is Śāriputra's coy reply, "[How] long have you been here?", wondering how many months and years had passed since [his] liberation of emptiness.

The fourth level is the goddess chastising [Śāriputra], asking whether the elder's realization of the liberation of emptiness has the attribute of lengthy duration. The fifth is the narrator's describing Śāriputra's silence. The sixth is the goddess's asking Śāriputra why he is silent. [Śāriputra] has been called an "elder" because of his long years [in the monastic community]. Among the ten disciples [Śāriputra] was foremost in discerning awareness, therefore she says, "great knowledge." Since the Virtuous One [Śāriputra] was already complete in the two meanings, why did he remain silent and not respond?

57c   The seventh level is Śāriputra's reply that liberation is devoid of perceptual attributes and cannot be spoken of; thus he remains silent. The eighth level is the goddess again chastising Śāriputra. Śāriputra knows only the wordless liberation and does not yet know equality. The reason he is scolded here is that within the underlying principle speaking is non-speaking and non-speaking is speaking—all *dharma*s are like this. Therefore, [the goddess] says, "Language and words all have the attribute of liberation." "Liberation is not internal" refers to the six sense organs; "nor is it external" refers to the six sense objects; "not in between" refers to the six consciousnesses. It can also be said that "internal" refers to samsara, nirvana is "external," and the factors of the Way are "in between." It can also be that in "neither internal nor external," "internal" refers to the teacher's own body, "external" refers to the Dharma that is taught, and "in between" refers to the sounds of their voices. All three locations are empty—what problem is there that would cause him not to answer?

The ninth is Śāriputra's asking if it is like this, then why was liberation in the past considered only to be the elimination of desire, anger, and delusion? The goddess answered that it was only for the spiritually arrogant who believe in existence that the Buddha taught liberation as the elimination of mental afflictions. For those who do not believe in existence and are not spiritually arrogant, the Buddha taught that mental afflictions are none other than liberation.

From "Śāriputra said, 'Excellent, excellent!'" is the third discussion, based on the question of [the goddess's] attainment. Having heard the goddess's eloquent explanation of emptiness as related above, [Śāriputra thought] that she surely must have personally experienced the ultimate fruits, and so he asked her, "Goddess, what have you attained, and through what realization [are you so eloquent]?" Her answer itself has two parts. The first is the actual answer, telling him that she does not exist and therefore has neither attainment nor realization. The second part is the interpretation. That is to say, if you think that you personally have attainments, then you will surely look down on others who do not have attainments. This would be to already have spiritual arrogance with regard to the Buddha-Dharma; therefore she has neither attainment nor realization.

From "Śāriputra asked the goddess, ['Which of the three vehicles do you pursue?']" is the fourth discussion, occasioned by [Śāriputra's] question about which of the three vehicles the goddess follows. Again, on hearing that [the goddess] is without attainment and without realization, [Śāriputra thinks that she] must surely be an ordinary person who is slowly working her way through the practice stages. Therefore he asks which of the three fruits she seeks. Another interpretation has it that, as with the above question and answer, [Śāriputra thinks that the goddess] must surely be a Mahayana [practitioner], and hence [Śāriputra] asks the question. Therefore he is again scolded.

The answer has two parts. The first is the answer in terms of the manifestation, explaining that because of her transformation [of sentient beings]
through the three vehicles, she too is of the three vehicles. What has Śāriputra
already decided to cause him to ask this question? Again, why has he completely made up his mind and decided that she must be a Mahayana [practi-
tioner]? The second part, from "Śāriputra, it is like a person entering a *cam-
paka* grove," gives the answer based on the source; this unfolds in two parts.
The first begins with the Great [Vehicle] and omits the Small [Vehicle], and
then concludes with the Great [Vehicle]. The second, from "Śāriputra, I have
been in this room [twelve years]," begins by asserting that there is no [teach-
ing of the] Small [Vehicle of the *śrāvaka*s and *pratyekabuddha*s] and [that
while she has been in Vimalakīrti's room the goddess has heard only of the]
Great [Vehicle]; this also concludes without the Small [Vehicle].

Another interpretation has it that it is for people that the Great [Vehi-
cle] is taught, and from "[Śāriputra,] I have been in this room [twelve years]"
is the second part, describing first the lack [of any teachings of the] Small
[Vehicle] and then concluding with [the Dharma of the] Great [Vehicle]. "I
have been in this room twelve years and from the beginning have not heard
58a the Dharma of the *śrāvaka*s or *pratyekabuddha*s taught." This means that
there is no [Dharma] of the Small [Vehicle taught by Vimalakīrti]. From "I
have only heard of the bodhisattva's [great kindness and great compassion]"
describes the Great [Vehicle Dharma taught by Vimalakīrti]. Another interpretation has it that from "I have been in this room [twelve years]" up to
"Dharma of the buddhas" explains only that within the room there is just the
great and not the small, and that from "This room always manifests eight
unprecedented and rare *dharma*s" clarifies the [nature of the Dharma as]
great through the eight unprecedented things. Another interpretation understands it as four pairs, but we won't use that here.

From "Śāriputra, this room always manifests [eight unprecedented and
rare *dharma*s]" concludes with the lack of the Small [Vehicle Dharma in
Vimalakīrti's room]. Another interpretation says that throughout and in the
conclusion there is only the [Dharma] of the Great [Vehicle] and none who
take delight in the Small [Vehicle]. Therefore the house is great and described
in five levels. However, when asked whether she had been in the house a long
or short time, [the goddess] definitely did not answer by stating the number

of years but said only, "[as long] as the elder's liberation," and [she] did not allow [Śāriputra's] conceptions. What does it mean that she now herself says she has been [in Vimalakīrti's room] for twelve years? In interpreting this, we can say that first she wished to remove his conceptions and so did not state the number of years. Now, however, because she had already explained the nature of the undetermined by saying "[as long] as the elder's liberation," she gives the real answer. Why, then, did she say that she had been in the house for twelve years? She said that she had been in the house for twelve years because she wished to negate the two vehicles' attachment to the matter of "twelve years" as real. Another interpretation is that it might be the case that Vimalakīrti has actually been in the room for twelve years.

From "Śāriputra said, 'Why do you not change your female body?'" is the fifth discussion, occasioned by the question of [the goddess changing her] body. [Śāriputra] is now hearing about her manifestations within the three vehicles, but the source is none other than the Great [Vehicle]. Surely [the goddess] has accumulated unfathomable virtue and in fact should not have received a female body. Hence he asks why she does not transform her female body. This has three further parts: the first is the question and answer about the original nature of her body; the second, from "At that time the goddess [used her supernatural power and changed Śāriputra to be like a goddess]," is the question and answer about the transformed body; the third part, from "At that time the goddess withdrew her supernatural power," is another question and answer about [the goddess] returning to her original body.

The first part, the question and answer about the original nature of her body, itself has two parts. The first is Śāriputra's question; the second is the goddess's answer. The answer has four parts. The first is the direct answer that shows that ultimate truth is originally without the perceptual attributes of male or female. Therefore [the goddess said], "I have been looking for [the attribute] of a female body but have not found it—what is there to transform?" The second part is an example that throws the question back to Śāriputra. The third is Śāriputra's reply to her example. The fourth is the goddess bringing [her original statement] together with the example and showing that all *dharma*s are empty and lacking in anything that could be transformed.

From "At that time [the goddess used her supernatural power and changed Śāriputra to be like a goddess]" is the second part, the question and answer about the transformed body; this has four further parts. The first is the narrator describing the transformation of the two bodies. The second is [the goddess] asking Śāriputra, "Why don't you transform your female body?" The third is Śāriputra's reply, "I do not know how you have now transformed me into a female body"; how, then, could he change back into a male [body]? It could also be said that this is not a transformation of a real *dharma*—emptiness is without anything that can be transformed. The fourth part is the goddess's responding instruction to Śāriputra. This has three lines. In the first [the goddess] tells Śāriputra that because [his female body] is already nonexistent he is not able to transform it; all female [bodies] are also empty and thus not able to transform. The second line says that all [females] are empty and thus not female although they manifest female [bodies]. The third cites the Buddha's words as the summary proof.

58b

From "At that time the goddess withdrew [her supernatural power]" is the third part, more questions and answers about [the goddess] returning to her original body; the import of this is fourfold. The first is the narrator describing the goddess's body returning to its original [female attribute]. The second is the goddess asking Śāriputra where the physical form of a female exists. The third is Śāriputra's answer that [the physical form of a female] is primordially unborn and undying; therefore it neither exists nor does not exist. The fourth is the goddess using the emptiness of the underlying principle to conclude that, [as with the physical form of a female,] the various *dharma*s are all empty and unborn; she then cites the Buddha's words as proof. This can be understood.

From "Śāriputra asked the goddess" is the sixth discussion, occasioned by the question of where [the goddess] will be born. Those present who saw her perfect mastery of supernatural powers greatly revered her in their hearts and assumed that she was close to the ultimate [reward], and that after her death she would surely be born in a place of beauty and marvel. Therefore [Śāriputra] asked, "After you die [here], where will you be born?"

Śāriputra's question is about a buddha's birth being for the sake of transforming [beings] but without actual birth or extinction—how is it that the goddess does not pass away or be reborn? The goddess replied that sentient beings are all like the Buddha in not passing away or being reborn—how could the Buddha be alone in this? Another interpretation says that Śāriputra understands the gist [of what the goddess] is saying, that if, like the Buddha's birth, [the goddess's birth] is for the sake of transforming [beings], then she is without passing away and rebirth. Therefore, the goddess responds accordingly, saying that, like the Buddha, no sentient beings are born or extinguished—how could she be alone in this?

From "Śāriputra asked the goddess, 'Will it be long before you attain [supreme and perfect] *bodhi*?'" is the seventh discussion, born of [Śāriputra's] question [to the goddess about her] attainment of the ultimate fruit. When in the sixth [discussion], above, [Śāriputra] heard [the goddess] say that she too has a birth like that [of a buddha], he thought that she must be a very evolved practitioner and not far from attaining *bodhi*. Hence he arrived at this question. This itself has three parts. The first explains non-attainment with regard to nonexistence. The second, from "Śāriputra said, 'What about the buddhas who are now [attaining *bodhi*],'" explains non-attainment with regard to existence. The third, from "The goddess said, [Śāriputra, have you attained arhatship?]", explains non-attainment with regard to both existence and nonexistence.

The first part also has four parts. The first is Śāriputra's question. The second is the goddess's answer that she will attain *bodhi* when Śāriputra once again becomes an ordinary person. The third is "Śāriputra said, 'That I become an ordinary person is impossible.'" The fourth is "The goddess said, 'My attaining of [supreme and perfect] *bodhi* is likewise impossible.'" *Bodhi* is empty, therefore it is "without any place of abiding." Likewise, the practitioner is also empty and so there is no one who can attain [*bodhi*].

From "Śāriputra said, ['What about the buddhas who attain *bodhi*?']" is the second part, explaining non-attainment with regard to existence. This has exactly one question and answer.

The question is that if there is no one who attains [*bodhi*], then what can be said about the many buddhas who have already attained [*bodhi*] and those who will attain it? The answer is that all of this is explained within conventional cause and condition; it is not that *bodhi* has a past, future, or present, or that [*bodhi*] really has the attribute of attainment.

From "The goddess said, ['Śāriputra, have you attained arhatship?']" explains non-attainment with regard to emptiness and existence; this has three parts. The first is the goddess asking Śāriputra if he has attained arhatship.   58c

The second is Śāriputra's answer, "There is nothing that is attained, and there-fore I have attained it." With regard to emptiness, there is no attainment—attainment is taught with regard to the conventional. The third is the god-dess's response accordingly, that the many buddhas and bodhisattvas are also like this—with regard to emptiness there is no attainment, but with regard to the conventional there is attainment. There is no real attainment.

From "At that time Vimalakīrti [said to Śāriputra]" is the third part [of the fourth explanation that removes the fourth doubt]; this gives Vimala-kīrti's praise of the goddess's virtues and is the summary conclusion of [the discussion of] the meaning of the absence of perceptual attributes. This has three further parts. The first is the praise of [the goddess's] past actions; the second, from "She already is able to disport," is the praise of her present virtues; the third, from "Because of her original vows," is praise of her cur-rent unbounded benefiting of beings. This can all be understood.

Chapter Eight

The Way of the Buddha

This chapter describes how bodhisattvas cultivate the wrong [path] and thereby thoroughly penetrate the way of the Buddha; hence the title of the chapter. This is the second [chapter] that deals with the transformation of [people of] middling capacity, as explained above [at the beginning of the third chapter of this *Commentary*]. When those of middling capacity hear in the earlier [chapter] "The Inconceivable" that most of the Māra kings in the worlds of the ten directions are bodhisattvas who, dwelling in inconceivable liberation, use their skillful means to manifest as Māra kings and teach and transform sentient beings, they have doubts. The way of the Tathāgata should only spread what is right by means of what is right. It should not use what is wrong to master what is right. How is it, then, that [bodhisattvas] become Māra kings and thereby master the way of a buddha? This chapter is given in order to explain this.

This is unpacked in three parts. The first, from the beginning up to "This is thorough penetration of the way of the Buddha," is the initial explanation that within their hearts [bodhisattvas cultivate] great compassion devoid of perceptual attributes, yet externally they manifest the practices of the wrong [path] and, in accordance with beings' spiritual capacities, use their skillful means to save them—this is called the bodhisattva's thorough penetration of the way of the Buddha. This dispels the doubt about the inappropriateness of using what is wrong in order to penetrate what is right.

The second part, from "At this, Vimalakīrti asked Mañjuśrī, 'What is the seed of the Tathāgata?'", is a demonstration that the defilements are the seed of the Tathāgata.

The third part, from "At that time there was a bodhisattva in the assembly named Universally Manifested Form Body," describes Vimalakīrti's numerous and varied manifestations of the inconceivable; this concludes the [discussion of how] practicing what is wrong leads to penetration of what is right.

The first part itself is made up of two exchanges of questions and answers. The first exchange establishes the name [of the chapter]; the actual two, the question and answer, can be understood. The latter exchange actually explains how practicing what is wrong leads to penetration of what is right. This also has the two [parts of a] question and answer, and there are four divisions within the answer. The first is the initial three lines that clarify how practicing what is wrong leads to penetration of what is right from the standpoint of evil fruits. The second division, from "manifests greed and desire," describes how practicing what is wrong leads to penetration of what is right from the standpoint of of evil causes. The third, from "manifests flattery and deception," clarifies how practicing what is wrong leads to penetration of what is right with regard to various standpoints. The fourth is the one line that concludes this part, "Mañjuśrī, [if the bodhisattva is able to practice the wrong path in this manner, this is to penetrate the way of the Buddha]."

"[The bodhisattva] cultivates the [deeds that lead to the hell of the] five interminable sufferings, yet there is no worry or anxiety." This means that [the bodhisattva] enables others to attain the fruit of non-worry and non-anxiety. The following lines are similar and can be interpreted thus. One interpretation understands it to only refer to [the bodhisattva's] own mind: although [the bodhisattva] manifests [the deeds that lead to the hell of the five] interminable sufferings externally, within his mind there is no worry or anxiety. The following lines also have the same [meaning].

The second division, from the standpoint of [evil] causes, is further divided into two parts; the first concerns the three poisons, and the latter concerns the six obstacles. This shows that although [the bodhisattva] manifests the three poisons and six obstacles, he is not in opposition to the three virtues and the six perfections. The third and fourth divisions can be understood.

From "At this, Vimalakīrti [asked Mañjuśrī, 'What is the seed of the Tathāgata?']" is the second part, a demonstration that the defilements are the seed of the Tathāgata. One interpretation takes it that the reason this is explained again is that sentient beings, having heard earlier that the practice of what is wrong leads to penetration of what is right, will have further doubts. [They will think that] it is like this only because of [the bodhisattva's] wish to transform beings, but in fact it is not so—the correct argument is that buddhahood is achieved solely through virtue. So it is now shown that virtue arises from evil; there is no virtue that arises by itself. Therefore it says that the defilements are the seed of the Buddha—how could virtue alone [be the seed]?

This has two parts: the first is the actual statement that defilements are the seed of the Tathāgata; the second, from "Kāśyapa exclaimed, 'Excellent, [excellent, Mañjuśrī!]'", is Kāśyapa's expression of complete agreement.

The first part has two exchanges of questions and answers, which itself has two parts: the first question and answer is the actual explanation that defilements are the seed of the Tathāgata; the subsequent exchange further clarifies what it means that defilements are the seed of the Tathāgata. The first exchange has three parts: 1) the question, 2) the answer, and 3) the conclusion.

[The first part deals with the question.] The reason [Vimalakīrti] asked Mañjuśrī was because of the doubts beings would have, thinking that Vimalakīrti's practice of what is wrong would not lead to the penetration of what is right. Therefore [Mañjuśrī] was made to explain it to Vimalakīrti.

The second part is [Mañjuśrī's] answer: "Having a body is the seed." This means that a body [that lives] within the three existences is the seed. "The five hindrances" are desire, anger, dullness, agitation, and doubt. "The six entrances" are the six sense organs. "The seven consciousnesses" are the three *dhyāna*s [of the form realm], the three empty [regions of the formless realm], and the deities and humans of the desire realm added together to make seven. The fourth *dhyāna* [of the form realm] is a state of concentration devoid of perceptual attributes, and the [state of neither thinking] nor not thinking [in the formless realm] is the state of concentration characterized by cessation [of all mental activity] (*nirodha-samāpatti*), so they are not included. The three lower destinies [below the formless realm, that is, the realm of form, and the two destinies of deities and humans in the desire realm] can be seen and known. "The eight heterodox [*dharma*s]" oppose the eightfold right [*dharma*s of the eightfold noble path]. The "nine afflictions" refer to dislike of one's virtuous friends, affection for one's enemies, and dislike of oneself through the three worlds [of past, present, and future], for a total of nine afflictions.

From "To summarize [this]" is the third part, the conclusion.

From "Why is this?" is the second exchange of a question and answer, further clarifying what it means that the defilements are the seed of the Tathāgata; this has the two parts of the question and the answer. The question is not elaborated; it simply asks why it is that defilements are the seed of the Tathā-gata. The answer has three further parts. The first gives a doctrinal explanation, explaining a one-sided extreme of non-attainment. This describes how those of the two vehicles fear and avoid the defilements; because they only see the uncon-ditioned and enter the stage of certainty, they are not able to finally arouse [the

59b aspiration for] the great way of [highest and perfect] *bodhi*. Hence it says that defilements are the seed of the Tathāgata. For this reason as well, one inter-pretation is the opposite, i.e., that this part explains attainment.

The second part [of the answer] is from "For example, it is like the dry lands of a high plateau." This gives a metaphor in order to explain both extremes of attainment and non-attainment. This explains that because those of the two vehicles have a one-sided belief in the stage of certainty, they fear and avoid the mental afflictions and are not able to generate the seed of *bodhi*. Because ordinary people are not yet established in the two supports, if they encounter the [right] conditions they are able to generate the mind that is the seed of the Tathāgata.

From "Thus you should know" is the third part, the conclusion. It has a doctrinal explanation as well as a metaphor; this can be understood.

From "At that time, Mahākāśyapa exclaimed, 'Excellent, [excellent, Mañjuśrī!]'" is the second part, Kāśyapa's praise and description of Mañjuśrī's teaching. [Kāśyapa] again laments his own cutting off the capac-ity [for awakening, as he did at the beginning of Chapter Six]. This also has three parts. The first is his summary praise of [Mañjuśrī's] teaching as not false. The second, from "The field of troubling defilements," is the actual expression [of Mañjuśrī's] earlier words. The third, from "Therefore, Mañjuśrī," is the conclusion. These can be understood.

"Respond" is to say that ordinary people will surely attain the fruits of buddhahood—they are able to respond to the Buddha's benevolence. There-fore it says that [ordinary people] "respond" [to the Buddha-Dharma]. Those of the two vehicles are not like this, and so they do not "respond."

From "At that time there was a bodhisattva in the assembly [named Uni-versally Manifested Form Body]" is the third part of this chapter, describing Vimalakīrti's numerous and varied manifestations of the inconceivable; this concludes the [discussion of how the] practice of what is wrong leads to pen-etration of what is right. This is unpacked in two divisions. The first is the question posed by Bodhisattva Universally Manifested [Form Body]; the second is Vimalakīrti's reply in verse. This, [the third part of this chapter, is also] the fourth of the five discussions born of [Vimalakīrti's] emptying his room.

The first division is the question of Bodhisattva Universally Manifested [Form Body]. The Virtuous One wore the white robes of a layman, yet his room was small and narrow and there was nothing in it. Where were his father, mother, relatives, and all the requisite furnishings? If we look deeper into this question, there is an inner purpose. The essence of Vimalakīrti is inconceivable, yet within the path of response manifestations he appears the same as a layman.

Fearing that the confused will see his appearance but not understand [that it is merely a manifestation] along the path [in response to the needs of sentient beings], this question was asked.

Vimalakīrti's answer, the second division [of the third part of this chapter], has a total of forty-two verses divided into three parts. The first part consists of the twelve verses from "The perfection of discerning awareness is the bodhisattva's mother" up to "His victory banner flies over the seat of enlightenment." This part describes how, with regard to his essence, the bodhisattva is solely related to the many and various factors of the path and is without [actual] kinsfolk [or retinue] in the world.

The second is the twenty-seven verses from "Although [the bodhisattva] knows that there is neither origination nor extinction." This part describes how, with regard to his manifestations, although there is neither [origination nor extinction, nonetheless] great beings make their existence appear through their inconceivable skill. It is exactly through their inconceivable [skills] that they negate the confusion of those people.

The three verses from "In this way, innumerable paths [are traveled without restriction]" comprise the third part, together concluding [the discussion] of the essence and manifestation [of the bodhisattva].

There are some who divide these verses and interpret them in detail, but here I simply understand them according to the text.

The "seven purities" are: 1) purity of morality, 2) purity of mind, 3) purity of views, 4) purity in overcoming doubts, 5) purity in discrimination, 6) purity of practice, and 7) purity of nirvana. The "seven treasures" are faith, morality, learning, renunciation, awareness, conscience, and shame.

59c

Chapter Nine

Entering the Dharma Gate
of Nonduality

This chapter explains the bodhisattva's entering the Dharma gate of non-duality; hence the title of the chapter.

This chapter and the next take up the transformation of [beings] of inferior capacity; it is the third part of the six chapters that altogether deal with the transformation of [beings] of the three capacities. The earlier chapter "Contemplating Sentient Beings" said that bodhisattvas contemplate sentient beings as empty, like a fifth element. When [beings] of inferior capacity hear this they give rise to doubts—if this is so, then bodhisattvas are the same as [followers of] the two vehicles in that their primary [practice] is the contemplation of emptiness. Why, then, should bodhisattvas be honored [above those of the two vehicles]? Therefore, in order to dispel these doubts this chapter explains the bodhisattva's cultivation of the nondual contemplation.

This is to say that although it is the same contemplation of emptiness, [bodhisattvas'] contemplation of emptiness is not the same [as that practiced in the two vehicles]. The reason is that in the contemplation [practiced in] the two vehicles there is the belief in emptiness and existence; hence [followers of the two vehicles] abandon existence and realize emptiness. They seek only their own salvation and do not include the transformation of others. For this reason, although it is called the contemplation of emptiness, in fact it is a contemplation of perceptual attributes. The bodhisattvas' contemplation includes existence without losing sight of emptiness. It includes emptiness and perfects the ten thousand transformations. Emptiness is none other than existence; existence is none other than emptiness—there is no bias for existence or nonexistence, they are equally nondual. Therefore, this is called the true contemplation of emptiness—how could this be called the same as [the contemplation practiced in] the two vehicles? Abandon this [notion].

This chapter unfolds in three main parts. The first part describes Vimala-kīrti's urging each [bodhisattva] to explain [how one enters the Dharma gate of nonduality]. The second part describes each [bodhisattva's] explanation of [how one enters the Dharma gate of nonduality]. The third part, from "When the teaching had been given in these words," explains the benefits obtained [at that time].

The second of the three parts, the explanations given by each [bodhi-sattva], also unfolds in three parts. The first part depicts the various bodhi-sattvas using words to expound wordlessness.

The second part, from "[After] the various bodhisattvas had thus [given their explanations]," shows Mañjuśrī using words to reject words. The third, from "At this, Mañjuśrī asked Vimalakīrti," shows Vimalakīrti wordlessly expounding wordlessness.

All three of these sections reveal that there is neither depth nor shal-lowness within the principle of wordlessness. Sentient beings, however, upon hearing each of the various bodhisattvas using words to expound wordless-ness, will think that the underlying principle can surely be expounded with words. Hence Mañjuśrī uses words to reject words. Beings will then reckon that although the underlying principle is wordless, there are words that are able to dispel [words]. Therefore Vimalakīrti is silent and does not speak, thereby dispelling the notion that [words are] able to dispel [words].

"Birth and extinction are a duality." This means that the underlying principle is essentially without the distinction of birth and extinction, and therefore is nondual. The various passages after this are similar and can be understood.

"The one attribute and the absence of perceptual attribute are a duality." The "one attribute" is none other than the absence of attribute; wishing to reject dualities, however, it says, "one attribute." The confused, however, will see them as a duality because of their attachments.

"The exhaustible and the inexhaustible are a duality." The conditioned is impermanent, therefore it is exhaustible. The unconditioned is eternal, therefore it is inexhaustible. If we talk about it in terms of the one empti-ness, there is no duality.

60a

"The [differentiation of the] four categories [of elements] and the cate-gory of space is a duality." The four categories are the four great [elements];

the category of space is the great [element] of space. It also [can mean that] the one emptiness is without duality.

"Emptiness, the absence of perceptual attributes, and wishlessness constitute dualities." The [cultivation of the liberations of emptiness, absence of perceptual attributes, and wishlessness in the] three realms are the cultivation of the one emptiness; those who have not yet arrived [at this understanding] take them to be three [separate cultivations].

"Virtuous [actions], sinful [actions], and neutral [actions] constitute dualities." "Virtuous [actions]" means good actions within the desire realm. "Sinful [actions]" means the ten evil deeds. "Neutral [actions]" refers to the [neutral] actions of the form and formless realms. All three actions are of one attribute, without duality.

"Generation from the self and what arises [from others] are a duality." "Generation from the self" means oneself and "what arises" refers to others; they are nondual.

"The attributes of the attainable are a duality." To "attain" refers to the self; the "attribute" [of what is obtained] refers to other [things]. If the self is without the attribute of being attainable, then who is it that could grasp and reject?

From "[After] the various bodhisattvas had thus [given their explanations]" is the second part of the explanations [concerning nonduality] given by each [bodhisattva], showing Mañjuśrī using words to reject words. This itself has two parts. The first is the inquiry to [Mañjuśrī] about how a bodhisattva [enters the Dharma gate of nonduality]; the second is Mañjuśrī's answer.

From "At this, Mañjuśrī asked [Vimalakīrti]" is the third part, showing Vimalakīrti silently rejecting words. This itself has three parts: the first is Mañjuśrī's question; the second is Vimalakīrti's non-answer; the third is Mañjuśrī's exclamation of praise and explanation. But if the ultimate is without words, Mañjuśrī should also have been silent—why, then, did he exclaim words of praise and explanation? By way of explanation, I say that the underlying principle is, in fact, like this[—that is, without words]. If, however, Mañjuśrī had not given his explanation, those with confused minds would wonder if Vimalakīrti's silence was [simply] not answering and they would not know that he was showing the ultimate to be without words. Therefore

Mañjuśrī, wishing to convey this to beings, exclaimed words of praise and explanation.

From "When the teaching on nonduality [had been given]" is the third part of the chapter, explaining the benefits that were obtained [at that time].

Chapter Ten

The Buddha Accumulated Fragrances

This is the second part of the section describing the transformation of people of inferior capacity. When people of inferior capacity hear in the earlier chapter on "The Way of the Buddha" that [bodhisattvas] practice what is wrong and thereby penetrate what is right, they think that this must be just words—that it is not in fact true. Hence [this chapter] now uses food, although an obstacle, and through [Vimalakīrti's] requesting a meal from the land of the Buddha Accumulated Fragrances and extensively performing the deeds of a buddha, shows how [those of inferior capacity] should understand that the practice of what is wrong leads to penetration of what is right, and that having faith there will be a sign. Hence the title of this chapter is "The Buddha Accumulated Fragrances."

This chapter unfolds in two main parts. The first is actually using food to demonstrate that the practice of what is wrong leads to penetration of what is right; the second describes the benefits attained.

The first part further unfolds in ten items. The first shows Śāriputra thinking about food. The second, from "Vimalakīrti, knowing his thoughts," is Vimalakīrti scolding him. The third, from "If you want food," is [Vimalakīrti's] assent to [get what Śāriputra] wants. The fourth, from "Then Vimalakīrti entered into *samādhi*," reveals the place where there is food. The fifth, from "Vimalakīrti asked the assembly of bodhisattvas," depicts Vimalakīrti asking the host of bodhisattvas who [among them] was able and worthy of going to get the food.

The sixth, from "At this, Vimalakīrti, [without rising from his seat,]" shows Vimalakīrti sending a conjured bodhisattva [to get the food]. The seventh, from "When the many great beings saw the conjured bodhisattva," describes how the bodhisattvas of the Multitude of Fragrances [world] saw the conjured bodhisattva and exclaimed that it was unprecedented. The eighth, from "At this, the Tathāgata Accumulated Fragrances [gave his bowl to the conjured bodhisattva]," describes the Buddha Accumulated Fragrances bestowing the food and sending [the conjured bodhisattva] back [to Vimalakīrti's room]. The ninth, from "Vimalakīrti said to Śāriputra," depicts Vimalakīrti giving the food to the assembly and thereby actually demonstrating how the practice of what is wrong can lead to mastery of what is right. The tenth, from "At that time, Vimalakīrti asked the bodhisattvas from the Multitude of Fragrances [world]," shows Vimalakīrti and the bodhisattvas from the Multitude of Fragrances [world] exchanging questions and answers that describe how beings are transformed in the two realms.

The first item is Śāriputra thinking about food—according to the rules of the Buddha-Dharma, [*bhikṣus*] should eat by midday, and so he thought, "It is already noon, what are all of these bodhisattvas going to eat?" It would have been inappropriate to just think about himself, so [Śāriputra] thought about all the "bodhisattvas."

The second item is [Vimalakīrti's] scolding [of Śāriputra]; he chastised him by raising the eight liberations. The eight liberations [are taught so that] one will weary of the desire realm; they also enable people to sunder their fetters. Śāriputra had already undertaken their cultivation, so why was he now desirous of food while yet listening to the Dharma?

The third item is [Vimalakīrti's] assent to get [Śāriputra] what he wanted. The fourth item reveals the place where the food is. These can be understood.

The fifth item shows Vimalakīrti asking who is able and worthy to go [and get the food]; this has four parts. The first is Vimalakīrti's asking. The second is Mañjuśrī keeping the assembly from answering because he wished to reveal Vimalakīrti's power. The third is Vimalakīrti's wishing to encourage those [whose practice] was not yet complete, and so [after Mañjuśrī silenced the assembly, Vimalakīrti] asked, "Isn't [this great assembly] embarrassed [that no one will go]?" The fourth part is Mañjuśrī's wishing to encourage the newly trained [bodhisattvas], and so he quoted the Buddha, saying, "We should not belittle those who have yet to learn."

From "At this, Vimalakīrti, [without rising from his seat]" is the sixth item, showing Vimalakīrti sending a conjured bodhisattva [to get the food]. This has three further parts. The first describes [Vimalakīrti] creating the conjured bodhisattva. The second, from "[Vimalakīrti] then said to him," gives [Vimalakīrti's] instructions to [the conjured bodhisattva] in how to conduct himself [when he reaches the world of the Buddha Accumulated Fragrances]. The third, from "Then, the conjured bodhisattva," describes the [conjured bodhisattva] receiving the teachings and rising to the upper regions. This can be understood.

From "When those [many] great beings [saw the conjured bodhisattva]" is the seventh item, showing the bodhisattvas of the Multitude of Fragrances [world] seeing the conjured bodhisattva and exclaiming that it was unprecedented. This has four parts. The first shows the bodhisattvas of the Multitude of Fragrances [world] exclaiming that [the sight of the conjured bodhisattva] was unprecedented and asking the World-honored One [of their own world to explain it]. The second, from "That buddha spoke these words," shows the buddha of the Multitude of Fragrances [world] answering. The third, from "Those bodhisattvas said," is a further inquiry about Vimalakīrti's power. The fourth, from "That buddha said, ['Vimalakīrti's powers] are very great,'" is that buddha's answer, and describes Vimalakīrti's supernatural power as very great and his transformation of beings as without limit.

From "At this, the Tathāgata Accumulated Fragrances [gave his bowl to the conjured bodhisattva]" is the eighth item, showing [the Buddha Accumulated Fragrances] giving the food and sending [the conjured bodhisattva] back [to Vimalakīrti's room]. This itself has seven parts. The first depicts the giving of the food. The second, from "Then those nine million [bodhisattvas]," shows the bodhisattvas of the upper region asking to accompany [the conjured bodhisattva and go to see] the Buddha. The third part, from "The Buddha said, 'You may go,'" is granting their request. The fourth, from "Then the conjured bodhisattva [took the bowl and food]," shows [the conjured bodhisattva] together with the bodhisattvas from the Multitude of Fragrances [world] coming [back to the Sāha world]. The fifth, from "Vimalakīrti magically created [nine million lion thrones]," describes how Vimalakīrti attended to his guests. The sixth, from "The conjured bodhisattva [gave the bowl full of fragrant food to Vimalakīrti]," depicts Vimalakīrti receiving the food. The seventh, from "The fragrance of the food wafted throughout [Vaiśālī]," describes how people and gods all gathered [at Vimalakīrti's house] when they smelled the fragrant and wonderful aroma.

The first two can be understood. The third part, allowing [the bodhisattvas to] go, itself has two parts. The first is simply granting permission.

60c

221

The second is the instructions [of the Buddha Accumulated Fragrances], which is further divided into three parts. The first is the instruction to withdraw the fragrance of their bodies; the second is the instruction to leave behind their true form; the third is the instruction to not harbor feelings of disdain. The latter four parts [of the eighth item, which depicts the Buddha Accumulated Fragrances giving the food and sending the conjured bodhisattva back to Vimalakīrti's room,] can also be understood.

From "Vimalakīrti said to Śāriputra," the ninth item, shows [Vimalakīrti] giving the food to the assembly and thereby actually demonstrating how the practice of what is wrong can lead to mastery of what is right. This is further divided into five parts. The first describes Vimalakīrti encouraging [everybody in the assembly] to eat. The second, from "The other śrā-vakas [thought]," is a question about whether there is enough food. The third, from "The conjured bodhisattva said," is his reply [that the amount of food] is inexhaustible. The fourth, consisting of the twelve characters from "At this, the bowl of food [satisfied the entire assembly]," is the actual description of how [the food in the bowl] was not depleted. The fifth part, from "All of those bodhisattvas," is the actual description of the benefits attained by those who ate the food.

From "At that time, Vimalakīrti asked the bodhisattvas from the Multitude of Fragrances [world]" is the tenth item, showing Vimalakīrti and the bodhisattvas from the Multitude of Fragrances [world] exchanging questions and answers that describe how beings are transformed in the two realms. This has eight parts. The first is Vimalakīrti asking how [beings are transformed] in the upper realms. The second, from "Those bodhisattvas [said]," has the bodhisattvas from the Multitude of Fragrances [world] explaining that [in their world] the transformation [of beings] takes place simply through a multitude of fragrances. The third part, from "Those bodhisattvas [asked Vimalakīrti]," is the bodhisattvas of the Multitude of Fragrances [world] inquiring about the Dharma [in this world].

The fourth part, from "Vimalakīrti said," is Vimalakīrti's reply that because the sentient beings in this world are strong, stubborn, and difficult to transform, [Śākyamuni Buddha] uses all manner of stern language to discipline them. "Difficult places" refers to the eight difficult places; "These are the places where foolish people are [born]" refers to the non-Buddhist paths and heterodox practices. "Meaningless speech" refers to flattering words used in order to please people. The remaining lines can be understood.

The fifth part, from "When those bodhisattvas had heard this explanation," shows the bodhisattvas of the upper regions praising the great beings who transform [living beings] in this world. The sixth part, from "Vimalakīrti said," gives Vimalakīrti's expression of affirmation for those bodhisattvas' praise. He says that one lifetime of transforming beings and bringing them benefits here [in the land of Śākyamuni], by means of the ten virtuous *dharma*s, surely surpasses one hundred thousand *kalpa*s of [lifetimes of] practice in that [Multitude of Fragrances world]. This has three parts. The first is the straightforward statement. The second, from "Therefore, in a single lifetime," is the actual description of why the merits of transforming [beings in other worlds] are not like [the merits of transforming beings in] this [world]. The third part, from "Why is this?", lists the ten virtuous [*dhar-* 61a *ma*s] and explains them. As for the ten virtuous [*dharma*s], the six perfections comprise six, liberation from the eight difficulties is the seventh, the Mahayana Dharma is the eighth, the various virtuous roots are the ninth, and the four means of attraction are the tenth.

The seventh part is from "Those bodhisattvas said" and shows the bodhisattvas of the upper region asking that if the hindrances and difficulties of this world are as numerous as Vimalakīrti said, what path do the bodhisattvas [here] practice in order to escape their transgressions and be born in a pure land? The eighth part, from "Vimalakīrti said," is Vimalakīrti's answer that there are eight *dharma*s. If the bodhisattvas here cultivate these *dharma*s, they are able to escape their transgressions and attain birth in their pure land. This itself has two parts. The first is the summary reply; the second, from "What is the reason?", lists the eight *dharma*s.

"They benefit sentient beings yet do not desire rewards. They take on various sufferings and afflictions in place of all sentient beings." This is great compassion. "They give all the merit they have produced to others." This is great kindness. These two together constitute the first *dharma*. "[The bodhisattvas] are impartial to sentient beings, humble and without obstruction" is the second [*dharma*]. "They regard all bodhisattvas as if they were buddhas" is the third [*dharma*]. "They have no doubts when they hear sutras [they have] not heard before" is the fourth [*dharma*]. "They are not in opposition to the *śrāvaka*s" is the fifth [*dharma*]. "They are not jealous of the offerings [received] by others and they are not boastful of their own gains; their minds are disciplined in these matters" is the sixth [*dharma*]. "They always reflect upon their own transgressions and do not speak of others' shortcomings" is the seventh [*dharma*]. "Singlemindedly they always seek the various merits" is the eighth [*dharma*].

From "When Vimalakīrti and Mañjuśrī explained this Dharma" is the second major division [of this chapter], describing the benefits attained by the great assembly.

Chapter Eleven

Practices of the Bodhisattva

In this chapter the Buddha explains to the bodhisattvas of the Multitude of Fragrances [world] the "practices of the bodhisattva" [in this world]; thus the title of the chapter.

From this chapter up to where it says "and all of the assembly saw it" in [the chapter] "Seeing Akṣobhya Buddha" is the second part of the main teaching, wherein [Vimalakīrti] goes to Āmrapālī and, together with the Buddha, explains the bodhisattvas' many and various profound practices, corroborating the teaching given in Vimalakīrti's room. The reason for this is that what was taught in the previous six chapters were all the essential practices, yet it is difficult to believe and accept. Vimalakīrti's essence is inconceivable, yet in the manifestation of one incarnation he appeared the same as a worldly layman who was a disciple [of the Buddha]. Perhaps the confused would see his form and not entirely believe his teachings. Therefore, when the affairs in Vimalakīrti's room were finished, he went to Āmrapālī and sought recognition from the ultimate person. Together with the Buddha they explained the bodhisattvas' many and various profound practices and corroborated the teaching given in Vimalakīrti's room, thereby causing beings to give rise to belief.

One interpretation has it that the main body of this scripture consists solely of that which was taught in Vimalakīrti's room. Therefore, from this chapter onward we have entered the dissemination of the teachings, because it takes place outside of Vimalakīrti's room. However, we will not follow [that interpretation] here.

This chapter unfolds in six main parts. The first, from the beginning up to "this auspicious sign," describes how auspicious signs appeared in Āmrapālī before [Vimalakīrti] visited the Buddha. The second, from "Thereupon, Vimala-kīrti said to Mañjuśrī," is the actual [description] of how they went together to the Buddha and paid their respects. The third part, from "At that time Ānanda spoke to the Buddha, saying," is a response to Ānanda's question about the fragrant scent, and straightaway shows that the power of the fragrant food [eaten by the bodhisattvas] is able to benefit beings. The fourth part, from "Ānanda spoke to the Buddha, saying, 'This is unprecedented!'", has the Buddha, in response to Ānanda's praise, extensively describing how the work of a buddha is not the same [in different buddha lands]. The fifth part, from "The bodhisattvas who enter these gates," is an attack on the bodhisattvas of the upper regions delivered to Ānanda. The sixth part, from "At that time, the bodhisattvas who had come from the Multitude of Fragrances world" to the end of the chapter, describes the bodhisattvas of the upper region requesting [the Buddha] to teach the Dharma and thereafter returning to their palace.

The first part, the appearance of auspicious signs, itself has three parts. The first is the appearance of the auspicious signs. The second part is Ānanda asking the Buddha the reason [for the appearance] of the auspicious signs. The third part is the Buddha's answer. These can be understood.

The second part, going to the Buddha and paying him respect, has two further aspects. The first is going to the Buddha and paying him respect. The second, from "Thereupon, the World-honored One," is the Tathāgata making the customary greetings and inquiries. The first aspect, paying respect [to the Buddha], has three parts. The first is Vimalakīrti exclaiming that they should go; the second is Mañjuśrī's exclamation in response; the third is actually going to pay their respects—these can all be understood.

"Now is exactly the right time [to visit the Buddha]" refers to the time when the spiritual capacity of beings and the transformative teachings are in accord with each other.

The second aspect, the Buddha's greeting and inquiries, is further divided into three parts. The first is his greeting; the second is the Buddha asking Śāriputra whether or not he has seen [what Vimalakīrti has done]; the third is Śāriputra's reply that he has seen it—again, these can be understood.

The third part, occasioned by Ānanda's inquiry about the fragrant scent, straightaway explains the power of the fragrant food to benefit beings; this further unfolds in seven parts. The first is Ānanda asking the Buddha what fragrance [he smells]. The second is the Buddha's immediate reply that it is the fragrance from the pores of the bodhisattvas. The third is Śāriputra telling Ānanda that their pores also emit this fragrance. The fourth is Ānanda asking where the fragrance comes from. The fifth is Śāriputra's reply. The sixth is Ānanda asking Vimalakīrti how long the power of the fragrance and the food would last. The seventh is Vimalakīrti's answer. These can be understood.

The reply concerning the power of the food has three parts. The first gives a reply about [how long the food] will benefit the body; the second, from "If a *śrāvaka* [. . . eats this food]," makes a reply about [how the food] will benefit the path; the third, from "It is like taking medicine," gives a metaphor as a concluding reply. If you investigate the text this can all be understood.

That the energy [from the food] will be depleted after seven days refers to the ordinary nature of food. "Entering the stage of certainty" refers to the inner ranks of ordinary disciples. "Mental liberation" refers to the fruits of arhatship. "Generated the intention" refers to those of the Mahayana attaining the inner ranks of the ordinary disciples. "Serene acceptance of non-arising" refers to the seventh stage. "The place of but [one more birth]" refers to the tenth stage.

The third part, the conclusion, opens [with a metaphor] and closes [by bringing the metaphor to bear on the issue at hand]; these can be understood.

Question: Is the fragrance from the pores of the bodhisattvas of the upper regions and the fragrance from Śāriputra's body [the same] fragrance or are they different? If they are [the same], then what is the Buddha's intention in praising [only] the bodhisattvas of the upper regions [when Ānanda asked what the fragrance was]? If they are different, what fragrance does Ānanda now smell? 61c

Interpretation: The fragrance is essentially one fragrance. There are two [reasons] that the Buddha only mentioned the bodhisattvas of the upper region here. The first is that the bodhisattvas of the upper region are the source of the fragrant food. The second is that [the Buddha] wants Śāriputra himself to reveal his own merit, and thereby cause the great assembly to arouse the mind [of *bodhi*].

Another question: When the bodhisattvas of the Multitude of Fragrances [world] were about to come [to this world], the Buddha Accumulated Fragrances gave them three injunctions. The first was to withdraw the fragrance of their bodies; the second was to leave behind their true form; the third was to not harbor feelings of disdain [for the denizens of this world]. However, what was the fragrance they were enjoined [to withdraw]? If it was their original fragrance, then the fact that there was a fragrance coming from the pores [of their bodies] at that time would mean that the bodhisattvas of the Multitude of Fragrances [world] had acted against their buddha's injunction.

There are two explanations. One has it that [the fragrance that the Buddha] prohibited here was an aroma that gives rise to mental afflictions, not a fragrance that causes one to enter the Way. Hence, in accord with that instruction, those fragrances that give rise to mental afflictions were withdrawn and not released. However, when the Buddha gave his injunctions, he simply said, "Withdraw the fragrances of your bodies." He did not distinguish the two [types] of fragrance. Moreover, how could it be that the bodhisattvas of the upper region have a fragrance that gives rise to mental afflictions? For these reasons we do not use this explanation.

Another interpretation has it that the fragrance is essentially the same fragrance [that causes one to] enter the Way. However, there is an appropriate time for [that fragrance] to be released and [a time for it] to be withheld. If [the bodhisattvas] had released their bodily fragrances before the great assembly had eaten the fragrant food, perhaps the beings might have given rise to attachment or heterodox views. Hence the injunction to withdraw [their fragrance]. Now, however, the great assembly has already eaten the fragrant food and each of them saw their own benefit and generated the aspiration for the Way. Therefore, in accordance with what is appropriate, [their bodily fragrances] were released and revealed together with the deeds of that buddha. All of this was in accord with the Buddha's original intentions—how could this be acting against the injunction of that buddha?

From "Ānanda spoke to the Buddha, saying, ['This is unprecedented!']" is the fourth part of this chapter, which shows the Tathāgata, in response to Ānanda's praise, extensively describing how the work of a buddha is not the same [in different buddha lands]. This is further divided into two parts. The first initially describes using what is right to penetrate what is right. The second, from "Ānanda, there are four Māras," gives the [example of a] wrong that leads to penetration of what is right to actually demonstrate the point that the practice of what is wrong leads to penetration of the Way of the Buddha, as discussed earlier in the chapter "The Way of the Buddha." Both have conclusions that can be understood. Thirteen things are given in the list of virtuous [things that constitute the work of buddhas in different lands]. These items are given in other commentaries and we won't record them here.

From "The bodhisattvas who enter these gates" is the fifth part of the chapter, an attack on the bodhisattvas of the upper regions delivered to Ānanda; this has three parts. The first is the initial admonishment of the bodhisattvas of the upper region, [telling them] to not harbor thoughts of superiority and inferiority. This describes how the bodhisattvas who enter these gates do not become happy even if they see purity, nor are they unhappy if they see impurity—they simply rejoice over the unprecedented [work] of the various buddhas. The [merits] of the buddhas are impartial and without duality; it is only for the sake of transforming beings that they manifest different [buddha] lands. All of the bodhisattvas of the upper regions likewise should not harbor thoughts of superiority about their [worlds] nor of the inferiority of this [world].

The second part, from "Ānanda, look [at the various buddha lands]," 62a gives Ānanda the two metaphors of land and space, and explains that the merits and discerning awareness are equal and without duality.

The third part, from "Ānanda said to the Buddha," is occasioned by Ānanda's reply that [the discerning awareness spoken of by the Buddha] is not within his sphere. That is to say, it explains that matters such as those [of which the Buddha has spoken] are only able to be attained and realized by bodhisattvas. This also corroborates Kāśyapa's lamentation regarding the severing of his capacity, which took place above in the chapter "The Way of the Buddha"—in regard to the path of the Tathāgata, these words are like dried-up seeds [for non-bodhisattvas].

From "At that time, the bodhisattvas who had come from the Multitude of Fragrances [world]" to the end of the chapter is the sixth part, showing the bodhisattvas from the Multitude of Fragrances [world] requesting the Dharma and returning to their palaces; this further unfolds in three parts. The first part, from the beginning up to "[bestow upon us a little of your Dharma so that when we return to that other world] we will remember the Tathāgata," shows them repenting their error and requesting the Dharma. The second, from "The Buddha said to those bodhisattvas," shows the Buddha explaining the Dharma for them. The third, from "When those bodhisattvas [heard the explanation of this Dharma]," shows the bodhisattvas of the Multitude of Fragrances [world] receiving the teaching and returning to their palaces.

With regard to the repentance of their transgression, however, they should have repented [the transgression] of all three injunctions [that they received from the Buddha Accumulated Fragrances]. Why did they only repent the error of generating thoughts of the inferiority [of this world]? Since they did not transgress the injunctions regarding their lovely fragrance and appearance they repented only of their thoughts of inferiority [about this world]. Moreover, when Śākyamuni had earlier criticized them he struck only at their [thoughts] of superiority and inferiority. Therefore, although there were transgressions and non-transgressions, they repented the errors they made with regard to the orders [they had received from the Buddha Accumulated Fragrances].

From "The Buddha said to those bodhisattvas" is the second part, the Buddha explaining the Dharma for them. This has four parts. The first is straightaway teaching them about the two kinds of Dharma gates of the exhaustible and the inexhaustible, saying, "You should study them." The "conditioned" are the perceptual attributes, therefore they are called "exhaustible."

The "unconditioned" is devoid of perceptual attributes, hence it is called "inexhaustible." The second part is from "What is it?" (i.e., the exhaustible). This gives the essential attributes of the exhaustible and the inexhaustible. The third is from "Like a bodhisattva, [one should neither exhaust the conditioned nor abide in the unconditioned]"; this is instruction on practice. The fourth is from "What does it mean to not exhaust the conditioned?" and explains the perceptual attributes of not exhausting and not abiding. The first three can be understood. The fourth part, though—the explanation of not exhausting and not abiding—has three parts. The first explains not exhausting the conditioned in terms of the gate of merits, and the second explains not abiding in the unconditioned in terms of the gate of discerning awareness. [The third concludes with an explanation of the two gates of merit and discerning awareness together.]

How, then, is merit distinguished from discerning awareness? "Merit" is the shared name for the ten thousand practices. "Discerning awareness" is the profound designation for penetrating the underlying principle. Within existence there is the illumination of the object and realization of right and wrong—thus it is called skillful means and belongs to the gate of merit. Investigating "not exhausting and not abiding," however, we find only exhortations to practice [in the realm of] existence. It has already been said that bodhisattvas contemplate emptiness and attain the eradication of entanglements. For bodhisattvas the two practices of emptiness and existence are like the two wings of a bird. Why, then, do we find only an exhortation about practice [in the realm of] existence?

Explanation: In the underlying principle things are just as they are. Followers of the two vehicles, however, only take emptiness as realization, and abandon the transformation of beings within [the realm of] existence. Hence this explains that physically remaining in samsara and transforming beings with impartiality is the buddha-mind. This is also the highest among prac-   62b
tices—therefore it is exhorted. That [the two practices of emptiness and existence] are like the two wings of a bird means that one is illuminated within the gate of discerning awareness. Within this teaching, however, it is all great beings that physically remain within samsara, serenely accept suffering, and save beings. This shows that the meaning is the same as the teaching on comforting and instructing [bodhisattvas who are ill] and disciplining [the mind, further] corroborating the teaching that was given in Vimalakīrti's room.

"Kindness" and "compassion" are the root of the bodhisattva's transformation of others, so they are listed first. "Generating the mind" to seek the "omniscience" of buddhahood is the root of one's own practice, hence it cannot be forgotten. The remaining lines can be understood.

"Do not belittle the unlearned or respect the learned as buddhas." To be kind to those below and respect those above is the great truth of heaven. For this reason, the non-Buddhist *Laozi* also says, "nonvirtuous people are the students of virtuous people. If you don't love your students or value your teachers—even if you are knowledgeable, you will be greatly confused." Again, the *Book* [*of History*] says, "When I look at everything under heaven, [any one of] the simple men and women may surpass me at some skill." So too, the *Hundred Verses* say, "The single virtue of a foolish person is the teacher of the knowledgeable." These four sayings differ slightly in expression but their meaning is the same: that is to say, it is clear that pride is the worst of evils.

"One will not be attached to one's own pleasure" means to not hold up one's own merits but only extol [other] people's virtues. Desiring to transform beings, one will "see samsara as a garden." Bestowing the Dharma upon people will return to benefit [the one who is teaching], therefore it says "[see those that come seeking] with the notion that they are excellent teachers." Not only giving the Dharma but [giving] material goods and food is also like this. "Perfecting one's own buddha land with the adornments of the numerous pure realms" means that cultivating the cause [of the pure land] like those other [buddhas] will perfect one's own buddha land.

"Remaining courageous of mind throughout countless *kalpa*s of samsara" is to say that one does not dislike or grow tired of dwelling in suffering and transforming beings. If you are not pure yourself, then you are not able to transform beings; therefore you must first free yourself from the triple world.

There are two understandings of "One will always seek the discerning awareness of no-thought." [The first] takes it that it says "no-thought" because when you are in the eighth level and above you have escaped the three retrogressions. The second says that the unafflicted mind is devoid of perceptual attribute and so all of the activity regarding objects is called "no-thought."

"One will have few desires [for the *dharma*s of the world], knowing what is sufficient." This is to say: don't exceed your lot. The non-Buddhist *Laozi* says, "No disaster is as great as not knowing what is sufficient; no fault is as extreme as the desire to attain" and "Knowing what is sufficient, there will be no humiliation; knowing when to stop, there will be no danger." Further, the *Spring and Autumn Annals* say, "Although the whip is long, it doesn't reach the horse's belly."

"Not rejecting worldly *dharma*s" is saying that even though you may be accomplished, do not go against the world or set yourself apart. This is the meaning of the saying in the non-Buddhist *Lunyu,* "Humble words, bold actions."

"Not going against rules of conduct" refers to the rules of conduct of the Way; it means to teach beings and enable them to receive heavenly rewards. It can also mean to manifest as Lord Brahmā and request the Buddha to preach the Dharma.

From "What does it mean to say that the bodhisattva does not dwell in the unconditioned?" explains not dwelling in the unconditioned in regard to the practice of discerning awareness. Followers of the two vehicles contemplate impermanence and enter nirvana, but bodhisattvas are not like that.

From "Further, to be complete in virtue [and merit]" is the third part, 62c the concluding explanation that brings together the two gates of merit and discerning awareness. This has three further parts. The first is the concluding explanation of the two gates of merit and discerning awareness. The next is a concluding explanation with regard to self-cultivation and the transformation of others: "Accumulating the myriad Dharma jewels, [the bodhisattva does not dwell in the unconditioned]." The third part, from "Good sirs, [bodhisattvas who cultivate the Dharma in this way,]" is the concluding exhortation to study rigorously; this can be understood.

From "When those bodhisattvas [heard the explanation of this Dharma]" is the third part, [in which the bodhisattvas of the Multitude of Fragrances world] receive the teaching and return to their palaces.

Chapter Twelve

Seeing Akṣobhya Buddha

This chapter gets its name because [the Buddha] enables the assembly to see the realm [of Akṣobhya Buddha]. If, however, we name the chapter according to the text, it could also be called "The Chapter on Contemplating the Tathāgata's Body." Here, though, the title is taken from the benefits attained, and so it is called the chapter "Seeing Akṣobhya Buddha."

As was explained above, from the beginning of this chapter up to "[the Wondrous Joy world returned to its original place] and all of the assembly saw it" is part of the main teaching. From "The Buddha said to Śāriputra, ['Did you see this Wondrous Joy world?']" at the end of this chapter belongs to [the third part of the scripture,] the dissemination [of the teachings].

[This chapter] unfolds in four parts. The first, from the beginning up to "If it is another vision, then it is called a false vision," shows that the Buddha's body is devoid of perceptual attributes and cannot be seen. The second part is from "Thereupon Śāriputra asked Vimalakīrti, ['Where did you die that you came to be born here?']." Following on Śāriputra's question to Vimala-kīrti regarding his place of origin, this part [of the text] further shows that the underlying principle is essentially without birth and extinction, thereby banishing the entanglements and attachment of beings. The third part is from "Then the Buddha said to Śāriputra." The Tathāgata shows that although there is no birth or death within the underlying principle, in the path of the conventional truth there is yet birth and death; for this reason he explains Vimalakīrti's place of origin. The fourth part, occasioned by the great assembly's respectful longing, is from "At that time the great assembly longed [to see the Wondrous Joy world]," wherein [the Buddha] actually enables them to see Vimalakīrti's original realm.

Now, the first part shows that the Dharma body is devoid of perceptual attributes and cannot be seen. The reason that this question comes up is found at the beginning of the previous chapter, "Practices of the Bodhisattva," where Vimalakīrti says to Mañjuśrī that they should go together to see the

Buddha. The great assembly did not know that within the underlying principle there is no buddha that can be seen. They also did not understand the meaning of the essence and its manifestation. Seeing the manifestation, they think that there truly is a buddha's body, just like they are now seeing. For this reason, Vimalakīrti's explanation is now used to show that the Buddha's body is devoid of perceptual attributes and cannot be seen; he produces all sorts of negations in order to banish beings' confusion [stemming from their] attachment to the manifestation and confusion about the essence.

The Buddha asks Vimalakīrti with what sort of perceptual attributes he wants to view the Tathāgata. There are three parts to Vimalakīrti's answer. The first is his immediate reply that the profound essence is devoid of perceptual attributes and cannot be seen. The second, from "[When] I contemplate [the Tathāgata]," gives specific explanations of [various] objects in regard to which [the Tathāgata] cannot be seen. The third part is the conclusion that [the Tathāgata] cannot be seen. This has the immediate purpose of explaining that the Dharma body is devoid of perceptual attributes and cannot be seen; more remotely, it corroborates the earlier chapter "Contemplating Sentient Beings." Why? Because the Buddha and Vimalakīrti are already masters of the Dharma; he is also a person of the singular ultimate. It is clear that beings transformed [by them] are empty, just as they too are empty.

63a

"As I view the true attributes of my own body, so too do I view the Buddha." This takes the emptiness of one's own body as comparable to the profound essence of the Buddha; the Dharma body is also like this—that is, devoid of perceptual attributes and unable to be seen. Within this there are four interpretations of the Dharma body. The first says that it is the permanently abiding body. The reason is that, although [in the overall time frame of the dissemination of the Buddha's teachings] this sutra comes before [sutras such as the *Mahāparinirvāṇa-sūtra* that explain the] "permanence" [of the Dharma body, and so on], the main body of the sutra consists only of the six chapters that were taught while in Vimalakīrti's room. There is nothing wrong with explaining permanence in the introductory section and the dissemination section. The second interpretation says that this sutra has not yet explained "permanently abiding"; this is the seven hundred incalculable bodies [produced by buddhas in order to liberate beings]. "Devoid of perceptual attributes and unable to be seen" refers to the underlying principle being without perceptual attribute. Now, if the underlying principle were not devoid of perceptual attributes, then, although [the Dharma body] is permanent, [it would appear to be] impermanent. What cannot be seen is the permanent Dharma of the Dharma body—it is not speaking of permanently abiding.

The third interpretation does not distinguish between the introduction, main section, and dissemination sections [of the sutra]. [This interpretation] simply says that this sutra, in short, explains "permanently abiding." Hence, although the outer level of the text appears to be about the underlying principle being devoid of perceptual attributes, the inner meaning points to the permanently abiding Dharma body. However, one might then wonder, why speak about [the nature of] the underlying principle?—in short, why would only this sutra explain the meaning of permanence when it has already been raised in earlier sutras? The fourth interpretation says that this sutra has already explained that the body of the Master of Transformation, [that is, the Buddha who transforms sentient beings,] is eternally abiding. However, the [sutras that teach the] meaning of the One Vehicle and the true cause have not yet been disclosed.

From "When I contemplate [the Tathāgata]" is the second part, specific explanations of objects in regard to which [the Tathāgata] cannot be seen. This has three parts. The first is the initial explanation [that the Tathāgata] cannot be seen with regard to the triple world. The second, from "I do not contemplate [the Tathāgata] as form," explains that [the Tathāgata] cannot be seen with regard to the five *skandha*s. The third part, from "[The Tathāgata] does not arise from the four elements," uses all kinds of negations to show that [the Tathāgata] cannot be seen. All of these [various arguments] show that the essence of [the Tathāgata] cannot be seen, and serve to dispel attachment to his manifestation and the confusion that the essence is simply this [manifestation]. Another interpretation says that from "When I contemplate [the Tathāgata]" up to "I do not contemplate him as the nature of consciousness" shows that the response body cannot be seen. From "[The Tathāgata] does not arise from the four elements" shows that the true body [of the Tathāgata] cannot be seen.

In "[When I contemplate the Tathāgata, he does not come in the past,]" "past" means "not yet come."

If these verses explain "not able to be seen" in regard to ultimate truth, then it means that ultimate truth is like this—that is, it cannot be seen. If it explains "not able to be seen" in regard to the absence of perceptual attributes of the profound essence, then it also means that the Dharma body, the profound essence, is also like this, as is Dharma.

"This shore" refers to samsara; "that shore" refers to nirvana; "the stream in between" refers to the factors of the path.

From "Thereupon Śāriputra asked Vimalakīrti, ['Where did you die that you came to be born here?']" is the second part [of this chapter]. Occasioned by Śāriputra's question to Vimalakīrti regarding his place of origin, this part [of the explanation] further shows that the underlying principle is essentially without birth and death, thereby banishing beings' doubt and attachment. This is so because within the explanation of the Buddha's body, Vimalakīrti has already said that he contemplates the Buddha's body as devoid of perceptual attributes, unable to be seen; just as in contemplating his own body the true attributes cannot be seen. This causes beings to doubt—if [Vimalakīrti's] own body is empty and cannot be seen, how is it that he has now personally taken birth and lives as a layman? Therefore, it is explained here that the essence of the underlying principle is without birth or death. Although this provisional explanation thus teaches that there is birth and death, bodhisattvas are born solely for the sake of transforming beings; they are not born because of karmic entanglements.

63b

Although this is the immediate context, more remotely this corroborates the point in the earlier chapter "Contemplating Sentient Beings," regarding the goddess's [discussion of the] the non-fixed existence of birth and death. That is, above the goddess simply states that there is no birth or death and so here, in the presence of the Buddha, Vimalakīrti is depicted as corroborating [the earlier teaching] that there is no birth or death. Although this provisional explanation thus teaches that there is birth and extinction, bodhisattvas are born solely for the sake of responding [to the needs of beings]; it is not because of karmic entanglements that they take birth and die.

The second part of this is the actual explanation that the essence of the underlying principle is without birth and death; this also has two parts. The first shows that there is neither birth nor death through a series of questions and answers about *dharmas*; the second part shows that there is neither birth nor death through a series of questions and answers about a simile. These can be understood.

From "Then the Buddha [said to Śāriputra]" is the third part. The Tathāgata shows that although there is no birth or death within the underlying principle, the conventional is not without [birth and death]; for this reason he
reveals [Vimalakīrti's place of] origin. This has three parts: the first is the
Tathāgata's actual revelation of [Vimalakīrti's place of] origin; the second is
Śāriputra's exclamation that [what the Buddha revealed to him] was unprecedented; the third part is the two exchanges of questions and answers between
Vimalakīrti and Śāriputra, which show that although the conventional is not
without birth and death, the birth of a bodhisattva is a birth only in response
[to the needs of sentient beings] and is not due to karmic entanglements.

From "At that time the great assembly longed [to see the Wondrous Joy
world]" is the fourth part of this chapter, wherein in response to the longing
of the great assembly, [Vimalakīrti] enables them to see [his place of] origin. Although this is the immediate reason [for showing them the Wondrous
Joy world], more remotely it corroborates the teaching given above in the
chapter "The Inconceivable."

[This section of the chapter] has four parts: the first is the Buddha direct-
ing [Vimalakīrti] to let [the assembly] see [the Wondrous Joy world]; the second is Vimalakīrti receiving [the Buddha's] directive and enabling [the assem-
bly] to see [the Wondrous Joy world]; the third is the Buddha exhorting the
great assembly to arouse the intention [to attain such a pure buddha land]; the
fourth is [the Wondrous Joy world] returning to its original place. The third
part, exhorting [the assembly] to arouse [the intention to attain such a pure
buddha land], is divided into three. The first is the direct exhortation; the second is the great assembly arousing the intention; the third is the Tathāgata
bestowing a prediction [of their future birth in that buddha land]; these can
be understood. This is where the attainment of benefits [by the assembly]
stops; hence we know that this is where the main teaching ends.

From "The Buddha asked Śāriputra, 'Do you see the see the realm Wondrous Joy and the Buddha Akṣobhya or not?" is the third major section of
this sutra, the dissemination of the teachings. This section unfolds in two
parts. The first is from here up to the end of the chapter "Dharma Offering,"
and is called the causes and conditions of the dissemination [of the teach-
ings]. The second is the single chapter "Entrustment," and is the actual commission to disseminate [the teachings].

The first part, the causes and conditions [of the dissemination], further unfolds in two parts. The first is from here up to "That is to make offerings to the buddhas of the past, present, and future" in the chapter "Dharma Offering," and consists of the actual praise of this sutra. Those [who accept and cultivate this sutra] will be honored [as though they were buddhas], and the places [where this sutra is found] will be valued as places [in which the Tathāgata is present]. The merit of those who receive and hold [this sutra] will be profound, and the rewards of those who disseminate [this sutra] will be great. Hence those who would disseminate [this sutra] are encouraged and sought out.

The second part is from "Heavenly Emperor, suppose this trimegachiliocosm [were filled with Tathāgatas]" in the chapter "Dharma Offering" up to the end of that chapter. This part explains how giving material wealth and offerings of great measure are not as worthy as an offering of the Dharma.

63c   The first part, the actual praise of this sutra, also has two parts. The first is Śāriputra's praise, which ends the chapter ["Seeing Akṣobhya Buddha"]. The second is Indra's praise; this is from the beginning of the chapter "Dharma Offering" up to "That is to make offerings to the buddhas of the past, present, and future."

The first part, Śāriputra's praise, has five further divisions. The first is the Buddha asking Śāriputra whether or not he saw [the buddha realm Wondrous Joy and the Buddha Akṣobhya]. The reason he asked this is because he thereby wished [Śāriputra] to praise what he had seen and to explain the dissemination [of this sutra]. The second is the direct answer, "Yes, I saw them." The third, from "World-honored One, I wish to make [all sentient beings attain such a pure land]," is [Śāriputra's] aspiration. The fourth division, from "World-honored One, we [have quickly attained wonderful benefits]," praises the people who spread this sutra—the Dharma is spread by people, thus they are praised. The fifth, from "Those sentient beings [who hear this sutra]," is the actual praise of the sutra.

The [fifth division] has two further sections: the first generally explains the profound merit obtained through the seven factors [of hearing, believing, understanding, accepting, holding, reading, and reciting] this sutra. The second section is from "If those who get hold [of this scripture]" and separately enumerates the light and heavy attributes of the rewards [obtained by those who receive this sutra]. This has six lines: the first line explains [the benefit] of receiving [this sutra]; the second, from "If one reads and recites [this scripture]," explains the profound attainment; the third, from "If one makes offerings [to such a person]," shows that such a person will be honored [as though a buddha]. The fourth line, from "If one copies and preserves [these sutra scrolls]," shows that the places [where this sutra] is found will be valued as places [in which the Tathāgata is present]; the fifth, from "If one hears this sutra," shows that the merit from becoming joyful [upon hearing this sutra] is profound; the sixth corroborates the above lines by saying that [understanding] even a small [portion of this scripture will lead to a prediction of future awakening].

Chapter Thirteen

Dharma Offering

This chapter describes the seeking, joyous, and sagely minds of those who disseminate this Dharma; hence the title of the chapter.

From the beginning of the chapter up to "That is, to make offerings to the buddhas of the past, present, and future" is Indra's praise, which is the second of the actual praises of this sutra. This section unfolds in four further parts: the first is the initial praise of the Dharma that is disseminated; it shows that the attributes of the underlying principle are definitive, clear, and leave nothing to be questioned. The second part is from "According to my understanding of the Buddha" and explains the attributes of the meritorious rewards of the seven factors [of hearing, believing, understanding, accepting, holding, reading, and reciting] this scripture. The third part, from "World-honored One," describes the vow to protect those who disseminate the sutra. The fourth, from "The Buddha said, 'Excellent, [excellent,]'" is the Tathāgata's expression of affirmation [of what Indra had said].

The first part can be understood.

From "Heavenly Emperor, suppose this trimegachiliocosm [were filled with Tathāgatas]" is the second part of the conditions of the dissemination [of this sutra], explaining how giving material wealth and making offerings of great amount is not as [worthy as] offering the Dharma. This unfolds in two parts. The first, from the beginning up to "Because of these causes and conditions the blessings are immeasurable," shows how an actual great measure of material offerings is not [the same as] an offering of the Dharma. The second part, from "The Buddha said to the Heavenly Emperor, 'In the past'", cites [an example] from the past in order to corroborate the present.

The first part, [describing] great amounts [of material offerings], has three further parts. The first shows the Buddha giving [an example of] a great measure [of material offering] and asking the Heavenly Emperor [whether such an offering would generate great merit]. The second part, from "Śakra Devānām Indra said," shows Indra's response. The third, from "The Buddha said to the Heavenly Emperor," is the conclusion.

The second part, citing the past and corroborating the present, unfolds in three parts. The first actually cites the events of the past. The second, from "Heavenly Emperor, was not King Jeweled Canopy of that time [an unusual person]?", ties together the past and the present.

The third part, from "Thus, Heavenly Emperor, should you know [what is essential]," is the concluding exhortation.

The first part, actually citing the events of the past, has three sections. The first starts off by giving the essential nature of a Dharma offering. The second, from "The Buddha [Medicine King] said, 'Good son, [the profound sutras explained by all the buddhas are the Dharma offering,']" actually gives the essential nature of the Dharma that is offered. The third is from "The Buddha said to the Heavenly Emperor, ['When Prince Moon Canopy heard this Dharma from Medicine King Buddha,']" and explains the rewards and benefits [of hearing this Dharma].

The first section can be understood. However, the second section, giving the essential nature of the Dharma that is offered, has two parts. The first is the initial presentation of the essential nature of the Dharma. The second, from "If one hears such sutras as this," describes the attributes of the offering. Another interpretation says that from the beginning up to "[Heavenly beings (*devas*), dragons (*nāgas*), spirits (*pretas*), and heavenly musicians (*ghandarvas*)] join together to praise them" gives the actual essential nature of the Dharma, and from "They enable sentient beings [to sit in the site of awakening]" gives the function [of a Dharma offering]; this [interpretation] is also acceptable.

"Difficult to believe, difficult to receive" means that it is not possible for the mind of an ordinary person to attain [this teaching]. "It cannot be attained solely through discriminating [thinking]" means that it cannot be known solely through the discrimination of discerning awareness; it is necessary to cultivate merit in order to assist in obtaining [these profound sutras]. One interpretation says that the underlying principle of the sutras is profound and subtle and cannot be attained by a discriminating mind. "They are contained in the Dharma storehouse of the bodhisattvas" means that the sutras include the Mahayana Dharma storehouse of the bodhisattvas. "*Dhāraṇī*" refers to "total retention," meaning that the sutras are sealed with the seal of total retention. They will not be forgotten and there will be no retrogression up through [completing] the six perfections. One interpretation says that from this point everything describes [the sutra's] benefit to beings. It shows that the inner minds of beings are sealed with the seal that is devoid of perceptual attributes, which causes them to not forget, to attain [the level of] nonretrogression, and to accomplish the six perfections.

"They well discrminate the meaning and are in accord with the Dharma of *bodhi*" praises the deeds of the profound sutras. One interpretation has it that this means that [the sutras] cause beings to be that way, [that is, able to well discriminate the meaning and be in accord with the Dharma of *bodhi*]. "Supreme among the host of sutras" means that the *vaipulya* [sutras that were] taught during a twelve-year period are supreme within the Tripiṭaka. "They enter great kindness and great compassion" praises the sutra for entering into great kindness and great compassion. One interpretation says that [this means that the sutras] cause practitioners to enter into great kindness and great compassion.

"They cut off the affairs of the hosts of Māras and various false views" praises the profound sutras for eliminating various wrongs. One interpretation says that [this means that] all are transformed and made to enter into the Way. "In accord with the Dharma of cause and condition" means that *dharmas* arise from cause and condition; thus they are without self-nature.

"Without self, sentient beings, or life span" is a provisional designation for emptiness. "[These sutras teach] emptiness, the absence of perceptual attributes, wishlessness, and non-production." This refers to the emptiness of real *dharmas*; it means that the profound sutras are in accord with the underlying principle of emptiness, devoid of perceptual attributes. One interpretation has it that [this means that these sutras] cause beings to understand this underlying principle.

From "Enables sentient beings [to sit in the site of awakening]" is the second part, explaining the function [of a Dharma offering]. That is to say, what function does the essential nature [of a Dharma offering] possess? It has the function of greatly benefiting beings.

From "If one hears such [sutras] as this" is the second part, describing the attributes of a [Dharma] offering. This has two further parts. The first is

64b   the initial explanation of the attributes with regard to the merit of the seven factors [of hearing, believing, understanding, accepting, holding, reading, and reciting this sutra]. Believing and cultivating these seven factors [with regard to this sutra] is what is called a Dharma offering. The second part, from "Further, [when one cultivates] the various *dharmas* [as taught]," explains the attributes with regard to what is attained when one practices in accordance with what has been taught. That is to say, it is not only the merit of practicing the seven factors that constitutes a Dharma offering. If you are further able to practice, as has been taught [in these scriptures], to understand cause and condition, the provisional and the true, the two kinds of emptiness [of self and phenomena], and you are also not confused with regard to the referents of the four reliances, and moreover put an end to all actions and volitions—"this is called a supreme Dharma offering."

"Relying on the meaning, not relying on the language" means to rely on the meaning of impermanence and not to rely on the language of permanence of the non-Buddhist paths. "Relying on knowing, and not relying on [differentiating] consciousness" means to rely on the knowledge of impermanence and not to rely on the false knowledge of permanence of the non-Buddhist paths. "Relying on the scriptures of definitive meaning, and not relying on the scriptures of non-definitive meaning" means to rely on those teachings that explain impermanence and not to rely on the teachings that explain permanence as found in the non-Buddhist paths. "Relying on the Dharma and not relying on the person" means to rely on the Dharma of impermanence and not to rely on those who teach the permanence of the non-Buddhist paths.

From "The Buddha said to the Heavenly Emperor, ['When Prince Moon Canopy heard this Dharma from Medicine King Buddha']" is the third part of the actual explanation of past matters, explaining the benefits attained when they heard about the Dharma offering. This has four parts. The first explains repaying the kindness for hearing this Dharma. The second, from "He spoke to the Buddha, saying, ['World-honored One, after the extinction of the Tathāgata,']" is [Prince Moon Canopy] making a vow to protect [the Dharma] and requesting [the Buddha's assistance]. The third part is from "The Buddha knew his thoughts" and shows the Tathāgata bestowing a prediction [of Prince Moon Canopy's ability to defend the Dharma in the future].

The fourth part, from "[The Buddha told the] Heavenly Emperor," is the actual description of the benefits [that Prince Moon Canopy] attained. This itself has two parts: the first is the personal benefit of Bhikṣu Moon Canopy; the second, from "Bhikṣu Moon Canopy, [through his defense of the Dharma, diligent practice, and zeal,]" describes the benefit of others.

From "Heavenly Emperor, was not King Jeweled Canopy of that time [an unusual person]?" is the second aspect of citing the past in order to corroborate the present, tying together past and present. From "Thus, Heavenly Emperor, [you should understand what is essential]" is the third part, the concluding exhortation.

Chapter Fourteen

Entrustment

This chapter depicts the Buddha's concerns and his entrustment of [the sutra]; this chapter gets its name because of his concern [and his entrustment of the sutra] to Ānanda.

This is the second aspect of the dissemination of the teaching, the actual commission to disseminate it. This unfolds in three parts: first it is given to Maitreya, next it is given to Ānanda, and finally various people joyfully accept it and put it into practice.

The first part, giving [the sutra] to Maitreya, has four more parts. The first is actually giving [it to Maitreya]. The second is Maitreya's accepting this teaching. The third, from "The Buddha said, 'Excellent, [excellent],'" is the Tathāgata's expression of affirmation [for Maitreya's acceptance]. The fourth part, from "At this, all of the bodhisattvas [put their palms together]," shows the rest of the bodhisattvas also accepting the teaching and making a vow to disseminate it.

The first part, actually giving [the teaching] to Maitreya, is further divided into three sections. The first is the actual bestowal of the sutra. The second, from "Sutras of this sort," is the exhortation to disseminate [the teaching]. The third, from "Maitreya, you should know," explains the errors that will be elim- 64c
inated through the dissemination [of this sutra]. Overall, this deals with an admonishment regarding three categories of two kinds [of bodhisattvas and their understanding of the profound Dharma]; these can be understood.

The second part, Maitreya's acceptance of the teaching, is from "Maitreya Bodhisattva, [upon hearing this teaching]"; this is further divided into three sections. The first is his acceptance of the admonishment to abandon the evils given in the third section above. The second, from "I will maintain the Tathāgata's [Dharma]," is his acceptance of the first aspect, the actual bestowal of the sutra. The third section, from "If, in the future," is his acceptance of the second aspect above, the exhortation to disseminate the teaching.

I will not explicate the third part, that is, the Tathāgata's expression of affirmation.

The fourth part, the rest of the skilled [bodhisattvas] making a vow to disseminate [the teaching], has two parts. The first shows the various bodhisattvas vowing to disseminate [the teaching]. The second depicts the four heavenly kings vowing to protect those who recite the sutra.

From "At that time, the Buddha spoke to Ānanda" is the second part of this chapter, bestowing [this sutra] to Ānanda. This is further divided into three parts. The first is the Buddha giving [it to Ānanda]. The second is [Ānanda's] receiving the teaching and inquiring as to its name. The third part is the Buddha's explaining to him [the name of the sutra].

From "When the Buddha had finished teaching this sutra" is the third part of this chapter, wherein various people joyfully accept it and put it into practice.

Glossary

anuttarā samyaksaṃbodhi: Complete, perfect awakening. *See also bodhi.*

arhat ("one who is worthy" of offerings): A saint who has completely eradicated the passions and attained liberation from the cycle of birth and death (samsara); arhatship is the highest of the four stages of spiritual attainment in the Hinayana, considered to be surpassed by the practitioners of the Mahayana. *See also* field of merit; Hinayana; samsara.

asura: A class of supernatural beings; a demigod.

attributes: See perceptual attributes.

bodhi: Awakening; the state of the highest perfection of wisdom.

bodhicitta: Lit., "mind (*citta*) of awakening (*bodhi*)," the aspiration or intention to attain awakening undertaken by a bodhisattva in order to help other sentient beings to liberation. *See also* bodhisattva.

bodhisattva ("awakening being"): One who has engendered the profound aspiration to achieve awakening (*bodhicitta*) on behalf of all sentient beings; the spiritual ideal of the Mahayana. *See also bodhicitta;* Mahayana; perfections.

bodhi tree: The tree under which a buddha attains awakening.

buddhahood: The state of becoming or being a buddha; the goal of the bodhisattva path.

buddha land: A cosmic world or realm in which a particular buddha dwells. Also called buddha realm.

deva: A class of supernatural beings; a god or divine being.

dhāraṇī: A powerful verbal incantation or mantra; a mnemonic device for the recollection of Buddhist doctrine.

dharma: Any phenomenon, thing, or element; the elements that make up the perceived phenomenal world.

Dharma: The truth, law; the teachings of the Buddha.

Dharma body (*dharmakāya*): The manifestation of the Buddha as ultimate reality or suchness. *See also* suchness.

Dharma-nature: The essential nature of all phenomena, the same as true suchness and the Dharma. *See also* Dharma body; suchness.

dhyāna: Meditation; a state of meditative concentration and absorption.

eighteen realms (*dhātu*s): The realms of sensory experience brought about by the inter-action of the six sense organs with their corresponding objects, and their resulting consciousnesses, totaling eighteen. *See also* entrances; sense organs; senses.

emptiness (*śūnyatā*): The absence of any independent or unchanging essence of the self and all phenomena (*dharma*s); all *dharma*s arise only through the interdependent origination of causes and conditions (*pratītyasamutpāda*). *See also* dharma.

entrances (*āyatana*s): The six sense organs of eyes, ears, nose, tongue, body, and mind and their six corresponding objects: form, sound, smell, taste, tangible objects, and mental objects, totaling twelve. *See also* sense organs; senses.

field of excellence. *See* "field of merit."

field of merit: Those saints who are worthy of respect and offerings (arhats), who will in turn generate merit for those who donate to them. *See also* arhat.

four continents: According to Buddhist cosmology, the four large land masses in the ocean around Mount Sumeru, one in each of the four cardinal directions, which comprise the world of human beings. *See also* Mount Sumeru.

four elements: The four physical elements that constitute material things (*dharma*s)—earth, fire, water, and wind. *See also* dharma.

four heavenly kings: The guardian gods of the four cardinal directions, rulers of the four continents. *See also* four continents.

four immeasurables (*brahma-vihāra*s): Four mental states or qualities to be cultivated by bodhisattvas—kindness (*maitrī*), compassion (*karuṇā*), joy (*muditā*), and equa-nimity (*upekṣā*). Also called four unlimited states of mind.

four majestic postures: The four basic physical postures of walking, standing, sitting, and lying down; a Buddhist practitioner strives to maintain mindfulness in all of these postures. *See also* mindfulness.

four noble truths: The basic doctrine of Buddhism: 1) the truth of suffering, 2) the truth of the cause of suffering, 3) the truth of the cessation of suffering, and 4) the truth of the path that leads to nirvana. *See also* nirvana.

gandharva: A heavenly musician.

garuḍa: A mythological being in the form of a giant bird.

Hinayana ("Small Vehicle"): A term applied by Mahayana Buddhists to various early schools of Buddhism whose primary soteriological aim is taken to be individual salvation. Hinayana followers are grouped into the two categories of *śrāvaka*s and *pratyekabuddha*s and there are four stages of spiritual attainment, culminating in arhatship. See also arhat; Mahayana; *pratyekabuddha; śrāvaka;* stream-enterer.

kalpa: An eon, an immensely long period of time.

kiṃnara: A class of mythological beings, half bird and half human, that make celestial music.

lion's roar: A metaphor for great eloquence in teaching the Dharma.

Mahayana ("Great Vehicle"): A form of Buddhism that developed in India around 100 B.C.E. and which exalts as its religious ideal the bodhisattva, a great being who aspires to awakening on behalf of all sentient beings. *See also* bodhisattva.

mahoraga: A class of snake-like mythological beings.

Maitreya: The future Buddha, currently still a bodhisattva. *See also* bodhisattva.

Mañjuśrī: The bodhisattva who represents wisdom. *See also* bodhisattva.

Māra: The Evil One, the personification of the realm of desire; a symbol of the afflictions that hinder progress on the path to buddhahood. *See also* buddhahood.

mindfulness: A fundamental Buddhist practice of maintaining awareness and clear observation during all one's activities, physical or mental, in order to develop insight into the impermanent nature of all things.

Mount Sumeru: In Buddhist cosmology, the highest mountain rising from the center of the world, surrounded by an ocean in which the four continents that comprise the world of human beings are situated. *See also* four continents.

nirvana: Liberation from samsara, a state in which all passions are extinguished and the highest knowing attained; *bodhi,* awakening. *See also bodhi;* samsara.

One Vehicle (*ekayāna*): The Buddha vehicle, the Mahayana teaching that leads to complete awakening and attainment of buddhahood, contrasted with the teachings of the two Hinayana vehicles. The One Vehicle includes and transcends all three vehicles of the *śrāvaka, pratyekabuddha,* and bodhisattva paths. The *Commentary* notes that the *Vimalakīrti Sutra* was taught before the One Vehicle was taught. *See also bodhisattva; śrāvaka; pratyekabuddha;* vehicle.

pāramitā. See perfections.

perceptual attribute: The basic forms, features, or characteristics of phenomena (*dharmas*) such as color, sound, shapes, and the like. The absence of perceptual attribute is the nature of ultimate reality, nirvana, emptiness, suchness, etc. The Sanskrit equivalent of the majority of the twenty-plus instances of this term in Kumārajīva's translation of the *Vimalakīrti Sutra* is *animitta,* usually translated as "signless." In the *Commentary* the term appears nearly five times as often and is of great concern, for buddhas and bodhisattvas are all devoid of perceptual attribute yet the *Vimalakīrti Sutra* describes them as having particular names, forms, living in particular buddha lands, performing actions, etc. *See also* buddha land; *dharma;* emptiness; nirvana; suchness.

perfections (*pāramitās*): Six qualities to be perfected by bodhisattvas on their way to complete awakening—1) charity or giving (*dāna*), 2) discipline or morality (*śīla*), 3) forbearance or patience (*kṣānti*), 4) exertion or perseverance (*vīrya*), 5) meditation (*dhyāna*), and 6) discerning awareness (*prajñā*). *See also* bodhisattva.

prajñā: Discerning awareness; one of the perfections. *See also* perfections.

pratyekabuddha ("solitary enlightened one"): One of the two kinds of Hinayana sages, along with *śrāvaka*s, who seek to reach the stage of arhat and attain nirvana. A *pratyekabuddha* attains liberation through direct observation and understanding of the principle of interdependent origination (*pratītyasamutpāda*) without the guidance of a teacher, and does not teach others. *See also* arhat; Hinayana; *śrāvaka*.

Śākyamuni: The historical Buddha, who lived in India in the fifth century B.C.E. and whose life and teachings form the basis for Buddhism.

samādhi: A mental state of concentration, focusing the mind on one point.

samsara: The cycle of existence, the continuous round of birth and death through which beings transmigrate; the world of suffering, contrasted with the bliss of nirvana. *See also* nirvana.

Śāriputra: A principal disciple of the Buddha. In several Mahayana sutras such as the *Vimalakīrti Sutra* the figure of Śāriputra serves as an example of the inferior learning and understanding of the Hinayana *śrāvaka* path. *See also* Hinayana; *śrāvaka*.

sense organs: The six sense organs of the eyes, ears, nose, tongue, body, and mind. *See also* eighteen realms; entrances; senses.

senses: The sense perceptions that correspond to the six sense organs—visual, auditory olfactory, gustatory, tactile, and mental perceptions. *See also* entrances; eighteen realms; sense organs.

*skandha*s: Psychophysical elements or forces; the five elements of form, feeling, conception, mental process, and consciousness that comprise the personality and give rise to the mistaken view of a permanent, inherent self.

skillful means (*upāya*): The various methods and means used by buddhas and bodhisattvas to guide and teach sentient beings, adapted to their different capacities.

śramaṇa: Mendicant, monk; another name for a Buddhist monk, originally applied to those who maintained an ascetic practice.

śrāvaka ("auditor"): Originally, a disciple of the Buddha, one of those who heard him expound the teachings directly; later, the term came to refer to one of the two kinds of Hinayana followers, along with *pratyekabuddha*s, to distinguish them from followers of the Mahayana. *See also* Hinayana; Mahayana; *pratyekabuddha*.

stream-enterer (*srota-āpanna*): The first of the four stages of spiritual attainment in the Hinayana; one who has entered the stream of the Dharma by destroying various wrong views. *See also* Hinayana.

suchness: Ultimate reality; the state of things as they really are. Insight into the suchness of all phenomena, i.e., as empty of inherent self-existence, arising only through interdependent origination, is perfect knowing (*prajñā*). *See also* emptiness; *prajñā*.

sutra: A Buddhist scripture, a discourse of the Buddha. Capitalized, the term refers to one of the three divisions of the Tripiṭaka. *See also* Tripiṭaka.

Tathāgata: An epithet for a buddha, meaning one who has gone to (*gata*) and come from (*āgata*) suchness (*tathā*), i.e., the embodiment of the truth of suchness. *See also* suchness.

Three Jewels: Buddha, Dharma (the teachings), and Sangha (the monastic community), also called the three refuges.

Tripiṭaka: The three divisions or "baskets" (*piṭaka*s) of the Buddhist canon: the Sutras, discourses and teachings of the Buddha; the Vinaya, codes of monastic discipline; and the Abhidharma, scholastic treatises on the Buddhist teachings.

triple world: The three realms of samsaric existence: the realm of desire (*kāmadhātu*), i.e., the world of ordinary consciousness accompanied by desires; the realm of form (*rūpadhātu*), in which desires have been eliminated but the physical body remains; and the formless realm (*ārūpyadhātu*), in which the physical body no longer exists. *See also* samsara.

underlying principle: The original or primordial way or truth of all things; emptiness; suchness. This concept is very important in the Sinitic understanding of the *Commentary* but does not appear in Kumārajīva's translation of the *Vimalakīrti Sutra*. *See also* emptiness; suchness.

vehicle (*yāna*): The various Buddhist paths of practice. The two vehicles of the *śrāvaka* and *pratyekabuddha*, contrasted with the bodhisattva vehicle of the Mahayana. *See also* Hinayana; Mahayana; One Vehicle; *pratyekabuddha; śrāvaka*.

Vinaya: Precepts and rules of conduct for monastics; along with the Abhidharma and the Sutras, one of the three divisions of the Tripiṭaka. *See also* Tripiṭaka.

Bibliography

Boin, Sara, trans. *The Teaching of Vimalakīrti (Vimalakīrtinirdeśa)*. London: Pāli Text Society, 1976. English translation of Étienne Lamotte's French translation of the *Vimalakīrti Sutra* (see below).

Hanayama, Shinshō, trans. *Shōtoku Taishi bunka kyōbun Yuimagyōgisho zenyaku*. Kyoto: Hyakkaen, 1971.

—. *Yuimagyōgisho*. In *Kokuyaku Issaikyō*, vol. 16. Tokyo: Daitō Shuppansha, Shōwa 39 (1964). Revised edition Heisei 4 (1992).

Idumi, Hokei, trans. "Vimalakirti's Discourse on Emancipation," *The Eastern Buddhist*, vol. 2, no. 6 (1923): 358–366; vol. 3, no. 1 (1924): 55–69; vol. 3, no. 2 (1924): 138–153; vol. 3, no. 3: 224–242; vol. 3, no. 4 (1925): 336–349; vol. 4, no. 1 (1925): 48–55; vol. 4, no. 2 (1927): 177–190; vol. 4, no. 3 (1927–1928): 348–366.

Lamotte, Étienne, trans. *L'enseignement de Vimalakīrti*. Louvain: Bibliothèque du Muséon, 1962.

Luk, Charles (Lu Ku'an Yü), trans. *The Vimalakīrti Nirdeśa Sūtra*. Berkeley, CA: Shambhala Publications, 1972.

McRae, John R., trans. *The Vimalakīrti Sutra*. Berkeley, CA: Numata Center for Buddhist Translation and Research, 2004.

Taishō University Institute for Comprehensive Studies of Buddhism. *Vimalakīrtinirdeśa and Jñānālokālaṃkāra: Transliterated Sanskrit Text Collated with Tibetan and Chinese Translations*. Tokyo: Taishō University Press, 2004.

Thurman, Robert A. F., trans. *The Holy Teaching of Vimalakīrti: A Mahāyāna Scripture*. University Park, PA and London: Pennsylvania University Press, 1976.

Watson, Burton, trans. *The Vimalakirti Sutra*. New York: Columbia University Press, 1997.

Index

A

Abhirati 6, 147

affliction(s) 13, 68, 82, 93, 114, 121, 127, 159, 171, 202, 223
    mental 68, 82, 92, 120–121, 126, 127, 131, 141, 142, 152, 160, 172, 179, 183, 185, 203, 212, 228
    nine 211
    ten 13

Āgamas 98

Ajita Keśakambala 89

Akṣobhya 6, 147, 225, 235, 239, 240

alms, almsbowl, almsgiver(s), alms-giving 78, 79, 81, 83, 84, 85, 86, 87, 89, 90, 92, 93

Āmrapālī 7, 8, 21, 22, 23, 24, 147, 152–154, 225

analysis, analytic xiv, xv, xvi, 32, 33, 71, 114

Ānanda 6, 7, 8, 9, 21, 22, 23, 55, 63, 64, 112–115, 225–227, 228–229, 249, 250

Aniruddha 100–101

anuttarā samyaksaṃbodhi (*see also* awakening, perfect, supreme; *bodhi;* enlightenment) 134

apparition(s) (*see also* spirits) 94, 127

arhat, arhatship (*see also* holy one; sage) 28, 53, 105, 181, 186, 197, 198, 207, 227

aspiration(s) 5, 15, 18, 37, 43, 44, 48, 57, 96, 126, 136, 169, 185, 186, 228, 240

for awakening, *bodhi* (*see also bodhicitta; bodhi,* mind) 46, 84, 139, 189, 191, 193, 212

asura(s) 21

attachment(s) 4, 9, 34, 49, 60, 78, 80, 82, 88, 92, 94, 103, 110, 118, 124, 126, 128, 151, 155, 156, 157, 158, 159, 160, 161, 168, 171, 173, 178, 179, 180, 182, 185, 200, 205, 216, 228, 235, 236, 237, 238
    four 117–118

austerities 77

awakening 27, 28, 29, 122, 129, 130, 212
    aspiration for, mind of (*see also bodhicitta; bodhi,* mind) 84, 131, 189, 191, 193
    future 122, 241
    perfect, supreme 52, 134, 144, 189, 193
    seven factors of 186
    site of 128–132, 244, 245
    true 3, 130, 158

awareness 37, 52, 141, 213
    discerning (*see also prajñā*) xvi, 14, 15, 18, 19, 30, 37, 47, 48, 49, 52, 59, 60, 63, 66, 68, 95, 96, 140, 142, 149, 150, 151, 178, 182–183, 186, 187, 194, 202, 213, 229, 230, 231, 232, 233, 244

B

bhikṣu(s) 8, 9, 20, 21, 95, 96, 97, 102, 103, 106, 107, 112, 220

*bhikṣunī*s 9

Index

BDK English Tripiṭaka
(First Series)

Abbreviations

Ch.: Chinese
Skt.: Sanskrit
Jp.: Japanese
Eng.: Published title

Title	Taishō No.
Ch. Changahanjing (長阿含經) Skt. Dīrghāgama	1
Ch. Zhongahanjing (中阿含經) Skt. Madhyamāgama	26
Ch. Dachengbenshengxindiguanjing (大乘本生心地觀經)	159
Ch. Fosuoxingzan (佛所行讚) Skt. Buddhacarita Eng. *Buddhacarita: In Praise of Buddha's Acts* (2009)	192
Ch. Zabaocangjing (雜寶藏經) Eng. *The Storehouse of Sundry Valuables* (1994)	203
Ch. Fajupiyujing (法句譬喩經) Eng. *The Scriptural Text: Verses of the Doctrine, with Parables* (1999)	211
Ch. Xiaopinbanruoboluomijing (小品般若波羅蜜經) Skt. Aṣṭasāhasrikā-prajñāpāramitā-sūtra	227
Ch. Jingangbanruoboluomijing (金剛般若波羅蜜經) Skt. Vajracchedikā-prajñāpāramitā-sūtra	235
Ch. Daluojingangbukongzhenshisanmoyejing (大樂金剛不空眞實三麼耶經) Skt. Adhyardhaśatikā-prajñāpāramitā-sūtra	243
Ch. Renwangbanruoboluomijing (仁王般若波羅蜜經) Skt. Kāruṇikārājā-prajñāpāramitā-sūtra (?)	245

Title	Taishō No.
Ch. Banruoboluomiduoxingjing (般若波羅蜜多心經)	251
Skt. Prajñāpāramitāhṛdaya-sūtra	
Ch. Miaofalianhuajing (妙法蓮華經)	262
Skt. Saddharmapuṇḍarīka-sūtra	
Eng. The Lotus Sutra (Revised Second Edition, 2007)	
Ch. Wuliangyijing (無量義經)	276
Ch. Guanpuxianpusaxingfajing (觀普賢菩薩行法經)	277
Ch. Dafangguangfohuayanjing (大方廣佛華嚴經)	278
Skt. Avataṃsaka-sūtra	
Ch. Shengmanshizihouyichengdafangbianfangguangjing	353
(勝鬘師子吼一乘大方便方廣經)	
Skt. Śrīmālādevīsiṃhanāda-sūtra	
Eng. The Sutra of Queen Śrīmālā of the Lion's Roar (2004)	
Ch. Wuliangshoujing (無量壽經)	360
Skt. Sukhāvatīvyūha	
Eng. The Larger Sutra on Amitāyus (in The Three Pure Land Sutras, Revised Second Edition, 2003)	
Ch. Guanwuliangshoufojing (觀無量壽佛經)	365
Skt. Amitāyurdhyāna-sūtra	
Eng. The Sutra on Contemplation of Amitāyus (in The Three Pure Land Sutras, Revised Second Edition, 2003)	
Ch. Amituojing (阿彌陀經)	366
Skt. Sukhāvatīvyūha	
Eng. The Smaller Sutra on Amitāyus (in The Three Pure Land Sutras, Revised Second Edition, 2003)	
Ch. Dabanniepanjing (大般涅槃經)	374
Skt. Mahāparinirvāṇa-sūtra	
Ch. Fochuiboniepanlüeshuojiaojiejing (佛垂般涅槃略説教誡經)	389
Eng. The Bequeathed Teaching Sutra (in Apocryphal Scriptures, 2005)	
Ch. Dicangpusabenyuanjing (地藏菩薩本願經)	412
Skt. Kṣitigarbhapraṇidhāna-sūtra (?)	
Ch. Banzhousanmeijing (般舟三昧經)	418
Skt. Pratyutpannabuddhasammukhāvasthitasamādhi-sūtra	
Eng. The Pratyutpanna Samādhi Sutra (1998)	

Title	Taishō No.
Ch. Yaoshiliuliguangrulaibenyuangongdejing (藥師琉璃光如來本願功德經) Skt. Bhaiṣajyaguruvaiḍūryaprabhāsapūrvapraṇidhānaviśeṣavistara	450
Ch. Milexiashengchengfojing (彌勒下生成佛經) Skt. Maitreyavyākaraṇa (?)	454
Ch. Wenshushiliwenjing (文殊師利問經) Skt. Mañjuśrīparipṛcchā (?)	468
Ch. Weimojiesuoshuojing (維摩詰所説經) Skt. Vimalakīrtinirdeśa-sūtra Eng. *The Vimalakīrti Sutra* (2004)	475
Ch. Yueshangnüjing (月上女經) Skt. Candrottarādārikāparipṛcchā	480
Ch. Zuochansanmeijing (坐禪三昧經)	614
Ch. Damoduoluochanjing (達磨多羅禪經)	618
Ch. Yuedengsanmeijing (月燈三昧經) Skt. Samādhirājacandrapradīpa-sūtra	639
Ch. Shoulengyansanmeijing (首楞嚴三昧經) Skt. Śūraṅgamasamādhi-sūtra Eng. *The Śūraṅgama Samādhi Sutra* (1998)	642
Ch. Jinguangmingzuishengwangjing (金光明最勝王經) Skt. Suvarṇaprabhāsa-sūtra	665
Ch. Rulengqiejing (入楞伽經) Skt. Laṅkāvatāra-sūtra	671
Ch. Jieshenmijing (解深密經) Skt. Saṃdhinirmocana-sūtra Eng. *The Scripture on the Explication of Underlying Meaning* (2000)	676
Ch. Yulanpenjing (盂蘭盆經) Skt. Ullambana-sūtra (?) Eng. *The Ullambana Sutra* (in *Apocryphal Scriptures*, 2005)	685
Ch. Sishierzhangjing (四十二章經) Eng. *The Sutra of Forty-two Sections* (in *Apocryphal Scriptures*, 2005)	784
Ch. Dafangguangyuanjuexiuduoluoliaoyijing (大方廣圓覺修多羅了義經) Eng. *The Sutra of Perfect Enlightenment* (in *Apocryphal Scriptures*, 2005)	842

Title	Taishō No.
Ch. Dabiluzhenachengfoshenbianjiachijing (大毘盧遮那成佛神變加持經)	848
Skt. Mahāvairocanābhisambodhivikurvitādhiṣṭhānavaipulyasūtrendra-rājanāmadharmaparyāya	
Eng. *The Vairocanābhisaṃbodhi Sutra* (2005)	
Ch. Jinggangdingyiqierulaizhenshishedachengxianzhengdajiao-wangjing (金剛頂一切如來眞實攝大乘現證大教王經)	865
Skt. Sarvatathāgatatattvasaṃgrahamahāyānābhisamayamahākalparāja	
Eng. *The Adamantine Pinnacle Sutra* (in *Two Esoteric Sutras*, 2001)	
Ch. Suxidijieluojing (蘇悉地羯囉經)	893
Skt. Susiddhikaramahātantrasādhanopāyika-paṭala	
Eng. *The Susiddhikara Sutra* (in *Two Esoteric Sutras*, 2001)	
Ch. Modengqiejing (摩登伽經)	1300
Skt. Mātaṅgī-sūtra (?)	
Ch. Mohesengqilü (摩訶僧祇律)	1425
Skt. Mahāsāṃghika-vinaya (?)	
Ch. Sifenlü (四分律)	1428
Skt. Dharmaguptaka-vinaya (?)	
Ch. Shanjianlüpiposha (善見律毘婆沙)	1462
Pāli Samantapāsādikā	
Ch. Fanwangjing (梵網經)	1484
Skt. Brahmajāla-sūtra (?)	
Ch. Youposaijiejing (優婆塞戒經)	1488
Skt. Upāsakaśīla-sūtra (?)	
Eng. *The Sutra on Upāsaka Precepts* (1994)	
Ch. Miaofalianhuajingyoubotishe (妙法蓮華經憂波提舍)	1519
Skt. Saddharmapuṇḍarīka-upadeśa	
Ch. Shih-chu-pi-p'o-sha-lun (十住毘婆沙論)	1521
Skt. Daśabhūmika-vibhāṣā (?)	
Ch. Fodijinglun (佛地經論)	1530
Skt. Buddhabhūmisūtra-śāstra (?)	
Eng. *The Interpretation of the Buddha Land* (2002)	
Ch. Apidamojushelun (阿毘達磨俱舍論)	1558
Skt. Abhidharmakośa-bhāṣya	

Title	Taishō No.
Ch. Zhonglun (中論) Skt. Madhyamaka-śāstra	1564
Ch. Yüqieshidilun (瑜伽師地論) Skt. Yogācārabhūmi	1579
Ch. Chengweishilun (成唯識論) Eng. *Demonstration of Consciousness Only* (in *Three Texts on Consciousness Only,* 1999)	1585
Ch. Weishisanshilunsong (唯識三十論頌) Skt. Triṃśikā Eng. *The Thirty Verses on Consciousness Only* (in *Three Texts on Consciousness Only,* 1999)	1586
Ch. Weishihershilun (唯識二十論) Skt. Viṃśatikā Eng. *The Treatise in Twenty Verses on Consciousness Only* (in *Three Texts on Consciousness Only,* 1999)	1590
Ch. Shedachenglun (攝大乘論) Skt. Mahāyānasaṃgraha Eng. *The Summary of the Great Vehicle* (Revised Second Edition, 2003)	1593
Ch. Bianzhongbianlun (辯中邊論) Skt. Madhyāntavibhāga	1600
Ch. Dachengzhuangyanjinglun (大乘莊嚴經論) Skt. Mahāyānasūtrālaṃkāra	1604
Ch. Dachengchengyelun (大乘成業論) Skt. Karmasiddhiprakaraṇa	1609
Ch. Jiujingyichengbaoxinglun (究竟一乘寶性論) Skt. Ratnagotravibhāgamahāyānottaratantra-śāstra	1611
Ch. Yinmingruzhenglilun (因明入正理論) Skt. Nyāyapraveśa	1630
Ch. Dachengjipusaxuelun (大乘集菩薩學論) Skt. Śikṣāsamuccaya	1636
Ch. Jingangzhenlun (金剛針論) Skt. Vajrasūcī	1642
Ch. Zhangsuozhilun (彰所知論) Eng. *The Treatise on the Elucidation of the Knowable* (2004)	1645

Title	Taishō No.
Ch. Putixingjing （菩提行經） Skt. Bodhicaryāvatāra	1662
Ch. Jingangdingyuqiezhongfaanouduoluosanmiaosanputixinlun （金剛頂瑜伽中發阿耨多羅三貌三菩提心論）	1665
Ch. Dachengqixinlun (大乘起信論) Skt. Mahāyānaśraddhotpāda-śāstra (?) Eng. *The Awakening of Faith* (2005)	1666
Ch. Shimoheyanlun (釋摩訶衍論)	1668
Ch. Naxianbiqiujing (那先比丘經) Pāli Milindapañhā	1670
Ch. Banruoboluomiduoxinjingyuzan (般若波羅蜜多心經幽賛) Eng. *A Comprehensive Commentary on the Heart Sutra* (*Prajñāpāramitā-hṛdaya-sūtra*) (2001)	1710
Ch. Miaofalianhuajingxuanyi (妙法蓮華經玄義)	1716
Ch. Guanwuliangshoufojingshu (觀無量壽佛經疏)	1753
Ch. Sanlunxuanyi (三論玄義)	1852
Ch. Dachengxuanlun (大乘玄論)	1853
Ch. Zhaolun (肇論)	1858
Ch. Huayanyichengjiaoyifenqizhang (華嚴一乘教義分齊章)	1866
Ch. Yuanrenlun (原人論)	1886
Ch. Mohezhiguan (摩訶止觀)	1911
Ch. Xiuxizhiguanzuochanfayao (修習止觀坐禪法要)	1915
Ch. Tiantaisijiaoyi (天台四教儀)	1931
Ch. Guoqingbailu (國清百録)	1934
Ch. Zhenzhoulinjihuizhaochanshiwulu (鎮州臨濟慧照禪師語録) Eng. *The Recorded Sayings of Linji* (in *Three Chan Classics*, 1999)	1985
Ch. Foguoyuanwuchanshibiyanlu (佛果圜悟禪師碧巖録) Eng. *The Blue Cliff Record* (1998)	2003
Ch. Wumenguan (無門關) Eng. *Wumen's Gate* (in *Three Chan Classics*, 1999)	2005

Title	Taishō No.
Ch. Liuzudashifabaotanjing (六祖大師法寶壇經)	2008
Eng. *The Platform Sutra of the Sixth Patriarch* (2000)	
Ch. Xinxinming (信心銘)	2010
Eng. *The Faith-Mind Maxim* (in *Three Chan Classics,* 1999)	
Ch. Huangboshanduanjichanshichuanxinfayao (黃檗山斷際禪師傳心法要)	2012A
Eng. *Essentials of the Transmission of Mind* (in *Zen Texts,* 2005)	
Ch. Yongjiazhengdaoge (永嘉證道歌)	2014
Ch. Chixiubaizhangqinggui (勅修百丈清規)	2025
Eng. *The Baizhang Zen Monastic Regulations* (2007)	
Ch. Yibuzonglunlun (異部宗輪論)	2031
Skt. Samayabhedoparacanacakra	
Eng. *The Cycle of the Formation of the Schismatic Doctrines* (2004)	
Ch. Ayuwangjing (阿育王經)	2043
Skt. Aśokāvadāna	
Eng. *The Biographical Scripture of King Aśoka* (1993)	
Ch. Mamingpusachuan (馬鳴菩薩傳)	2046
Eng. *The Life of Aśvaghoṣa Bodhisattva* (in *Lives of Great Monks and Nuns,* 2002)	
Ch. Longshupusachuan (龍樹菩薩傳)	2047
Eng. *The Life of Nāgārjuna Bodhisattva* (in *Lives of Great Monks and Nuns,* 2002)	
Ch. Posoupandoufashichuan (婆藪槃豆法師傳)	2049
Eng. *Biography of Dharma Master Vasubandhu* (in *Lives of Great Monks and Nuns,* 2002)	
Ch. Datangdaciensisancangfashichuan (大唐大慈恩寺三藏法師傳)	2053
Eng. *A Biography of the Tripiṭaka Master of the Great Ci'en Monastery of the Great Tang Dynasty* (1995)	
Ch. Gaosengchuan (高僧傳)	2059
Ch. Biqiunichuan (比丘尼傳)	2063
Eng. *Biographies of Buddhist Nuns* (in *Lives of Great Monks and Nuns,* 2002)	

Title	Taishō No.
Ch. Gaosengfaxianchuan (高僧法顯傳) Eng. *The Journey of the Eminent Monk Faxian* (in *Lives of Great Monks and Nuns,* 2002)	2085
Ch. Datangxiyuji (大唐西域記) Eng. *The Great Tang Dynasty Record of the Western Regions* (1996)	2087
Ch. Youfangjichao: Tangdaheshangdongzhengchuan (遊方記抄: 唐大和上東征傳)	2089-(7)
Ch. Hongmingji (弘明集)	2102
Ch. Fayuanzhulin (法苑珠林)	2122
Ch. Nanhaijiguineifachuan (南海寄歸内法傳) Eng. *Buddhist Monastic Traditions of Southern Asia* (2000)	2125
Ch. Fanyuzaming (梵語雜名)	2135
Jp. Shōmangyōgisho (勝鬘經義疏) Eng. *Prince Shōtoku's Commentary on the Śrīmālā Sutra* (2011)	2185
Jp. Yuimakyōgisho (維摩經義疏) Eng. *Expository Commentary on the Vimalakīrti Sutra* (2012)	2186
Jp. Hokkegisho (法華義疏)	2187
Jp. Hannyashingyōhiken (般若心經秘鍵)	2203
Jp. Daijōhossōkenjinshō (大乘法相研神章)	2309
Jp. Kan-jin-kaku-mu-shō (觀心覺夢鈔)	2312
Jp. Risshūkōyō (律宗綱要) Eng. *The Essentials of the Vinaya Tradition* (1995)	2348
Jp. Tendaihokkeshūgishū (天台法華宗義集) Eng. *The Collected Teachings of the Tendai Lotus School* (1995)	2366
Jp. Kenkairon (顯戒論)	2376
Jp. Sangegakushōshiki (山家學生式)	2377
Jp. Hizōhōyaku (秘藏寶鑰) Eng. *The Precious Key to the Secret Treasury* (in *Shingon Texts*, 2004)	2426
Jp. Benkenmitsunikyōron (辨顯密二教論) Eng. *On the Differences between the Exoteric and Esoteric* *Teachings* (in *Shingon Texts*, 2004)	2427

Title	Taishō No.
Jp. Sokushinjōbutsugi (即身成佛義) Eng. *The Meaning of Becoming a Buddha in This Very Body* (in *Shingon Texts*, 2004)	2428
Jp. Shōjijissōgi (聲字實相義) Eng. *The Meanings of Sound, Sign, and Reality* (in *Shingon Texts*, 2004)	2429
Jp. Unjigi (吽字義) Eng. *The Meanings of the Word Hūṃ* (in *Shingon Texts*, 2004)	2430
Jp. Gorinkujimyōhimitsushaku (五輪九字明秘密釋) Eng. *The Illuminating Secret Commentary on the Five Cakras* *and the Nine Syllables* (in *Shingon Texts*, 2004)	2514
Jp. Mitsugoninhotsurosangemon (密嚴院發露懺悔文) Eng. *The Mitsugonin Confession* (in *Shingon Texts*, 2004)	2527
Jp. Kōzengokokuron (興禪護國論) Eng. *A Treatise on Letting Zen Flourish to Protect the State* (in *Zen Texts*, 2005)	2543
Jp. Fukanzazengi (普勧坐禪儀) Eng. *A Universal Recommendation for True Zazen* (in *Zen Texts*, 2005)	2580
Jp. Shōbōgenzō (正法眼藏) Eng. *Shōbōgenzō: The True Dharma-eye Treasury* (Volume I, 2007) *Shōbōgenzō: The True Dharma-eye Treasury* (Volume II, 2008) *Shōbōgenzō: The True Dharma-eye Treasury* (Volume III, 2008) *Shōbōgenzō: The True Dharma-eye Treasury* (Volume IV, 2008)	2582
Jp. Zazenyōjinki (坐禪用心記) Eng. *Advice on the Practice of Zazen* (in *Zen Texts*, 2005)	2586
Jp. Senchakuhongannenbutsushū (選擇本願念佛集) Eng. *Senchaku Hongan Nembutsu Shū: A Collection of Passages* *on the Nembutsu Chosen in the Original Vow* (1997)	2608
Jp. Kenjōdoshinjitsukyōgyōshōmonrui (顯淨土眞實教行証文類) Eng. *Kyōgyōshinshō: On Teaching, Practice, Faith, and* *Enlightenment* (2003)	2646
Jp. Tannishō (歎異抄) Eng. *Tannishō: Passages Deploring Deviations of Faith* (1996)	2661

Title	Taishō No.
Jp. Rennyoshōninofumi (蓮如上人御文)	2668
Eng. *Rennyo Shōnin Ofumi: The Letters of Rennyo* (1996)	
Jp. Ōjōyōshū (往生要集)	2682
Jp. Risshōankokuron (立正安國論)	2688
Eng. *Risshōankokuron or The Treatise on the Establishment of the Orthodox Teaching and the Peace of the Nation* (in *Two Nichiren Texts,* 2003)	
Jp. Kaimokushō (開目抄)	2689
Eng. *Kaimokushō or Liberation from Blindness* (2000)	
Jp. Kanjinhonzonshō (觀心本尊抄)	2692
Eng. *Kanjinhonzonshō or The Most Venerable One Revealed by Introspecting Our Minds for the First Time at the Beginning of the Fifth of the Five Five Hundred-year Ages* (in *Two Nichiren Texts,* 2003)	
Ch. Fumuenzhongjing (父母恩重經)	2887
Eng. *The Sutra on the Profundity of Filial Love* (in *Apocryphal Scriptures,* 2005)	
Jp. Hasshūkōyō (八宗綱要)	extracanonical
Eng. *The Essentials of the Eight Traditions* (1994)	
Jp. Sangōshīki (三教指帰)	extracanonical
Jp. Mappōtōmyōki (末法燈明記)	extracanonical
Eng. *The Candle of the Latter Dharma* (1994)	
Jp. Jūshichijōkenpō (十七條憲法)	extracanonical